The Virtue of Nonviolence

SUNY series in Constructive Postmodern Thought

David Ray Griffin, editor

The Virtue of Nonviolence

From Gautama to Gandhi

Nicholas F. Gier

STATE UNIVERSITY OF NEW YORK PRESS

Published by
State University of New York Press, Albany

Printed in the United States of America

For information, address State University of New York Press,
90 State Street, Suite 700, Albany, NY 12207

Production by Marilyn P. Semerad
Marketing by Jennifer Giovani

Library of Congress Cataloging-in-Publication Data

Gier, Nicholas F., 1944–

The virtue of nonviolence : from Gautama to Gandhi / Nicholas F. Gier.
p. cm.—(SUNY series in constructive postmodern thought)
Includes bibliographical references and index.
ISBN 0-7914-5949-7 (alk. paper)
1. Nonviolence—Philosophy. 2. Nonviolence—Religious aspects.
I. Title. II. Series.
HM1281.G54 2003
303.6'1—dc21 2003042553

10 9 8 7 6 5 4 3 2 1

In Memory of My Brother

DeWayne Howard Gier
July 31, 1945–December 29, 1991

May He Rest in Peace

Contents

	Acknowledgments	ix
	Series Introduction	xi
	Introduction	1
ONE	**Gandhi as a Postmodern Thinker**	8
	Gandhi as Premodernist	9
	The Modernist Gandhi	11
	Two Forms of Postmodernism	18
	A Postmodern Gandhi	22
TWO	**Nonviolence in Jainism and Hinduism**	28
	Absolute Nonviolence in Jainism	29
	Gandhi and Jainism	31
	Relative Nonviolence in Hinduism	34
	Gandhi's View of the *Bhagavad-gītā*	36
THREE	**Vedānta, *Ātman,* and Gandhi**	39
	Bhikhu Parekh's Advaitin Gandhi	40
	Ramashray Roy's Nondual Gandhi	42
	Metaphors of Self and World	46
FOUR	**The Buddha and Pragmatic Nonviolence**	51
	Nonviolence in Buddhism	52
	Gandhi's Misconceptions about Buddhism	54
	Gandhi, Self-Suffering, and the Buddha	57
	The Mahātma and the Bodhisattva	58
	The Buddhist Self as Functional	61
	Gandhian and Buddhist Humanism	63
FIVE	**Experiments with Truth**	66
	Aristotle on Practical Reason	67
	Yi and *Phronēsis*	69
	Dharma and the Middle Way	73
	The Eight-Fold Path	76
	Experiments with Truth	78
SIX	**The Aesthetics of Virtue**	81
	A Confucian Critique of Greco-Roman Ethics	82
	Rational versus Aesthetic Order	86

A Confucian Aesthetics of Virtue 89
A Fusion of Making and Doing 92
Conclusions 98

SEVEN **Gandhi, Confucius, and Virtue Aesthetics** 100
Confucius versus Gandhi 101
Instructive Similarities 105
A Gandhian Aesthetics of Virtue 109

EIGHT **Rules, Vows, and Virtues** 113
Rules and Virtues 114
Virtue and Virility 119
Vows and Virtues 123
Gandhi's Vows 126
Gandhi's Virtues 131

NINE **The Virtue of Nonviolence** 136
Character Consequentialism 137
The Means–Ends Relation 142
Is Nonviolence a Virtue at All? 144
Is Nonviolence an Enabling Virtue? 146
The Virtues, Pleasure, and Moral Freedom 150
Happiness, Joy, and Pleasure 151

TEN **The Saints of Nonviolence: Buddha, Christ, Gandhi, King** 156
Saintly Gentleness and Tough Love 157
Utility, Duty, or Infused Charity? 159
The Charismatic Saint 164
Mahātma, *Megalopsychia,* and the Flawed Saint 168
Buddha, Christ, and Duress Virtue 174

Notes 177

Glossary of Foreign Terms 205

Selected Bibliography 209

Note on Supporting Center 215

Index 217

SUNY Series in Constructive Postmodern Thought 223

Acknowledgments

In India I would thank Rashmi Puri and Ashok Ratan of Panjab University for their constant guidance and encouragement in my first exposure to Gandhi's writings. Professor Puri was my host during a sabbatical stay at Panjab University in Chandigarh in 1992. Next I am grateful to Mahendra Kumar of the Gandhi Peace Foundation in New Delhi and the editor of *Gandhi Marg,* the premier journal of Gandhi scholarship. Professor Kumar hosted me for two visits in New Delhi in 1995 and 1999. I would also like to thank the librarians at the Gandhi Library at Rajkot and the Nehru Museum Library for their aid in locating books and articles.

The Departments of Philosophy and Studies in Religion at Queensland University provided office space and library privileges for two summer stays in 1995 and 1999.

I am indebted to Soka Gakkei International in Japan and the United States for their invitations to speak in Tokyo, Osaka, Santa Monica, Seattle, and Boston, and their keen interest in my Buddhist interpretation of Gandhi's ethics of nonviolence. My visit to Soka University and their Institute of Oriental Philosophy in March 2002 was a memorable experience.

In 1993 the Niwano Peace Foundation provided a grant for three months of study and research in Kyoto. The Markkula Center for Applied Ethics at Santa Clara University also provided me with a fellowship to attend their Seminar on Civic Virtue in 1997–98. Chapter 6 would not have been possible without their encouragement and support.

At the University of Idaho I would like to thank the Martin Institute of Peace Studies and Conflict Resolution for research and travel grants. I am also grateful to the university administration for granting me two sabbaticals (1992 and 1999) and one leave of absence (1995) to pursue my Gandhi research. Students in my Hinduism and Jainism classes as well as those in Peace and Asian Thought made substantial contributions.

I also received constructive criticism from Michael Myers at Washington State University and Nicholas Yonker, my undergraduate mentor at Oregon State University. David DeMoss offered some corrections to my understanding of Aristotle in chapter 5. Charles Rice did a great job of proofreading the entire manuscript.

Most of all I am indebted to Cynthia Townley of the University of Nevada at Las Vegas for offering a critique of nonviolence as an enabling virtue. Her fine arguments against this position are integrated into the fourth section of chapter 9. The central arguments of the book are much stronger because of her insightful contributions.

I would like to thank Mahendra Kumar for allowing me to use the material in the following articles published in *Gandhi Marg:* "Gandhi, *Ahimsa,* and the Self," 5, no. 1 (April–June 1993): 24–38 (integrated into chapter 2); "Gandhi: Premodern, Modern, or Postmodern?" 17, no. 3 (October–December 1996): 261–281 (essentially the current chapter 1); "Gandhi, the Buddha, and *Ātman:* A Response to Roy," 21, no. 4 (January–March 2000): 447–459 (a good portion of chapter 3); and "Gandhi and the Virtue of Non-Violence," 23, no. 3 (October–December 2001): 261–284 (the original draft of chapters 8 and 9). I am grateful to Roger T. Ames for allowing me to revise "The Dancing Ru: A Confucian Aesthetics of Virtue," *Philosophy East & West* 51, no. 2 (April 2001): 280–305 as chapter 5. I would like to thank the editors of the *Seikyo Times* for permission to use material from "The Virtue of Non-Violence: A Buddhist Perspective," February 1994, pp. 28–36. The editors of *International Philosophical Quarterly* have graciously allowed me to adapt my article "*Ahimsa,* the Self, and Postmodernism," 35, no. 1 (March 1995): 71–86. Dr. Yoichi Kawada of the Oriental Institute of Philosophy in Tokyo has given me permission to revise "Gandhi and Mahayana Buddhism" (in Japanese), *Journal of Oriental Studies* 35, no. 2 (1996): 84–105 as chapter 4. And finally Sarah Wilkins at Taylor & Fancis (www.tandf.co.uk) has allowed me to revise "Confucius, Gandhi, and the Aesthetics of Virtue," *Asian Philosophy* 11, no. 1 (March 2001): 41–54 as the current chapter 7.

Finally, I want to acknowledge the Indian artist who created the artwork on the cover: Brij Kul Deepak. (The third figure in the painting is Abduhl Ghaffar Khan, better known as the Frontier Gandhi. He is mentioned on pages 107, 108, and 171.) Deepak is both a peace artist and a toymaker. Deepak has conducted toy workshops for children around the world. He always uses natural materials and fashions the toys after ancient Indian prototypes. Examples of his artwork and information about his workshops can be seen at www.class.uidaho.edu/ngier/deepak/home.htm.

Introduction to SUNY Series in Constructive Postmodern Thought

The rapid spread of the term *postmodern* in recent years witnesses to a growing dissatisfaction with modernity and to an increasing sense that the modern age not only had a beginning but can have an end as well. Whereas the word *modern* was almost always used until quite recently as a word of praise and as a synonym for *contemporary,* a growing sense is now evidenced that we can and should leave modernity behind—in fact, that we *must* if we are to avoid destroying ourselves and most of the life on our planet.

Modernity, rather than being regarded as the norm for human society toward which all history has been aiming and into which all societies should be ushered—forcibly if necessary—is instead increasingly seen as an aberration. A new respect for the wisdom of traditional societies is growing as we realize that they have endured for thousands of years and that, by contrast, the existence of modern civilization for even another century seems doubtful. Likewise, *modernism* as a worldview is less and less seen as The Final Truth, in comparison with which all divergent worldviews are automatically regarded as "superstitious." The modern worldview is increasingly relativized to the status of one among many, useful for some purposes, inadequate for others.

Although there have been antimodern movements before, beginning perhaps near the outset of the nineteenth century with the Romanticists and the Luddites, the rapidity with which the term *postmodern* has become widespread in our time suggests that the antimodern sentiment is more extensive and intense than before, and also that it includes the sense that modernity can be successfully overcome only by going beyond it, not by attempting to return to a premodern form of existence. Insofar as a common element is found in the various ways in which the term is used, *postmodernism* refers to a diffuse sentiment rather than to any common set of doctrines—the sentiment that humanity can and must go beyond the modern.

Beyond connoting this sentiment, the term *postmodern* is used in a confusing variety of ways, some of them contradictory to others. In artistic and literary circles, for example, postmodernism shares in this general sentiment but also involves a specific reaction against "modernism" in the narrow sense of a movement in artistic-literary circles in the late nineteenth and early twentieth centuries. Postmodern architecture is very different from postmodern

1. The present version of this introduction is slightly different from the first version, which was contained in the volumes that appeared prior to 1999.

literary criticism. In some circles, the term *postmodern* is used in reference to that potpourri of ideas and systems sometimes called *new age metaphysics,* although many of these ideas and systems are more premodern than postmodern. Even in philosophical and theological circles, the term *postmodern* refers to two quite different positions, one of which is reflected in this series. Each position seeks to transcend both *modernism,* in the sense of the worldview that has developed out of the seventeenth-century Galilean-Cartesian-Baconian-Newtonian science, and *modernity,* in the sense of the world order that both conditioned and was conditioned by this worldview. But the two positions seek to transcend the modern in different ways.

Closely related to literary-artistic postmodernism is a philosophical postmodernism inspired variously by physicalism, Ludwig Wittgenstein, Martin Heidegger, a cluster of French thinkers—including Jacques Derrida, Michel Foucault, Gilles Deleuze, and Julia Kristeva—and certain features of American pragmatism.[2] By the use of terms that arise out of particular segments of this movement, it can be called *deconstructive, relativistic,* or *eliminative* postmodernism. It overcomes the modern worldview through an antiworldview, deconstructing or even entirely eliminating various concepts that have generally been thought necessary for a worldview, such as self, purpose, meaning, a real world, givenness, reason, truth as correspondence, universally valid norms, and divinity. While motivated by ethical and emancipatory concerns, this type of postmodern thought tends to issue in relativism. Indeed, it seems to many thinkers to imply nihilism.[3] It could,

2. The fact that the thinkers and movements named here are said to have inspired the deconstructive type of postmodernism should not be taken, of course, to imply that they have nothing in common with constructive postmodernists. For example, Wittgenstein, Heidegger, Derrida, and Deleuze share many points and concerns with Alfred North Whitehead, the chief inspiration behind the present series. Furthermore, the actual positions of the founders of pragmatism, especially William James and Charles Peirce, are much closer to Whitehead's philosophical position—see the volume in this series entitled *The Founders of Constructive Postmodern Philosophy: Peirce, James, Bergson, Whitehead, and Hartshorne*—than they are to Richard Rotry's so-called neopragmatism, which reflects many ideas from Rorty's explicitly physicalistic period.

3. As Peter Dews points out, although Derrida's early work was "driven by profound ethical impulses," its insistence that no concepts were immune to deconstruction "drove its own ethical presuppositions into a penumbra of inarticulacy" (*The Limits of Disenchantment: Essays on Contemporary European Culture* [London and New York: Verso, 1995], 5). In his more recent thought, Derrida has declared an "emancipatory promise" and an "idea of justice" to be "irreducible to any deconstruction." Although this "ethical turn" in deconstruction implies its pulling back from a completely disenchanted universe, it also, Dews points out, implies the need to renounce "the unconditionality of its own earlier dismantling of the unconditional" (6–7).

paradoxically, also be called *ultramodernism,* in that its eliminations result from carrying certain modern premises—such as the sensationist doctrine of perception, the mechanistic doctrine of nature, and the resulting denial of divine presence in the world—to their logical conclusions. Some critics see its deconstructions or eliminations as leading to self-referential inconsistencies, such as "performative self-contradictions" between what is said and what is presupposed in the saying.

The postmodernism of this series can, by contrast, be called *revisionary, constructive,* or—perhaps best—*reconstructive.* It seeks to overcome the modern worldview not by eliminating the possibility of worldviews (or "metanarratives") as such, but by constructing a postmodern worldview through a revision of modern premises and traditional concepts in the light of inescapable presuppositions of our various modes of practice. That is, it agrees with deconstructive postmodernists that a massive deconstruction of many received concepts is needed. But its deconstructive moment, carried out for the sake of the presuppositions of practice, does not result in self-referential inconsistency. It also is not so totalizing as to prevent reconstruction. The reconstruction carried out by this type of postmodernism involves a new unity of scientific, ethical, aesthetic, and religious intuitions (whereas poststructuralists tend to reject all such unitive projects as "totalizing modern metanarratives"). While critical of many ideas often associated with modern science, it rejects not science as such but only that *scientism* in which only the data of the modern natural sciences are allowed to contribute to the construction of our public worldview.

The reconstructive activity of this type of postmodern thought is not limited to a revised worldview. It is equally concerned with a postmodern world that will both support and be supported by the new worldview. A postmodern world will involve postmodern persons, with a postmodern spirituality, on the one hand, and a postmodern society, ultimately a postmodern global order, on the other. Going beyond the modern world will involve transcending its individualism, anthropocentrism, patriarchy, economism, consumerism, nationalism, and militarism. Reconstructive postmodern thought provides support for the ethnic, ecological, feminist, peace, and other emancipatory movements of our time, while stressing that the inclusive emancipation must be from the destructive features of modernity itself. However, the term *postmodern,* by contrast with *premodern,* is here meant to emphasize that the modern world has produced unparalleled advances, as Critical Theorists have emphasized, which must not be devalued in a general revulsion against modernity's negative features.

From the point of view of deconstructive postmodernists, this reconstructive postmodernism will seem hopelessly wedded to outdated concepts, because it wishes to salvage a positive meaning not only for the notions of selfhood, historical meaning, reason, and truth as correspondence, which were central to modernity, but also for notions of divinity, cosmic meaning, and an enchanted nature, which were central to premodern modes of thought. From the point of view of its advocates, however, this revisionary postmodernism is not only more adequate to our experience but also more genuinely postmodern. It does not simply carry the premises of modernity through to their logical conclusions, but criticizes and revises those premises. By virtue of its return to organicism and its acceptance of nonsensory perception, it opens itself to the recovery of truths and values from various forms of premodern thought and practice that had been dogmatically rejected, or at least restricted to practice, by modern thought. This reconstructive postmodernism involves a creative synthesis of modern and premodern truths and values.

This series does not seek to create a movement so much as to help shape and support an already existing movement convinced that modernity can and must be transcended. But in light of the fact that those antimodern movements that arose in the past failed to deflect or even retard the onslaught of modernity, what reasons are there for expecting the current movement to be more successful? First, the previous antimodern movements were primarily calls to return to a premodern form of life and thought rather than calls to advance, and the human spirit does not rally to calls to turn back. Second, the previous antimodern movements either rejected modern science, reduced it to a description of mere appearances, or assumed its adequacy in principle. They could, therefore, base their calls only on the negative social and spiritual effects of modernity. The current movement draws on natural science itself as a witness against the adequacy of the modern worldview. In the third place, the present movement has even more evidence than did previous movements of the ways in which modernity and its worldview *are* socially and spiritually destructive. The fourth and probably most decisive difference is that the present movement is based on the awareness that *the continuation of modernity threatens the very survival of life on our planet.* This awareness, combined with the growing knowledge of the interdependence of the modern worldview with the militarism, nuclearism, patriarchy, global apartheid, and ecological devastation of the modern world, is providing an unprecedented impetus for people to see the evidence for a postmodern worldview and to envisage postmodern ways of relating to each other, the rest of nature, and the cosmos as a whole. For these reasons, the failure of the previous antimodern movements says little about the possible success of the current movement.

Advocates of this movement do not hold the naively utopian belief that its success would bring about a global society of universal and lasting peace, harmony, and happiness, in which all spiritual problems, social conflicts, ecological destruction, and hard choices would vanish. There is, after all, surely a deep truth in the testimony of the world's religions to the presence of a transcultural proclivity to evil deep within the human heart, which no new paradigm, combined with a new economic order, new child-rearing practices, or any other social arrangements, will suddenly eliminate. Furthermore, it has correctly been said that "life is robbery": A strong element of competition is inherent within finite existence, which no social-political-economic-ecological order can overcome. These two truths, especially when contemplated together, should caution us against unrealistic hopes.

No such appeal to universal constants, however, should reconcile us to the present order, as if it were thereby uniquely legitimated. The human proclivity to evil in general, and to conflictual competition and ecological destruction in particular, can be greatly exacerbated or greatly mitigated by a world order and its worldview. Modernity exacerbates it about as much as imaginable. We can therefore envision, without being naively utopian, a far better world order, with a far less dangerous trajectory, than the one we now have.

This series, making no pretense of neutrality, is dedicated to the success of this movement toward a postmodern world.

David Ray Griffin
Series Editor

Introduction

Language at best is but a poor vehicle for expressing one's thoughts in full. For me nonviolence is not a mere philosophical principle. It is the rule and the breath of my life.... It is a matter not of the intellect but of the heart.

—M. K. Gandhi

Truth and nonviolence are no cloistered virtues but applicable as much in the forum and the legislatures as in the market place.

—M. K. Gandhi

True morality consists, not in following the beaten track, but in finding out the true path for ourselves and in fearlessly following it.

—M. K. Gandhi

Ahiṃsā *is my God and Truth is my God. When I look for* Ahiṃsā, *Truth says, "Find it through me." When I look for Truth,* Ahiṃsā *says, "Find it through me."*

—M. K. Gandhi

Gandhi's greatest contribution to the concept of nonviolence *(ahiṃsā)* was to build a bridge, principally through action and only afterward by thought, between its application for the social good as well as individual spiritual development. This involved synthesizing Vedic and ascetic views of nonviolence and making *ahiṃsā* a powerful moral and political tool. Gandhi transformed *ahiṃsā*'s earlier world-denying expressions into a world-affirming sociopolitical principle, one that drove an imperial power from India. Gandhi claimed that *ahiṃsā* is not "a resignation from all real fighting. ...On the contrary, ...nonviolence...is more active and more real fighting against wickedness than retaliation whose very nature is to increase wickedness."[1]

The essence of Gandhi's philosophy is the principle of "soul force" *(satyāgraha),* and his main contention was that soul force will always, at least morally and spiritually, win over brute force. It is the thesis of this book that *satyāgraha* can best be interpreted in terms of the power of personal virtue. Mark Juergensmeyer is right in his contention that *satyāgraha* "signifies a style of ethics that is not rule-bound but exploratory in nature."[2] Juergensmeyer argues that Gandhi's so-called "epic fast" in 1932 against a separate franchise for the untouchables was not genuine *satyāgraha,* primarily because Gandhi initiated the fast with an inflexible position that did not take into consideration the fact that most of the untouchables supported a separate electorate. (The other problem with this fast, as well as all the others characterized as "unto death," was its coercive nature.) Gandhi's mistake was to apply the principle of universal suffrage to a situation that called for examining cultural particularities rather than applying a hard and fast rule. Typically, Gandhi's experiments with truth tested universal rules against the exigencies of any given situation, and in many instances some rules, even those against noninjury, were suspended. Chapter 6 will examine the contextual and exploratory nature of Gandhi's ethics in terms of the practical reason of ancient virtue ethics. Here I will agree with Juergensmeyer that *satyāgraha* is not only a political strategy but a "way of knowing."[3]

One of the goals of constructive postmodernism is to overcome the Cartesian dichotomy of inner and outer and reaffirm the fusion of personal virtue and sociopolitical action. Gandhi stands as one of history's most eminent examples of this ideal. Gandhi's thoroughly contextual and personal ethics made him very suspicious of abstract moral reasoning, the primary contribution of modern ethical theories such as Kantianism and utilitarianism. Constructive postmodernism can be found in major nineteenth-century thinkers, primarily the Romantics and the German *Lebensphilosophen,* and Gandhi said that John Ruskin convinced him to see the error of separating private interest and public interest, a division characteristic not only of modernist thinkers but also his own Indian ascetic tradition. From Ruskin Gandhi derived his own moral maxim that the good of the individual is the good of all *(sarvōdaya),* a principle that should not be interpreted in a utilitarian way.

In his article "The '*Satyā*' in *Satyā*graha" Jay Garfield offers a Buddhist interpretation of Gandhi's soul-force and claims that his concept of *satyā* is very different than the Buddhist view. He states that "for Gandhi *satyā* is grounded in the permanence of *ātman* and its centrality for action, in the union of the personal *ātman* with the godhead, and in the revealed truth of the Hindu scriptures."[4] While Gandhi certainly took the Hindu scriptures very seriously, his own experiments with truth would always trump any revealed truth. Furthermore, I will argue that even though Gandhi uses the language of Vedānta, it is a Pāli Buddhist view of the self as a process rather than permanent substance that best suits his political activism and pragmatic concept of nonviolence. Gandhi's experiments with truth imply the intimate connection between moral actions and the particular facts of the world that informs the mindful action of a Buddhist *satyāgrahi.* Garfield himself admits that Gandhi would agree with the following proposition: "Effective action requires not just (or perhaps not at all) a grasp of theory, not just a harmony of action with the fundamental nature of reality, but also awareness of the concrete details of the immediate context of action. A firm grasp of the details of the action-context and insistence on the particular facts against obfuscation or error is constitutive of *satyāgraha.*"[5]

A principal thesis of this book is that Vedāntist philosophy, particularly the Advaita Vedānta with which Gandhi is usually associated, cannot support this "action-context" ethics. As Raghavan Iyer states, "Gandhi's radical reinterpretation of Hindu values in the light of the message of the Buddha was a constructive, though belated, response to the ethical impact of the early Buddhist Reformation on decadent India."[6] This is the first book-length attempt to work out the full implications of Iyer's observation. I will also take advantage of Luis O. Gomez's observation that the Buddhist ethics is distinctive in its "recognition of the indispensable link between nonviolence and self-cultivation,"[7] which is of course the driving force of all virtue ethics. I will also argue, contrary to some critics of virtue theory, that self-cultivation, especially for Gandhi and socially committed Buddhists, does not at all ignore other-regarding virtues such as justice and compassion. Indeed, Gandhi claims that "there is not a single virtue that aims at, or is content with, the welfare of the individual only"; and "nonviolence is not merely a personal virtue; it is also a social virtue to be cultivated like the other virutes."[8]

This book has three major goals: (1) to conceive of the ethics of nonviolence from a virtue perspective; (2) to give Gandhi's philosophy a Buddhist interpretation; and (3) to ally Gandhi with the constructive postmodern school of thought. My intent is not to foreclose on the possibility of a Hindu or Jain reading of Gandhi's work; rather, I argue that there are some distinct advantages in thinking of Gandhi as a Buddhist, especially with regard to the concept of self. (Although Gandhi would have been more sympathetic to the Māhāyanist self, I contend that the Pāli *jīva* serves virtue theory and the ethics of nonviolence much better.) In another book in this series, I have argued that Buddhism, along with Confucianism, anticipates many of the elements of constructive postmodernism,[9] so the second and third goals of this book are joined in this general way. Finally, I will argue that virtue ethics is the best option for constructive postmodernism. Other contemporary philosophers have attempted full-scale defenses of virtue ethics, so I see my task as applying some of their insights, adding my own, and initiating a discussion about the virtue of nonviolence.

Feminist and deconstructive postmodern critics appear to have placed the final nail in the coffin of the traditional idea of ethics as obedience to a moral code. (A detailed critique of rule ethics is found in chapter 8.) For postmodernists universal moral laws are the ethical expression of logocentric and essentialist thinking and are more intelligibly conceived as abstractions from particular moral decision making. Feminists are more specific in their claim that this type of morality represents one of the most pervasive forms of patriarchy—to wit: the tyranny of the divine father who created the rules and the earthly fathers who have enforced them. Both deontological and utilitarian perspectives also assume a disembodied, impersonal self, which is a pale and misleading shadow of our own engaged personal agency. The most constructive response to this crisis in moral theory has been the revival of virtue ethics, an ethics that has the advantages of being personal, contextual, and, as I will argue, normative as well. These and other aspects of virtue theory make it thoroughly consistent with the program of constructive postmodernism.

In his book *From Morality to Virtue* Michael Slote criticizes Kant for his moral asymmetry.[10] Kant believes we have a duty to contribute to the well-being of others but no corresponding duty to promote our own well-being. Slote grants that Kant does believe in a duty to develop our own talents, not to harm ourselves, and obviously to preserve our lives, but we have no duty to promote our own happiness or well-being. Slote also critiques utilitarianism for its reductionism and, at least in its Singerian form, unreasonable moral demands such as a voluntary equalization of living standards. Alaisdair MacIntyre argues that utilitarianism cannot distinguish between the clear qualitative difference between the internal value of the virtues and the extrinsic value of ordinary pleasures, a difference crucial to what we will call "character" consequentialism in chapter 9. This means that I will not be supporting Slote's program of giving the virtues intrinsic value independent of their consequences.

It is impossible to force all of Gandhi's ideas into a Procrustean bed, so that means that Vedāntist or theistic rule ethics are also options for his ethics of nonviolence. Furthermore, Gandhi's commitment to the Indian ascetic tradition and to a Hindu dialectic of extremes is not compatible with either the Buddhist Middle Way or the moderation of classical virtue theory. Hindus are sometimes inclined, as Wendy Doniger describes it, to pursue a Doctrine of Golden Extremes, between excessive eroticism at one end and excessive asceticism at the other.[11] In 1946, when the controversy about his sleeping with his grandniece Manu erupted, Gandhi asked his good friend C. F. Andrews for advice. Andrews diplomatically suggested that Gandhi should be much more moderate in his testing of *brahmacharya,*[12] but Gandhi continued to the extreme rather than aiming for the mean. The more contemporary commentators stress this aspect of Gandhi's philosophy, the more difficult it will be to build a widely acceptable theory of nonviolent political activism.

At least six book-length studies and one journal volume have been devoted to *ahiṃsā,* but none of them have related the principle to the ontology of self.[13] In his *Ahiṃsā: Non-Violence in Indian Tradition,* the best book on the subject, Uno Tähtinen notes the differences among the Upaniṣadic, Jain, and Buddhist doctrines of self, but he concludes that these differences are "irrelevant for the practice of non-violence."[14] It seems to me, however, that one's view of the self obviously affects one's social practices. If individual agency is unreal, as Advaita Vedānta maintains, then it is difficult to see how a dynamic and engaged practice of *ahiṃsā* can be possible. On the other hand, if the self is real but exhorted to detach itself from other selves and from an unredeemable nature (the Jain and Sāṃkhya-Yoga view), then it is uncertain how either real engagement with others or ecological values can be supported. A principal thesis of this book is that Buddhism and Confucianism, primarily because of their relational view of the self and positive view of nature, are better able to present *ahiṃsā* as a positive virtue in the framework of a comprehensive social ethics.

Gandhi did not have a consistent doctrine of the self—his fervent individualism was always in tension with his Hindu pantheism—and I believe that contemporary Gandhians should take a middle way between these extremes. Regarding the self, one might think that Christianity must have influenced Gandhi's views. Except for his use of the phrases "special creation of God" and "image of God,"[15] this does not seem to have been the case. Raghavan Iyer contends that the principal European influence on Gandhi was Socrates, from whom he derived a view of an inviolable and fiercely independent conscience. (Gandhi translated Plato's *Apology* into Gujarati.) In an impressive two-page analysis, Iyer demonstrates that there is no Indian equivalent to Socrates's *daimon,*[16] an "inner voice" that claims, as Gandhi said often during his campaigns, an authority higher than the laws of the land. One could propose that Gandhi's idea of self-suffering—that it is better to suffer injury than to inflict it—also comes from Socrates, although its Indian origins in *tapasā* are clearly evident.

It is not very clear if Gandhi's idea of conscience is consistently Socratic. One passage on Gandhi's "inner voice" contains an odd mix of popular Christianity and situation ethics: "The 'Inner Voice' may mean a message from God or from the Devil, for both are wrestling in the human breast. Acts determine the nature of the voice."[17] (This Manichean dualism of good and evil is one of the most troublesome aspects of Gandhi's religious philosophy.) Another passage gives Gandhian conscience an infallible divine sanction: "For me the Voice of God, of Conscience, of Truth or the Inner Voice,..mean one and the same thing.... For me the Voice was more real than my own existence. It has never failed me, and for that matter, any one else."[18] These passages reveal a persistent tension between a thoroughly humanistic Gandhi—compatible with Buddhism, Confucianism, and Aristotelianism—and a Christian or Vaiṣṇava Gandhi, in which the grace of an omnipotent God is prominent.

Contrary to the cultural solipsism of some current postmodern schools I believe that we can still affirm a common humanity. The rank Orientalism of Rudyard Kipling's "East is East and West is West and never shall the twain meet" is not only odious but wrong. Asian and European thought is converging today just as it met on common ground in ancient times. The new translations of Asian texts are consummate scholarly creations and they are further witness to the truth of Hans-Georg Gadamer's principle of *Horizontsverschmelzung,* that no matter how different the cultures it is still possible to meet and to communicate. For example, Roger T. Ames's and Henry Rosemont's introduction to their new translation of the *Analects* is a most insightful and sensitive appreciation of distinctive features of the Chinese way of thinking and writing. Chinese thought can be best described as a process philosophy, one found not only in Buddhism, but also in Europe with Heraclitus and his descendants: Hegel, the *Lebensphilosophen,* Bergson, James, Whitehead, and Hartshorne. Gandhi was an active and enthusiastic synthesizer of European and Asian thinking, and one of the tasks of this book is to reinterpret Gandhi as a process thinker, a mode of thought integral to constructive postmodernism. A process view of the self is the only way one can make intelligible his claim that humans can turn from violent to nonviolent action. In subsequent chapters I will demonstrate that a substance view of the self cannot support the idea of moral progress, let alone the revolution in human thought that Gandhi intended.

Something must be said at the outset about the terms *pragmatism, utilitarianism,* and *relativism.* Regrettably, all three terms are commonly conflated. There is a significant difference between the pragmatic criterion of "what works" and the hedonic calculus. And, as I will show throughout the book, "what works" is primarily tied to objective personal and environmental factors that are not just personal whim or the results of impersonal calculations. For example, if Gandhi followed the hedonic calculus, he would have immediately stopped his sexual experiments with his grandniece for the greater good of his crucial campaign of 1946–47 in Bengal. He was convinced, however, that his goal of spiritual purity, rather than the reduction of mental anguish in his supporters and general efficiency in his political campaign, was the overall best strategy. Iyer is completely correct when he claims that Gandhi's "keen alertness to detail can...be accompanied by a cultivated lack of interest in immediate results."[19] In this observation we see not only the operation of Buddhist mindfulness but also a character consequentialism that always maximizes the long-term benefits of personal virtue and integrity over mere hedonic results.

During this controversy over Manu, Acharya Kripalani suggested that Gandhi may have been violating the principle of *loka sangraha* (conservation of the social good) and he urged that "this consideration...must not be absent from your calculations in this experiment of yours."[20] Sleeping with Manu was part of his spiritual discipline and he was convinced that his inability to stop the violence in Bengal was due to his failure to become a true *brahmachāri*. By purifying himself with Manu, he was certain that he could convince the people of his absolute sincerity and the necessity of the Bengali Muslims and Hindus to lay down their arms and embrace each other as brothers and sisters. What worked for Gandhi was definitely not the same as what maximized utility. Indeed, following one's own truth may lead to much suffering, not pleasure. Gandhi also made it clear that what might work for him would not necessarily work for others. What was suitable and appropriate for Gandhi was related primarily to the objective conditions of his life and the requirement that people have the courage to face their sexual temptations squarely and honestly right in the presence of the opposite sex.

Chapter summaries and anticipations will be found in chapter 1. Before turning to detailed discussion and analysis, something must be said about the Gandhian texts and their inconsistencies. Gandhi repeatedly warned people that he was an activist and not a scholar. Except for perhaps his autobiography and *Hind Swaraj*, Gandhi wrote not for posterity but for what the exigencies of the time required. As he once said, "My words and deeds are dictated by prevailing conditions. There has been a gradual evolution in my environment and I react to it as a *satyāgrahi*."[21] (Again we can see Gandhi's contextual pragmatism, certainly not a Kantianism or a utilitarianism.) His experiments with truth forced him to constantly revise his thinking, so he advised readers to take his current statements, not his past remarks, as their guide. For commentators this situation provides both challenges and relief. The challenge is the difficultly of pouring over thousands of pages and finding an intelligible thread of discussion. The relief is that anyone who reads the texts carefully and responsibly can come up with contending interpretations that have value and contemporary application. It is my hope that my reading of Gandhi has produced both.

Chapter 1

Gandhi as a Postmodern Thinker

Formerly I used to resent the ignorance of my opponents. Today I can love them because I am gifted with the eye to see myself as others see me and vice versa.

—M. K. Gandhi

A dawning realization that I have no idea what "postmodernism" means has led me to wonder whether I ever knew what I meant by "modernism."

—Richard Rorty

Gandhi is usually seen as a forceful critic of modernism and it is generally assumed that he proposed a return to premodern modes of thought. While this was a reasonable hypothesis to his contemporaries and most commentators since his death, it is now time to reevaluate Gandhi's philosophy in light of postmodern modes of thought. Radhakrishnan's first impression of Gandhi was that he possessed a "medieval attitude of mind,"[1] but he later saw that he was mistaken. In this book I will not only be revising my first reactions to him as premodernist, but I shall also go beyond my second impressions of him as a modernist thinker. I believe that a postmodern Gandhi can be defended and that he may offer significant contributions to a postmodern view of self, ethics, religion, and political philosophy. I shall also suggest that it is a constructive rather than a deconstructive postmodernism that suits him best.

Let me say at the outset that I am not equating, as Gandhi may have done, modernism with modernization in the sense of industrialization and urbanization. Modernism is also not necessarily European and premodernism is not primarily Asian. (Recognizing the profound effect of Euro-American thinkers on him, Gandhi did not see his own reform program as one that would divide East from West.) Furthermore, modernism is not something new and recent and premodernism something old and ancient. Finally, I contend that we can also discern the beginnings of a postmodernist response among the ancient philosophers, most notably Confucius, Zhuangzi, and Gautama Buddha.[2] Some commentators claim that Śaṅkara is a forerunner of postmodern thought,[3] but it seems to me that Brahman as the ultimate, undifferentiated substance is a premodern assumption.

Gandhi as Premodernist

The crisis of the modern world has led many to believe that the only answer is to return to the traditional forms of self and community that existed before the Modern Age. Such a move would involve the rejection of science, technology, and a mechanistic cosmology. Ontologically the modern worldview is basically atomistic, both at the physical and the social level. The cosmos is simply the sum total of its many inert and externally related parts, just as modern society is simply the sum total of social atoms contingently related to other social atoms. (The modern state is simply the social atom writ large on an international scale, acting as dysfunctionally as the social atom does in smaller communities.) The modernist view of time is also linear, with one event happening after the other, with no other purpose than simply to continue that way. The modernist view of the sacred has been to reject it altogether, or to place God in a transcendent realm far removed from the material world. The latter solution is the way that some Christian theologians have reconciled themselves with mechanistic science.

By contrast the premodern vision of the world is one of totality, unity, and, above all, purpose. These values were celebrated in ritual and myth, the effect of which was to sacralize the cycles of seasons and the generations of animal and human procreation. The human self, then, is an integral part of the sacred whole, which is greater than and more valuable than its parts. And, as Mircea Eliade has shown in *Cosmos and History,* premodern people sought to escape the meaningless momentariness of history (which Eliade called the "terror of history") by immersing themselves in an Eternal Now. Myth and ritual facilitated the painful passage through personal and social crises, rationalized death and violence, and controlled the power of sexuality. One could say that contemporary humankind is left to cope with its crises with far less successful therapies or helpful institutions.

When Gandhi says that "in order to restore India to its pristine condition, we have to return to it,"[4] most commentators have taken this to mean that he has joined the premodernist revolt against modernism. The pristine India was for him the village communities where a vast majority of Indians still live today. In the villages Gandhi found people who "overflowed with faith" and "whose wisdom was boundless."[5] Because of his confidence in these people, he called for a dismantling of centralized state authority and a return to what he called "village republicanism." He also supported the caste system as long as the scourge of untouchability was removed. Otherwise Gandhi insisted that the son should follow the father's occupation, as long as that job did not involve immoral activity. A critic once countered that, according to this logic, Abraham Lincoln should not have aspired to become president of the United States. Gandhi answers that, as long as he keeps his profession, the scavenger can otherwise be anything that he wants to be.[6]

Modern philosophy generally separates fact and value, the "is" and the "ought," science and faith, politics and religion, the public from the private, and theory from practice. Gandhi rejects each of these distinctions in what again appears to be a return to premodern modes of thought. Even more pointed is his disavowal of modern technology, mechanized industry, centralized bureaucratic administration, and the rule of science in all areas of life. Most of us would probably agree with Gandhi that the modern state does indeed swallow up individual persons, even as it is, ironically, celebrating their autonomy, and that it has also destroyed the intimate ties of traditional community life. Gandhi reaffirms his own Hindu tradition that the goal of human life should be truth and virtue rather than wealth and power. According to *The Laws of Manu,* the attainment of family and prosperity is only a stage on life's way, a stage that is eventually replaced by the person who takes vows of nonviolence, nonpossession, and chastity.

In addition to the terror of history, many premodern peoples also saw the body and senses as a hindrance to the spiritual life. This view was sometimes connected, as it was in Advaita Vedānta, with the view that the natural world as a whole is illusory or at most only a derivative reality. Again Gandhi appears to be in agreement with premodernism on the first point. (He never speaks of the world as unreal or illusory, so his connection to Advaita Vedānta, as I will argue later, is problematic.) Gandhi frequently affirms a strict dualism between soul and body, and he speaks constantly of a Manichean battle between our spiritual natures and our animal natures. The body is given to us because of our karma: "We are enslaved in the body because of our sinful deeds."[7] The body is "a filthy mass of bones, flesh and blood"; and "when it is under the control of God it is a jewel, but when it passes into the control of the Devil, it is pit of filth."[8]

Gandhi's Manicheanism is pervasive and it may have come from Christian influences as well as his own Indian tradition: "In God there is no duality. But as soon as we descend to the empirical level, we get two forces—God and Satan, as Christians call them."[9] Gandhi claims that we are necessarily violent because of life in a body, so that is why we should aim to be rid of it or at least train ourselves to become impervious to its needs. Interestingly enough, a mind-body dualism characterizes much of modern thought, but it is formulated in a much more subtle and sophisticated form. Cartesian dualism does not impute evil to the body, so Gandhi's dualism is definitely more premodern than modern—it is more Manichean than Cartesian—and it stands as the greatest obstacle to a postmodern interpretation of his thought. Curiously, Gandhi rejects the synthetic dialectic of opposites embedded in his own tradition—namely, that both good and evil are found in the Godhead—for a Manichean exclusion of opposites.

When Gandhi speaks of a person's spiritual development, he argues that it is not a passive and static affair, but it involves making war on the enemy's camp. True to the Manichean spirit, the enemy is first and foremost the body: "The spirit in me pulls me one way, the flesh in me pulls in the opposite direction. ...This struggle resolves itself into an incessant crucifixion of the flesh so that the spirit may become entirely free."[10] When Gandhi writes about his philosophy of education, he calls for a harmony of intellect, heart, and body,[11] a view that obviously conflicts with the passages just cited. Furthermore, Nair Pyarelal's analysis of *brahmacharya* as involving the unity of one's entire life, including the spirit and the body, reflects Tantrism rather than Manicheanism.[12] (Indeed, the Tantric tradition is the most provocative answer to the ascetic rejection of the body.) As interpreters of Gandhi, we should take every opportunity to stress the aspects of his thought that emphasize the unity of heart, mind, body, and spirit.

As we now look beyond Gandhi as a premodernist, it is important to note that, although he admired the achievements of the ancient India, he realized that he could not take the *dharma* of another age as his own. Distinctively modern, or even postmodern, is Gandhi's principle that each society, as each individual, has its own truth, and that simply reviving ancient truths was not only anachronistic but unworkable. As Bhikhu Parekh states, "Every *yuga* or age had its own distinctive problems and needed to come to terms with them in its own way. For [Gandhi] as for Hindus in general the past was a source of inspiration and self-confidence, never a model or blueprint for the present."[13] The integration of past truths combined with a constructive critique of modernism is the principal methodological goal of constructive postmodernism.

The Modernist Gandhi

Modernism has been described as a movement from *mythos* to *logos*, and this replacement of myth by logic has been going on for at least 2,500 years. Almost simultaneously in India, China, and Greece, the strict separation of fact and value, science and religion was proposed by the Lokāyata materialists, the Greek atomists, and the Chinese Mohists. These philosophies remained minority positions, but it is nevertheless essential to note that the seeds for modernist philosophy are very old. The Greek Sophists stood for ethical individualism and relativism; they gave law its adversarial system and the now accepted practice that attorneys may "make the weaker argument the stronger"; they inspired Renaissance humanists to extend education to the masses as well as to the aristocracy; and they gave us a preview of a fully secular modern society. Even though maintaining teleology and the unity of fact and value, Socrates, Plato, and Aristotle affirmed ethical individualism and rationalism, and Aristotle supported representative government, held by many as one of the great achievements of the modern world.

One of Gandhi's most basic assumptions was his firm belief in the integrity of the individual: "The individual is the one supreme consideration";[14] "[I]f the individual ceases to count, what is left of society?"[15] Gandhi said that he feared the power of the state, because "it does the greatest harm to mankind by destroying individuality, which lies at the root of all progress."[16] For Gandhi individuals must act on their own truth regardless of the consequences and regardless of whether others think they are in error. This proviso is foundational to Gandhi's experiments with truth. This affirmation of the integrity and reality of the individual is the principal reason why Gandhi cannot be related to Advaita Vedānta. If individuation is ultimately illusory, the very foundations of Gandhi's political ethics are dissolved.

It is important to observe that the doctrine of karma is modernist in assuming the concept of individual moral responsibility. It is also significant that individual karma is most consistently expressed in the Jain-Yoga-Sāṃkhya philosophies that anticipate the modernist idea of autonomous selves. Individual moral responsibility becomes problematic only in the *bhakti yoga* of the Hindu saviors' forgiveness of human sins and the distribution of the Bodhisattvas' excess merit. Some philosophers have struggled to make intelligible the idea of collective karma,[17] but the basic logic of karma dictates individual responsibility for individual acts and a corresponding individual resolution of guilt related to these acts. It is clear that even with his theistic tendencies Gandhi always affirms individual personal responsibility.

Gandhi's experiments with truth are distinctively modernist with their firm assumption that the individual is the final arbiter of action. To assert a source of authority outside of the Torah, Dikē, the Dharma, or the laws of any God is a sure sign of the modernist mind. (Sometimes, however, Gandhi does identify the inner voice as the command of God, so this gives us a premodern view of the matter.) Gandhi also rejects a premodern cyclical view of history in favor of a modernist view of linear moral progression. A very modernist Gandhi states, "The force of spirit is ever progressive and endless. … The remedy [from self-destruction] lies in every individual training himself for self-expression in every walk of life, irrespective of response of the neighbours."[18] This is not only progressive and individualistic, it also appears to undermine his premodern view that one should train in the profession of one's father.

The possibility of people's "inner voices" offering conflicting results raises the issue of relativism, a position associated with modernism but, again, one that is at least as old as Protagoras's dictum of *homo mensura*. Because of our finitude and fallibility, Gandhi firmly asserted that we can only attain relative truths. French postmodern philosophy is also criticized for its relativism, but the difference between it and Gandhi is that he believed in an absolute truth behind our failed attempts to reach it. Therefore, Gandhi's position on truth does not conform to French deconstruction, but it is more compatible with constructive postmodernism. Although he formulates his views in a much more sophisticated way, Charles Sanders Peirce shares Gandhi's dual commitment to falliblism and epistemological realism.[19] Peirce distanced himself from James and Dewey primarily because of their rejection of realism. Process philosophers Whitehead and Hartshorne also preserve epistemological realism while at the same time affirming the antiessentialist and process metaphysics that characterizes their form of constructive postmodernism.

Gandhi's conception of religion could be called modernist as well. He believed that all religions are equal, and all are to be tolerated. Gandhi was a fervent believer in prayer and he also chanted Rāma's name, but even these practices are sometimes given a modernist rendering. Gandhi said that for him Rāma was not the king of the *Rāmayāna* or an incarnation of Viṣṇu, but the name simply means "purity of conduct" and the "search for truth."[20] His usual explanation of prayer as communing with the "Higher Self"[21] could be interpreted as a Kantian-like appeal to conscience.

For Gandhi religion is a purely personal matter, and "there are as many religions as there are individuals."[22] One could also say that he is committed to the modernist reduction of religion to ethics. He has his own special version of this reductionist religion: religion is the search for truth, an endeavor even inclusive of atheists. Also modernist is his position that the state should not support religious organizations. But this did not prevent his holding that religion should be integrated into political action as its ethical ground and justification. This was a foundational belief for Gandhi and it was shared by political thinkers of the European Enlightenment. It is only some contemporary American critics who insist on a strict separation of religion and politics.

Gandhi scholar Ronald Terchek is very much committed to a modernist interpretation of Gandhi. In an interesting twist, Terchek offers a decidedly European rendering of what should be Gandhi's most Hindu concept.

Terchek suggests that *advaita* means the unity and equality of human beings, in the fully modernist sense of those terms.[23] Given Gandhi's very eccentric understanding of *advaita*, Terchek's position cannot be rejected outright. Terchek claims that complete moral autonomy, even if it means civil disobedience, was Gandhi's goal and, if this is so, then he is a fully modernist thinker. Terchek also believes that Gandhi's famous warning that "India is in danger of losing her soul" does not express a fear that Indians are losing their ancient premodern traditions; rather, it means that Indians will lose their moral autonomy in a dehumanizing bureaucratic state. Gandhi's principal fear was that people would not have enough self-determination to perform acts of civil disobedience. On each of these points I believe that Terchek has pressed Gandhi too far in a Euro-American and modernist direction. Although he rejects a postmodernist reading of Gandhi,[24] Terchek's qualifications of the traditional idea of autonomy look very much like a constructive postmodernist revision of the idea of self-legislation and the preservation of personal integrity. Indeed, it is this view of autonomy that is wedded to Gandhi's organic view of self, world, and society and Gandhi's view of the self as relational and social. I believe that this is thoroughly constructive postmodern worldview.

Gandhi's commitment to civil disobedience is intimately related to the issue of his professed anarchism. Gandhi called his village republicanism a form of "enlightened anarchy" in which "everyone is [her] own ruler."[25] He agrees with Thoreau that "government is best that governs least," and he believed that government is a necessary evil. (Before the Modern Age people generally followed Aristotle's assumption that human beings were social and political animals and that being ruled was a natural state of affairs.) If Gandhi's anarchism is modernist, then his utopianism is also modernist. Along with nationalism, militarism, and environmental degradation, utopianism is without doubt one of the great failures of modernism. Most utopian experiments have ended in innocuous failure, but some of them, especially the communist states, became, fulfilling the George Orwell's prophecies, totalitarian dystopias. Fortunately, especially for the future generations of these societies, the communist experiments collapsed within a single generation. The central problem with utopianism, the use of calculative reason in a systematic ordering of society, points to a fundamental flaw in the modern worldview.

One could also argue that even though he differed with other Indian nationalists, his own nationalism was modernist in its main points, especially if it is seen in connection with his anarchism and his utopianism. There is much truth in Huiyun Wang's claim that "Gandhi was...anti-modern subjectively and...a political modernizer objectively."[26] In the short text of *Hind Swaraj* the word "nation" is mentioned seventy-five times, and Gandhi believed that India, as a vast federation of village republics, could join the great family of nation states as an equal partner. The Gujarati text of *Hind Swaraj,* as Anthony J. Parel has pointed out, makes a significant difference between a genuine nation formed as community *(praja)* and a nation of individuals merely held together by state power *(rashtra)*.[27] As opposed to the received view that it was British administration and British railways that made India a nation, Gandhi claimed that "India has been one country right from ancient times."[28] Pilgrim saints, who walked the length and breadth of the Indian subcontinent, unified India centuries before it was linked by iron rails. Today millions of Indians still ply these British-built railways, not only to do business and visit relatives, but to continue the age-old pilgrimage to the sacred sites of Mother India.

The fact that Gandhi claims a premodern origin for the Indian nation does not necessarily mean that his political views are premodern. His views on nationhood are not modernist either, for the modern state, as we have seen, is viewed as analogous to the individual social atom magnified on the international level. As Parel states, "*[Hind Swaraj]* does not propound the *modern* concept of nation in so far as the latter is based on the notions of brute force, the priority of national interest, and a principle of exclusiveness based on either religion, or language, or race."[29] Even the relatively innocuous state apparatus of liberal democracy does not escape Gandhi's critical eye. Although it is theoretically designed to do so, liberal democracies do not empower individuals; rather, as Parekh so aptly phrases it, they abstract "power from the people, concentrate it in the state and then return it to them in their new [abstract roles] as citizens."[30]

Parel's and Parekh's views of Gandhi's political philosophy allow us to get our first glimpse of a postmodern Gandhi. His view of the nation state is arguably postmodern in that it offers India as a model for a new type of polity, one which has already proved itself, with some unfortunate exceptions, to be a success in bringing sixteen different major language groups and six world religions together, not by brute force, but by the rule of law and representative democracy. Gandhi's postmodern vision of nationhood is one based on decentralized local control, assimilation and tolerance of cultural differences, and above all, nonviolence. As we will see, "decentering" the self and national analogues of the self is the crux of all postmodern philosophy. Gandhi's position, however, definitely does not go as far as Derrida's view, which has been described as a "radical form of democracy, one without representation, and therefore one in which even individuals' representations of themselves would be drawn constantly into question."[31]

Returning to the issues of anarchism and utopianism, we can now see that some qualification is in order. Gandhi spoke fervently of his village communities as ideal states, but he was keenly aware of human fallibility and the limits of reason, especially the calculative reason of modern mass political organization. Joan Bondurant has also taken issue with those commentators who have interpreted Gandhi's anarchism along traditional lines. Most anarchist theories are based on the idea of mutual self-interest and a rejection of all external sanctions. But Gandhi's practice of nonviolence and self-suffering discourages self-interest and reintroduces constraint and coercion in a way unlike any other previous political theory. In addition to the two anarchist positions—violent overthrow of the authoritarian state or passive withdrawal from society altogether—Gandhi adds a third solution, which Bondurant believes solves the anarchist dilemma.

Anarchists have always opposed the state because they believe that the only way it could assert its authority was through violence. Gandhi's technique of *satyāgraha* offers a nonviolent way of restraining and persuading people to work for the common good. As Bondurant states, "Anarchists may claim a positive philosophy, but they, like other political theorists, have rarely sought a positive *technique* whereby a system could be realized."[32] Instead of using the term "anarchist," one could call Gandhi a "communitarian," a term that is commonly used by today's postmodern political thinkers. Gandhi's statement that Indians should "study [their] Eastern institutions in [a] spirit of scientific inquiry...[to] evolve a truer socialism and a truer communism,"[33] might be the synthesis of premodern and modern that we find in constructive postmodernism.

Gandhi's appeal to reason and scientific method also ties him to the modern worldview. Although he rejected scientism, the ideology that makes science the source of all truth, he was firmly committed to the method of rational inquiry and experimental testing. He said that we must reject truth claims, even those of scripture, that are "repugnant to reason or moral sense."[34] In his autobiography he is even more specific about the requirements of his scientific method: the scientist "conducts his experiments with the utmost accuracy, forethought and minuteness, [and] never claims any finality about his conclusions."[35] Richard B. Gregg states that Gandhi "is a social scientist because he follows social truth by the scientific method of observation, intuitional and intellectual hypothesis and experimental test."[36]

There is no sign in Gandhi, however, of the atomism and reductionism that characterizes much of the scientific mentality. The Cartesian method of reducing to clear and distinct simples to understand the whole is also missing from Gandhi. Furthermore, there is no evidence of a method of Cartesian doubt, which declared that there is only one subject of experience of which we are certain—namely, the human thinking subject. All other things in the world, including persons and other sentient beings, have now become objects of thought, not subjects in their own right. Cartesian subjectivism, therefore, gave birth simultaneously to modern objectivism as well. With the influence of the new mechanical cosmology the stage was set for uniquely modern forms of otherness and alienation. Gandhi would have been very sympathetic to the idea of the "reenchantment of science" proposed by today's constructive postmodernist thinkers.[37] In their view both teleology and an animate nature are revived in ways compatible with contemporary physics and with Gandhi's tendency to equate nature and life.

Gandhi's principal problem with modernism is its separation of fact and value. Ramashray Roy is the Gandhi scholar who, because of his vast knowledge of modern European philosophy, has been able to diagnose this problem most successfully. By separating the "ought" from the "is," human life loses its moral focus. The goal of modern life, especially in its most utilitarian forms, is simply the satisfaction of one desire after the other. Self-gratification is not only accepted but encouraged, and gradually higher purposes are replaced by lower ordinary ones.[38] In *Hind Swaraj* Gandhi equates modernism with sensual self-gratification, and condemns it primarily for this reason. The modern world view not only alienates us from nature, but also alienates our desires from any moral end. The teleology of the ancients, that which gave their life its ultimate meaning and purpose, has been eliminated in modernism.

Roy claims that "modernism attributes to man godly powers,"[39] which he has used to conquer nature and build weapons of mass destruction. In my other book in this series I have called this Titanism, a form of extreme humanism in which human beings have taken on divine prerogatives and, as a result of their hubris, have lost sight of their proper place in the world. The Faustian bargain of modernism has come at a great price: unlivable cities, devastation of the natural world, and the constant threat of deadly weapons everywhere. Ironically, the power promised by modernism has in many instances turned to impotence—either in complete hedonistic dissipation or the clash and mutual cancellation of personal and national power.

In his excellent book on Gandhi's political philosophy Bhikhu Parekh lists five "distinctively human powers"—self-determination, autonomy, self-knowledge, self-discipline, and social cooperation—that Gandhi would have required for any great civilization.[40] According to Gandhi, all five of these capacities are threatened by modern civilization, with the last three as the weakest and most vulnerable. Today's emphasis on the first two qualities is distinctively modern and Euro-American, but all five qualities are part of the European tradition beginning with the Greek and Christian philosophers. A lack of balance among the qualities makes contemporary culture especially unstable and violence prone. Except for the spiritual self-determination and autonomy of the yogis, which ultimately does not have a political or even a moral goal, these two characteristics have not been strong in Asian thought as well.

We can now see what Gandhi meant when he said that his attack on modern civilization was not an attack on the West, because each of his basic human powers is part of the European tradition. Europe and America can regain the moral ground that they lost by recognizing the importance of self-knowledge, self-discipline, and social cooperation. (Gandhi's concept of self-knowledge will be analyzed in chapter 5 and the virtues requiring self-discipline will be discussed in chapter 8.) The great irony is that Gandhi was initially inspired to recapture this lost ground by European thinkers (Socrates, Tolstoy, Ruskin, and Thoreau) and by English translations and expressions (theosophy as an example) of his own Indian tradition. By this analysis we can see once again how modernist and Western Gandhi really was. One could say that Socrates's and Thoreau's "soul-force" was stronger in an activist sense than the more passive "soul-force" of his Hindu tradition. Gandhi's own Vaiṣṇava tradition is known for its dynamic spirituality, but not for political confrontation, so Western activism must be an important key to Gandhi's idea of *satyāgraha* and progressive nonviolence.

We have already seen the possibility of a postmodern political philosophy in Gandhi, so let us see if we can take him beyond modernism to a more comprehensive and constructive postmodern philosophy. When Vivek Pinto calls Gandhi's work "critical traditionalism" and when Madhuri Sondhi suggests that Gandhi integrates Hindu *dharma* into modernism and that *Hind Swaraj* represents both a critique and an appropriation of modern ideas, both these authors are moving towards a constructive postmodern Gandhi.[41] Indeed, Thomas Pantham has already arrived at this interpretation: "[Gandhi's] project...is one of overcoming modernism without regressing to traditionalism. In his approach, there is a merging of the reconstruction of Indian tradition and the reconstruction of Western modernity."[42]

Two Forms of Postmodernism

The stage for a postmodern interpretation of Gandhi has been set, but we need better definitions of postmodernism than have been offered thus far in the Gandhian literature. We who embrace constructive postmodernism must also double our efforts to emphasize the fact that there is more to postmodernism than French deconstruction. (We are also confident that we can alleviate Richard Rorty's confusion expressed in the epigraph that heads this chapter.) Maduri Wadhwa defines postmodernism as "the adoption or adaptation of Western developmental models to indigenous systems"; or alternatively a "synthesis of old and new which is qualitatively new from the old and the new."[43] First, Wadhwa's first definition does hint at elements of constructive postmodernism. Second, we have already seen that modernism is not new, and that its roots go back at least 2,500 years. Third, modernism is not necessarily Western, because Jainism and Sāṃkhya-Yoga have views of moral and spiritual autonomy that are even more extreme than European views. One must remember that the Jain saint and the yogi do not merge with Brahman, as in the premodernist totality of the Upaniṣads and Vedānta, but are liberated to live a perfect life of total isolation from the world and from each other. Their liberated states are beyond good and evil and apart from all society and politics. Gandhi's this-worldly asceticism and political activism stands in stark contrast to this yogic tradition.

In his book *Presuppositions of India's Philosophies* Karl H. Potter focuses not only on conceptual similarities between the Indian ascetics and the Sophists' *homo mensura,* but also on the hubris of the Indian yogis. Agreeing with Heinrich Zimmer that asceticism is "an expression of an extreme will for power,"[44] Potter states, "Indian philosophy *does* in fact elevate power, control or freedom to a supereminent position.... The ultimate value...is not morality but freedom...complete control over one's environment...even control of the physical sources of power in the universe."[45] Potter even suggests that Europeans have better understood their limitations than their Indian counterparts. The modern scientific view of nature as "impersonal, neither in our control nor controlling us" is alien to the Indian mind, which has no doubt about "the power of the yogi to control not only his body but the bodies of others—indeed, the whole universe. ..."[46] There is, as I have argued in my other book in this series, an Indian Titanism as well as the technological Titanism of the West. The former is a benign form of Titanism, but it is nonetheless important to see the conceptual parallels. One might see Titanism as the culmination of all the negative implications of the modernist worldview.

What, then, is the postmodern response to Asian and European Titanism, and how do we define it correctly? Susanne Rudolph and Lloyd Rudolph point us towards an answer: we will find the postmodern Gandhi in the "contesting discourse" of the "counter-culture" voices against modernism that he found in Tolstoy, Ruskin, and Thoreau. (In the Indian tradition the most constructive countercultural force was Gautama Buddha, although not as successful as Gandhi claimed as bringing "an arrogant priesthood" to its knees.")[47] According to the Rudolphs, the use of "contesting discourse" allowed Gandhi to give truth a "contextual and experimental form."[48] The Rudolphs' contesting discourse might very well be conceived of as deconstructive discourse, which fragments and decenters the entrenched structures of the modern state and culture. In the jargon of French deconstruction, it is the "spacing" or distancing from a logocentric modern culture. Gandhi's experiments with truth can be seen as his way to dislodge and discredit the authority structures of British India and, therefore, to deconstruct the modernist, imperialist assumptions of British rule. Gandhi does this without falling back uncritically onto tradition, for he was also, at the same time, dismantling the brahmin-centered caste system of ancient India.

In his book *Gandhian Utopia: Experiments with Culture,* Richard G. Fox explicitly rejects the postmodernist approach to his discipline of anthropology. Some of his initial conclusions about Gandhi's method, however, sound like French deconstruction. For example, Fox acknowledges the fact that Gandhi is not the sole "author" of the Gandhian movement, just as Derrida claims that writers are never the sole authors of their own texts. Fox observes that Gandhi had many personal identities and that his experiments with truth intensified this fragmentation of self. If Fox is correct, it is on this very point that Gandhi stands furthest from his own Vedāntist tradition where there is only one true Self. The goal of Hindu philosophy might be seen as a radical recentering of the soul rather than its fragmentation. (This makes Vedānta premodern rather than postmodern.) Reviewing Fox's book, Douglas Allen states, "[Gandhi's] sense of discontinuous personhoods...[and] his different constructions of his identity as a person and of Indian culture, of his utopian ideals and practices and struggles, all must be understood as emerging from his experiments with truth—his ever-changing contingent confrontations with existing structures of domination."[49] Many commentators have despaired of Gandhi's inconsistencies and have concluded that Gandhi was either confused or unwilling to reconcile the various strands of his worldview. Fox, however, takes Gandhi's eclecticism as integral to his lifelong struggle to dismantle British rule in India. More fundamentally, we must see this phenomenon as a manifestation of Gandhi's experiments with truth, in which he was willing to give up even his own views if they did not test out in experience.

Although Fox asserts that Gandhi rejects integral personhood in favor of "discontinuous personhood," he does not give any evidence for this claim.[50] Even though he may be correct about Gandhi's changing identities throughout his career, we have seen that Gandhi's own view of self ranges from a Vedāntist *ātman* through a social, relational self to a modernist autonomous self. Fox's choice of the phrase "discontinuous personhood" is misleading, because Gandhi does believe, contrary to Derrida, in authorial intention, except that the locus of this intention is more social and collective. The theory of authorial intention has usually been connected to the "Great Person" theory of human creativity, but Fox wishes to establish a middle position between singular authorship and cultural determinism. Fox believes that great persons are "always authorized by little people" and that persons are "culturally defined" and not determined.[51] Fox is drawing on Paul Ricoeur and Ralph Mannheim for theoretical guidance and these moderate continental voices dovetail nicely with the American school of constructive postmodernism. My continental preference for the construction of social meanings is Maurice Merleau-Ponty, who offers a striking image of centripetal *Sinngebung* meeting the centrifugal forces of personal intention.

Although he is not aware of a postmodern alternative to the French school, Fox's position is clearly compatible with constructive postmodernism, a theoretical framework much more suitable to Gandhi as well. I just mentioned possible continental sources for this position, but it is usually connected with American pragmatism and contemporary process philosophy. This view attempts to reestablish the premodern harmony of humans, society, and God but without losing the integrity of the individual, the possibility of meaning, and the intrinsic value of nature. Constructive postmodernists believe that the French deconstructionists are throwing out the proverbial baby with the bath water. The latter wish to reject not only the modern worldview but any worldview whatsoever. The constructive postmodernist wants to preserve the concept of a worldview and proposes to reconstruct one that avoids the liabilities of both premodernism and modernism.

The ancient cosmology that most closely approximates the constructive postmodern view is the one found in Chinese philosophy. In their doctrine of the Cosmic Triad the Chinese gave equal value and integrity to human beings, earth and heaven. All have their own job to perform and none competes with the other with respect to these duties. Only rarely did the Chinese deify humans and humanize heaven in the way that Indian and Christian incarnational theologies have done. The deification of humans leads to spiritual Titanism, and in these views nature is usually left with little or no value. With regard to human nature Confucian philosophers do not consider reason to be the essence of persons and never describe the self as autonomous. Furthermore, Confucian thinkers do not conceive of substance or essence in the typical Indian or Greek way. When we interpret Gandhian cosmology as an organic holism rather than a Vedāntist monism, the two traditions become eminently more comparable. This connection between Confucianism and Gandhi is discussed in greater detail in chapter 7.

The other ancient philosopher who anticipates constructive postmodernism is Gautama Buddha. The Buddha's contribution to postmodernism comes primarily in his brilliant criticism of the substance metaphysics of Jainism and Hinduism. The Buddha rejected the idea of a permanent soul substance as a metaphysical fiction that has no basis in experience. As the ultimate point of craving and attachment, he also found it practically damaging to the spiritual life. The spiritual substance of the autonomous soul and the inert substance of the Newtonian atom constitute the ontological foundations of the modern worldview. The rejection of a spiritual self by many materialists has not lessened their commitment to human autonomy, although in some minds it may weaken their arguments for a moral basis for action.

When Gandhi says that we must reject "the theory of the permanent inelasticity of human nature,"[52] he seems to join the Buddha in the latter's critique of Indian philosophy. (This one passage is of course not enough to establish the antiessentialist credentials of Gandhi as a postmodern philosopher.) A consistently antiessentialist Gandhi would have rejected the *ātman* of the Upaniṣads, and all other Indian views of the self, because none of them, except the Buddhist, offers either the agency or elasticity that Gandhi requires in this particular passage. (When Gandhi states that "God is continuously in action without resting for a single moment," he affirms a process deity as well as a process self.[53]) Instead of aligning Gandhi with Derrida's complete decentering of the self, I propose that we associate him with the reconstruction of the self that we find in Buddhism, American pragmatism, and process philosophy. (I have defended the Buddha against nihilism and the complete deconstruction of the self elsewhere, and this work is summarized in chapter 4.[54]) If Gandhi had continued his study of American philosophy, he would have found American pragmatism much to his liking.[55]

A Postmodern Gandhi

We have seen that Gandhi wants to protect the individual from dissolution either in a premodern totality or the modern bureaucratic state. By some readings of French postmodernist literature, we should be equally anxious about the loss of individuality in its constant decentering and fragmentation of the self. Whereas the premodern view was that human beings are determined by a transcendent Other or dissolve into an immanent One, some modernist claims of autonomy demand that humans be fully self-defined and self-contained. Modernist ethics culminates in Immanuel Kant's strict provision that no heteronomous acts can have moral worth and even the "Holy One of the Gospels must be compared with our ideal of moral perfection before he is recognized as such."[56]

Ironically, although a different goal is reached, it appears that French postmodernism agrees with the idea of "other" constitution. For the French deconstructionists, the self does not make its own life any more than the author writes his own book. The constructive postmodernist, following Whitehead, Merleau-Ponty, or George Herbert Mead, combines self-and other-constitution and recreates a relational, social self that revives the best aspects of the relational self found in Buddhism, Hebrew religion, and Confucianism.[57] Gandhi also qualifies his individualism with other-constitution, and he definitely joins in this postmodern reconstruction of the self. As he once reminded a correspondent, "I value individual freedom, but you must not forget that man is essentially a social being."[58]

Also disconcerting is the possibility of a total loss of meaning that comes with a thorough application of Derrida's method.[59] The constructive postmodernists are also concerned about a logocentric society and the dominance of calculative and analytic reason, but instead of the elimination of reason altogether, they call for a reconstruction of reason. A working formula would be the following triad: *mythos* > *logos* as analytic reason > *logos* as synthetic, aesthetic, dynamic reason, (more on this in chapter 6). The best example of a reconstructed *logos* is found in the new "logic" of European art since the late nineteenth century. Cezanne rejected the classical (that is, logocentric) perspective and initiated a revolution that opened up new ways of looking at the world. Drawing on Japanese, African, and other non-European themes, these artistic revolutionaries synthesized the premodern and modern in the same way that Gandhi did in his social and political experiments. In a chapter entitled "The Reenchantment of Art: Reflections on the Two Postmodernisms," Suzi Gablick presents both deconstructive and reconstructive examples of contemporary art and finds that the latter movement is a continuation of the artistic revolution just described. Gablick states that "Reconstructionists...are trying to make the transition from Eurocentric, patriarchal thinking and the 'dominator' model of culture to a more participatory aesthetics of interconnectedness, aimed toward social responsibility, psychospiritual empowerment, deep ecological commitment, good human relations, and a new sense of the sacred...."[60] This view of art reintegrates premodern elements but emphatically rejects the modernist view of art for art's sake, which is yet another result of the alienation of the private and public that we find in modern culture. In chapter 7 we will see that Gandhi's aesthetic is in significant agreement with Gablick's position and that his aesthetics of virtue is part and parcel of the best ethics for constructive postmodernism.

While the theology of deconstruction calls for the "death of God" and the demise of meaning that definitely goes with it, constructive postmodern theology insists that religion and spirituality must recover their positive roles in society. It is again clear that Gandhi belongs with the constructive postmodernists rather than with the French school. (The only problem is Gandhi's unfortunate dualism of spirit and beast in human nature.) One could perhaps see the beginnings of Gandhi's postmodern theology in his adaptation of Tolstoy's *The Kingdom of God Is Within You*. One could also say that the proposition that "Truth is God" is an attempt to overcome the modernist critique of religion. Gandhi's postmodern religion is all-encompassing, because it includes truth-and virtue-seeking atheists as well as other religious people. Without using the term "postmodern," Huiyun Wang defines Gandhi's religion as "truth and non-violence rather than sacrament and priestcraft."[61] As such Gandhi's religion could be integrated nicely with his postmodern communitarianism. As we have seen above, such a polity would be based on "soul-force" not brute force. In Gandhi's village republicanism "there will be ever-widening, never-ascending circles...an oceanic circle whose centre will be the individuals...[and] the outermost circumference will not wield power to crush the inner circle."[62]

Gandhi's reasons for rejecting other Indian nationalists' programs can best be interpreted as constructive postmodern. Both the liberal constitutionalist Shri Gokhale and radicals such as Shri Tilak and B. B. Pal, who recommended violent means to the end of Indian independence, were thoroughly modernist in their worldviews. Both separated the inner from the outer, both proposed a rationalist methodology, and both ridiculed Gandhi's belief that legitimate political action must have a spiritual foundation. Answering questions at the 1930 Round Table Conference in London, Gandhi explained why he had to stand apart from these other nationalists. In South Africa he found that he was very good at marshaling facts and presenting a convincing case to his fellow Indians. He was dismayed, however, at their usual response: many quickly proposed violent solutions to their grievances. Gandhi concluded that his follower's minds were in the right place but their hearts were not prepared for the nonviolent action that was required. It was here that Gandhi discovered his most important philosophical principle: that good ends must always be matched with good means. This principle will be the key to distinguishing utilitarianism, where means are independent from ends, and character consequentialism, the theory that is wedded to the virtue of nonviolence in chapter 9.

Gandhi's fusion of means and ends, the inner and the outer, of religion and politics is neither premodern nor modern, but distinctively postmodern in the constructive sense. Tilak declared that "the ways of the Sadhu do not pay in politics" and that personal virtue was not necessary for successful political action.[63] Breaking with both the premodern Indian tradition of the isolated yogi and thoroughly modern nationalism, Gandhi ingeniously integrated the best of both. Constructive postmodernism can be seen as the result of a dialectical triad in which modernism negates premodernism, and then the constructive postmodernist, in a third stage of reintegration, gleans value from both. In stark contrast is the French postmodernist solution, which essentially intensifies the negation of the second moment of the triad. There is much truth in David Griffin's suggestion that deconstructive postmodernism can best be described as an "ultramodernism," implying as it does both extreme relativism and even nihilism.[64]

In the last section of chapter 3 we will analyze in some depth the various analogies that Gandhi uses to express the self-world relationship. The analogies that seem to place him in the premodernist camp are the drops-in-the-ocean, threads-in-the-cloth, and rays-of-the sun models. In each of these images I argue that the integrity of the individual, a fundamental axiom for Gandhi, is compromised. None of these models meets Gandhi's criterion that "corporate growth is therefore entirely dependent upon individual growth."[65] Only Gandhi's organic analogies offer sufficient protection for the individual while at the same time grounding the self's social relations. On the other hand, organic analogies have hierarchical implications that are problematic. For example, the dominance of brain over other bodily organs serves Gandhi's reformed caste system well, but it is does not support his equally strong egalitarianism. Central to the postmodern vision of process philosophy is Whitehead's "analogy of organism," in which every element of the universe is internally related and in which a noncoercive deity attempts to harmonize these elements into an aesthetic whole. If we focus the organic analogy at the cellular level, as some process philosophers do, it is much more amenable to egalitarian values. Again, if Gandhi is a postmodern thinker, Gandhi stands with Rāmānuja and Whitehead and not with Śaṅkara and Derrida.

One of the major moral theories of the Modern Age is utilitarianism and Jeremy Bentham was one of its principal proponents. Bentham declared that "pushpin is as good as poetry" and a utilitarian could conclude that the hedons of a vice such a gambling (especially if it brings in great state revenue) may outweigh the hedons of the traditional virtues. Both the Greek and Indian traditions held, however, that the good life of virtue and self-discipline was higher than the accumulation of material goods and gratification of desires. Traditional theories of value are deconstructed by the French postmodernist school, while the constructive postmodernists seek a reconstruction of traditional values. Here again we can see the operation of Gandhi's principle that good ends always require good means, and this is the reason why he always rejected utilitarian solutions.

I believe the most promising program for a postmodern view of ethics is the revival of virtue ethics. Earlier leaders of this movement, such as Alaisdair MacIntyre, have criticized the dismal state of contemporary moral theory, and they propose what appears to be a return to premodern forms of human society. (Ironically, MacIntyre appears very modern, perhaps even postmodern or more precisely Gandhian, in his view that people should fashion their own truths within the narrative flow of their own lives.) This book will propose that Confucius and the Buddha could be seen as the ancient forerunners of constructive postmodern virtue ethics. Such a view would allow us to reconstruct the truth of Socrates' dictum that knowledge is virtue and use this as an answer to the modernist claim that knowledge is power—yogic as well as technological. In *Hind Swaraj* Gandhi said, "Civilization is that mode of conduct which points out to man the path of duty. Performance of duty and observance of morality are convertible terms.

To observe morality is to attain mastery over our mind and our passion. So doing, we know ourselves. The Gujarati equivalent for civilization means 'good conduct.' "[66] In Anthony Parel's critical edition of *Hind Swaraj,* he notes that in discussion with Gandhi he said that what the Gujarati actually means is "a good way of life,"[67] phrasing that is even closer to virtue ethics. One could say that Gandhi's ethical program was to replace Vedic and Purāṇic ritual with the traditional virtues of courage, justice, and compassion. As Gandhi states, "Morality means acquisition of virtues such as fearlessness, truth, chastity, etc. Service is automatically rendered to the country in this process of cultivating morality."[68] Gandhi's virtues, including the virtue of nonviolence, will be the subject of chapters 8 and 9.

One of the great advantages of the revival of virtue ethics is that it offers a way out of the entrenched dichotomies of modern moral theory. As it does not address the issue of the origin of moral rules, it does not have to choose between ethical objectivism and ethical subjectivism. Nor does it have to choose between intentions and consequences. Philippa Foot, for example, believes that both are essential for her formulation of virtue theory.[69] The Kantian or Thomist who insists on intentions alone or the utilitarian who looks only to consequences generates strong counterintuitive, even absurd examples. The conflict between moral rationalism and moral voluntarism is also not an issue, especially with Confucians who never thought of making the distinction. Even Aristotle's difference between intellectual and moral virtue has been challenged, at least in Foot's attempts to demonstrate that wisdom is both. Contemporary virtue theorists have proved to be strong allies with those who wish to reconcile the unnecessary and destructive rift between reason and the passions. Ethics should preserve the unity of heart-mind and not perpetuate the conflict between the two.

Virtue ethics has unfortunately been viewed as premodern, conservative, even reactionary. With its focus on individual character development it has also been criticized for its lack of social concern. (When one notes the thoroughly social context of the Confucian self and its obligations, this objection loses much of its force.) Classical liberalism, one of the greatest achievements of modernism, is under increasing criticism for its social atomism and its indifference to cultural values. While the premodern agent is limited by prescribed roles, the modern selves are encouraged to free themselves from them. Conservative critics have rightly pointed out the high personal and social costs that this freedom has has exacted on society as a whole. Some liberal theorists, such as William Galston, have responded to this criticism and they believe that liberalism can meet the challenge. They are calling for a socially engaged self and a rededication to the liberal virtues.[70] Although conservative politicians and theologians have tried to capture virtue ethics as their own, there is nothing in a reconstructed theory that would support either sectarian politics or religion. The proposal that all of us dedicate ourselves to a common ensemble of virtues within the boundaries of the liberal state is well worth our serious consideration.

The modernist ethics of Kant and Mill have become philosophical dead ends, and the deconstructionist critique of these logocentric, dichotomized views offers no moral direction. It is time to think of virtue ethics as a constructive postmodern alternative, and work has already been done on Confucius and the Buddha as anticipating such an ethic. In *Thinking Through Confucius* Hall and Ames have done this for Confucius, and David Kalupahana has alluded to a constructive postmodern interpretation of Buddha ethics. The unity of fact, value, and the aesthetic is a premodern assumption that modern philosophy has torn asunder, but Whitehead's aesthetic cosmology shows that it can be brought back in a constructive postmodern form. With his balance of order and beauty and a strong social self, Whitehead's position is definitely not the anarchic aestheticism that we find in Oscar Wilde or French deconstruction.

Let us now summarize our conclusions. Although his mind–body dualism is a holdover from premodernism, Gandhi is not a premodern primarily because he firmly believes that no individual or culture can take on the *dharma* of another age. Gandhi's modernist sentiments regarding the inviolability of the individual are tempered by an equally strong sense of the unity of humanity and the social construction of personal identity. Most important, however, is Gandhi's rejection of all of modernism's famous distinctions, especially the ones between fact and value and means as separate from ends. Although some evidence of a deconstructive postmodernism may be discerned, Gandhi is best allied with the constructive school of postmodernism.

Chapter 2

Nonviolence in Jainism and Hinduism

I will desist from knowing or intentional destruction of all great lives [souls with two or more senses]. As long as I live, I will neither kill nor cause others to kill. I shall strive to refrain from all such activities, whether of body, speech, or mind.

—Mahāvīra

[Jain] anekāntavāda *is the result of the twin doctrine of satyā and ahiṃsā.*

—M. K. Gandhi

God versus Satan becomes Pure Soul versus Matter. God is Pure Soul. Satan is Pure Matter, the tempter, seducer, deluder and Jailor of the Soul.

—J. L. Jaini

The world of relationship is a world of attachment and aversion. But nonviolence is possible and possible only without interrelationship, because interrelationship is dependent on others and cannot be natural.

—N. D. Bhargava

Whereas [Gandhi's] view of ahiṃsā is based on the philosophy of action, that of the Jains is based on that of renunciation of action.

—A Jain writing to Gandhi

Gandhi's philosophy has usually been interpreted in terms of Jainism and Hinduism, the latter being his own family religion and the former having a profound influence through his friendship with the Jain saint Raichandcharya. The first two sections of this chapter will discuss Gandhi and Jainism and will demonstrate that their views on nonviolence are significantly different from Gandhi's. (Unfortunately, Gandhi and some Jains, such as J. L. Jaini quoted above, share a Manichean concept of body and soul.) In the third section we will see that the Hindus embraced *ahiṃsā* much later than the Jains and proposed significant exceptions to it. The final section will analyze Gandhi's interpretation of the *Bhagavad-gītā* and will remind readers that its view of nonattached action coincides with the Buddhist position.

Absolute Nonviolence in Jainism

Jainism offers us the first and unarguably the most extreme conception of nonviolence. (Commentators who claim that the Upaniṣadic references to *ahiṃsā* antedate Mahāvīra neglect the fact that the Jains have a history in India that is definitely pre-Aryan.) Jain thinkers have an incredible desire to categorize things that one can know and the result with regard to *ahiṃsā* is 432 types of violence, a sum derived by multiplying the sacred numbers $3 \times 3 \times 3 \times 4 \times 4$. Therefore, the restrictions on Jain actions are severe, and the precautions they must take are extraordinary—although the requirements for householders are not as strict. Jain householders may sweep their houses, grind their grain, and store water in jars. They may also protect their crops from pests and kill other persons in self-defense. This means, presumably, that Jains may fight in a just war, although this was done primarily because of political exigencies during the powerful Jain medieval kingdoms. For instance, King Khāravela of Kalinga went to war to recapture a Jain image from the Nandas who ruled Bihar.

Jain monks, however, must sweep the paths before them; they must pluck their hair (for cutting may kill lice); they may not eat after dark; they may not eat or drink anything that has life (fermented drinks, unstrained water, honey, figs, green vegetables or picked fruit); and they may not even use green leaves for serving food. The Jain monk may not dig in the ground, move in the water, light fires, fan the air, or even travel—all out of regard for the living beings residing in the four elements. (For example, the person who eats honey takes on the sin of burning seven villages.)[1] Mahāvīra preached that we may not even dream of killing a living being. In other words, a person is culpable for all injuries, even though they be only dreamed or thought and not yet committed.

The ancient view of a sympathetic continuum in which all things are internally related is one that the new ecological consciousness has rediscovered and affirmed. It also provided the basis for the Jain view of the equality of all souls. In the Jain *Uttaradhyayana Sūtra ahiṃsā* is defined as being "equal-minded to all creatures and regard[ing] them as one's own self. ..."[2] Compared to Hinduism and Buddhism, where there is a hierarchy of consideration (higher-minded creatures have priority over the lower), Jainism attempts to enforce a strict egalitarianism regarding the objects of injurious action. Simply put, every life unit *(jīva)* has equal value. (The exigencies of life force the absolutist Jains to subordinate one-sensed beings when they are exempted from household nonviolence.) Therefore, Jain *ahiṃsā* is based on the equality and universal kinship of all souls.

This egalitarianism is a great Jain achievement, but its philosophical foundations are conflicted. First, every Jain *jīva,* just as every Sāṃkhya *puruṣa,* is distinct and separate from every other, so a Jain cannot, strictly speaking, regard another self as one's "own self." Second, sympathy and reciprocity, along with equality, must be necessary conditions for *ahiṃsā*. Sympathy and reciprocity are possible only in a system of internal relations, in which the terms are dependent upon one another. (If A and B are externally related, neither enters into relations with the other; if A and B are internally related symmetrically, both are dependent upon one another.) Jain atomism, in so far as it pertains to personal salvation, is based on external relations, that is, the possibility of the soul to become completely independent from everything else in the cosmos.

It is problematically ironic that the Jain principle of equal treatment appears to be based on a sympathetic continuum of internal relations, but the Jain principle of liberation requires external relations. A Jain may, theoretically, be able to recognize another soul as equal, but it is difficult to see, given the Jains' insistence on absolute independence of the liberated soul, how souls can be truly sympathetic ("feeling with" is the literal meaning) with one another. In Buddhism and Chinese philosophy, on the other hand, we find that relatedness and interdependence are the very essence of reality, so that there is a near perfect match between ontology and ethics. Interdependence is of course central to Vedānta, but the problem with this view is that individual integrity may be compromised by its all-encompassing monism.

A contemporary Jain philosopher reaffirms the theory of absolute independence and its relation to *ahiṃsā*. N. D. Bhargava argues that *ahiṃsā* must be totally unconditional and unrelational, that its practice is successful only by disengaging from the world of "give and take." Bhargava contends that such a world, based as it is on possession and domination, is necessarily violent. In their practice of *ahiṃsā* Jain saints cannot depend upon the existence of others or the action of others, because nonviolent action is "independent of society." Bhargava states that "the world of relationship is a world of attachment and aversion. But nonviolence is possible and possible only without interrelationship, because interrelationship is dependent on others and cannot be natural."[3] The ultimate implication of Bhargava's position is a reductio ad absurdum: liberated Jain saints are the only ones who can practice nonviolence, but their isolated *lokas* are the only places in the universe where such practice has no meaning at all. Saints in the world, going from town to town for food and teaching, are still presumably in the world of "give and take" and still unable to fulfill the requirements of nonviolence as Bhargava defines it. While Bhargava finds interrelationship unnatural, both Buddhism and Chinese philosophy find it eminently natural.

Given Bhargava's position above it is not surprising that he defends the negative formulation of *ahiṃsā,* as opposed to the Buddha's (and Gandhi's) positive formulation that includes not only noninjury but sympathy, love, and compassion as well. Bhargava's reason is that "if we speak of love, we can [only] think of one form or the other of attachment. . . ."[4] Bhargava is certainly correct about the dangers of self-centered love, but his extreme caution on this point again reveals the radical nature of the Jain approach. By removing the self from its social and ecological relations, one can obviously remove most of the dangers of attachment and the injury that necessarily follows. But one also risks another danger: alienating people from one another and removing the content and meaning of a whole range of virtues that are arguably more important than *ahiṃsā* itself. With its flexibility and this-worldly emphasis, Gandhi's view of nonviolence is definitely more like the Buddhists. Gandhi believed that *ahiṃsā* without compassion is nothing, just as gold is an amorphous material without the goldsmith's artistic shape or the root is nothing without the magnificent tree.[5]

Gandhi and Jainism

The influence of Jainism on Gandhi was not as great as he or others have claimed. Stephen Hay's claim that Gandhi learned the importance of spiritual self-purification from Jainism is not convincing.[6] This goal is of course one that is common to the major religions of India. Gandhi's decision, on several occasions, to fast unto death, given its political motivations, is very different from the exclusively spiritual goal of the Jain fast-death *(sallekhanā).* In a letter to Gandhi, a Jain phrased the difference very aptly: "Whereas your view of *ahiṃsā* is based on the philosophy of action, that of the Jains is based on that of renunciation of action."[7] Gandhi responded, following the *karma yoga* of the *Bhagavad-gītā*, by saying that he had melded renunciation and action into one force. Anticipating the argument of chapter 4, George Kotturan claims that this is the equivalent of Gandhi's following the Buddha in integrating *ahiṃsā* "into a comprehensive world-affirming ethic."[8]

One might attribute this difference between Gandhi and the Jains to contrasting concepts of self: the isolation of the Jain self versus the relational and other-regarding elements of Gandhi's Buddhist-like compassion. Spiritual suicide would constitute the ultimate release of the Jain *jīva* from the corrupting influences of matter. Although we have seen that Gandhi is sympathetic to this view, we would prefer that he take a Buddhist position on this issue. Also Gandhi rationalizes self-injury as the Jains do: "Suffering injury in one's own person is...the essence of nonviolence and is the chosen substitute for violence to others."[9] Because of a nonsubstantial, dynamic, and somatic view of the self, a Buddhist would learn not to crave a pure self free from matter and would be more concerned about the karmic effects of suicide as the ultimate violence to the self. (For the Buddha the craving for an immortal self is far more serious than any sensual craving.) Incidentally, the fact that some Jains justify *sallekhanā* because one is reborn a god stands in tension with their criticism of Hindus who support animal sacrifice for the same reason. Furthermore, ethical consequentialism also plays a role in the Jain's belief that the suffering involved in *sallekhanā* burns away all karmic debt.[10]

In a response to queries about apparent inconsistencies—for example, holding to *advaita* and *dvaita* at the same time—Gandhi answered that he believed in Jain view of the many-sidedness *(anekāntavāda)* of reality, and that his "*anekāntavāda* is the result of the twin doctrine of *satyā* and *ahiṃsā*."[11] If one thinks of Gandhi's view of relative truth and how this would preclude one from thinking ill of others with differing beliefs, then the alliance with Jain *anekāntavāda* is a natural one. In the same passage Gandhi continues, "Formerly I used to resent the ignorance of my opponents. Today I can love them because I am gifted with the eye to see myself as others see me and vice versa." The Buddhist philosopher Śāntideva makes a similar point when he insists that we should always respect our enemies, even when they do us harm. Drawing on Śāntideva the Dalai Lama concludes that "tolerance can be learned only from an enemy; it cannot be learned from your guru."[12] From our opponents we learn that they have afflicted emotions just as we do and we should make a distinction between persons, who are all one and blameless in the Dharmakāya, and their blameworthy actions.

Ironically, *anekāntavāda* does not seem to have prevented Jains from holding a rather one-sided dualism, from imputing perfect knowledge to their Tīrthaṇkaras, and giving absolute value to *ahiṃsā*. This famous doctrine of many-sidedness—contrasted with the "one-sided" *(ekānta)* views of Vedānta and Sāṃkhya—is dramatically expressed in the story of the partial knowledge that five blind men have of an elephant. It is clear, however, that the omniscient Jinas are no longer blind, because they now know all aspects of all things at once. Even at the fourth level of a fourteen-stage spiritual practice, the Jain monk is "like a person born blind who sees the world for the first time on the sudden acquisition of eyesight, so the soul now sees the truth."[13] The epistemological mode of *anekāntavāda* is no longer operational, because at this stage, as P. S. Jaini states, the monk has an "absolutely undistorted view of reality."[14]

Surprisingly, P. S. Jaini offers a strong disclaimer on the point of epistemological tolerance in Jainism: "This practice *[anekāntavāda]* probably does not really increase tolerance of others' views; nevertheless it has generated a very well-informed (if not always valid) sort of criticism."[15] In a very sympathetic appraisal of Jainism, Christopher Chapple describes Jainism as a friendly form of religious fundamentalism, in which Jains are firmly committed to their own views and have no intention of ever changing them. At the same time *anekāntavāda* allows them to be tolerant of other views, which are seen as "incomplete" rather than "incorrect."[16] (The Jains' resistance to accepting other views is most likely the principal reason why Jainism survived in India, whereas Buddhists allowed far too much syncretism with Hinduism.) In stark contrast to these views, Gandhi is tolerant to the point of incoherence, sometimes stating that all religions are true and expressing his desire to convert to Islam or Buddhism—even though he found his own Hinduism good enough for his personal and political purposes.

Gandhi's view of the self is an interesting amalgam of the Socratic *daimon*, the Jain *jīva*, and the Upaniṣadic *ātman*. Unlike the Jains, the Vedantist Gandhi viewed the ideal self as inextricably bound up in its relations with others and society. But Jain individualism, most likely learned from Raichandcharya, may have persuaded Gandhi to revise Vedānta in a significant way. (Gandhi claimed that Raichand, a diamond merchant and early intellectual friend, was just as much an influence on him as Tolstoy and Ruskin.) Although nominally a Jain and taken by some even to be the twenty fifth Tīrthaṇkara (even Raichand indulged the thought), Raichand's view of the soul is much like Gandhi's: a mix of Jainism, Vedānta, and Vaiṣṇavism. The Raichand connection alerts us not to think of Advaita Vedānta every time Gandhi uses the word *ātman*. When Gandhi says that "*ātman* can be liberated only by itself," D. K. Bedekar is convinced that, because of Raichand's view that *ātman* is the individual Jain *jīva,* this statement could be read as, "[T]rue autonomy of the human spirit can only be attained by the human mind which breaks through snares and repressions."[17] Gandhi and Raichand parted ways on the question of social involvement, with Raichand advocating and living strict disengagement from the world. The influence of Raichand can help us appreciate, but not condone, Gandhi's relative ease in affirming both individualism and pantheism at the same time.

When Bhargava states that *ahiṃsā* is "the intrinsic nature of man," he seems to imply that *ahiṃsā* has absolute value. Gandhi appears to agree with Bhargava when he writes, in the words of Vedānta, that "*ahiṃsā* is the very nature of the *ātman*."[18] More frequently, however, he implies that *ahiṃsā* is a virtue that must be attained, and he claims that it is a means to a higher end, usually Truth or God.[19] In his interpretation of the *Gītā,* Gandhi connects *ahiṃsā* with selfless action *(anasakti),* and *ahiṃsā* is "a necessary preliminary...included in...[but] does not go beyond" *anasakti.*[20] Resisting the natural temptation to absolutize it, Gandhi has ascertained the proper place of *ahiṃsā* among the virtues. *Ahiṃsā* begins in self-restraint, self-purification, and selflessness and ends in love and compassion.

Making *ahiṃsā* a disposition rather than the essence of the soul preserves the essential element of freedom. Gandhi frequently spoke of the animal side of human nature, and how one must struggle to choose violence over nonviolence. If we are nonviolent by nature, then we cannot be praised for choosing peaceful actions. On the other hand, we cannot be completely devoid of a disposition for noninjury, for, as Gandhi says, "means to be means [they] must always be within our reach."[21] The language of "means within our reach" is support for the developmental view of the virtues that this book supports, as opposed to the recovery model of Jainism and Vedānta where a naturally nonviolent soul is recovered by spiritual practice. Furthermore, Gandhi frequently reminds us that true *ahiṃsā* towards an attacker must combine physical nonretaliation with love and compassion. (In other words, mere passivity without the proper disposition is not necessarily *ahiṃsā.*) Therefore, *ahiṃsā* appears to be a means to the end of the spiritual life, not an end in itself. The true proponent of nonviolence would hold, according to this view, that only Truth (in the sense of being true to yourself and your situation) has intrinsic value, and *ahiṃsā* is the principal means to Truth. (Incidentally, for Gandhi life is not the highest value because people should sacrifice their lives in the face of an aggressor, especially if it is to preserve their honor.) Emphasizing Gandhi's principle of the interchangeability of means and ends in chapter 7, we will finally reject the view that *ahiṃsā* is merely an enabling virtue.

Relative Nonviolence in Hinduism

We will characterize Hindu nonviolence as relative for a number of reasons: (1) the prohibition against killing is relative to the person, yogis and brahmins taking the vow most strictly; (2) it is also relative to the occasion, such as killing in war, in self-defense, and in sacrifice; and (3) it is relative to individual self-interest. Concerning the second reason, there is an interesting exception: one may not kill a brahmin even if he is attacking you. Regarding the third reason, the motivation for *ahiṃsā* is most important and it appears to be related to human security and eventually human salvation. Uno Tähtinen explains: "Ascetics may not have applied *ahiṃsā* basically because of the good of other beings, but because of their own spiritual good. Violence, even when socially pragmatic, is an expression of bad or mixed motives which harm the doer himself."[22] Tähntinen further explains that ordinary Aryans were more concerned about the violation of property, and bartered with the gods for power, cattle, and protection. This means that Vedic peoples conceived of nonviolence primarily in an instrumental way. The Aryans realized a simple truth: overwrought desires lead to injury and death and this affects everyone. The concept of *dharma* was valued because it controlled desires and in this way later Hindu texts could extol *ahiṃsā* as the essence of *dharma*.

Brian K. Smith claims that "the Vedic texts do not know the *ahiṃsā* doctrine."[23] Wendy Doniger joins Smith in rejecting the hypothesis that a preference for nonviolence grew in Vedic society because the priests became increasingly sensitive to the harm done to sacrificial animals. If it is true that even the Vaiṣṇavas did not give up animal sacrifice until the fifth century C.E.,[24] this is a very long time to decide not to cause pain to animals. (Animal sacrifice continues even today in goddess worship in Bengal and Nepal.) Indeed, there existed a very powerful rationale for understanding the violence of the sacrifice as the highest form of spiritual noninjury. The *Laws of Manu* argue that animal sacrifice is actually *ahiṃsā* because it represents the most sacred act.[25] More literally, the victim becomes divine: by paying the highest price, it is elevated to the highest level. This explanation makes most sense if we think of the original sacrifices as human beings and see the Vedic Puruṣa hymn as a poetic echo of those earliest times.

Most scholars believe that *ahiṃsā* is not mentioned in the Hindu texts until the Upaniṣads, where in the *Chāndogya* it is stated, "Mortification, the giving of alms, uprightness, refusal to do harm *(ahiṃsā)*, truthfulness—there are one's gifts to the priests"; and "he who has concentrated all his faculties on *ātman*, taking care to hurt no living things except in sacrifice...will reach the Brahman-world and will not return again."[26] Several points suggest themselves here: (1) the exception for the killing of sacrificial animals; (2) the fact that *ahiṃsā* is listed among principal virtues; (3) that truthfulness, Gandhi's highest value, is among those virtues; and (4) that meditation on the universal self is crucial to the perfection of *ahiṃsā* and the achievement of *mokṣa*. We have already seen that Gandhi has a rather eccentric view of *ātman* and one of the principal tasks of this book is to propose that Gandhians choose a Buddhist self for the ethics of nonviolence.

The nonsectarian *Kural*, sometimes called the Tamil Veda, is especially significant with regard to *ahiṃsā* and related issues. Dating from approximately 200 C.E., it demands strict vegetarianism and absolute noninjury, as well as having the most positive view of women in any Indian scripture. Interestingly enough, it contains criticism of Buddhist meat eating, and it also declares that forgiveness is a higher virtue than retaliation, and forgetting the infraction is even higher than forgiveness.[27] Only by forgiving and forgetting can a person become truly nonviolent. Even though it is a late text, the *Kural* may well preserve many pre-Aryan doctrines that are similar to Jainism. This further strengthens the thesis that Indian nonviolence is an indigenous principle.

Ahiṃsā as the "supreme virtue" *(paradharma),* as the "supreme happiness" *(parasukha),* or as the "highest dharma" *(ahiṃsā parmo* dharma*)* are phrases found frequently in the epic literature and the Purāṇas.[28] (The fact that *ahiṃsā* is related to happiness is relevant to our attempt, in chapters 8 and 9, to make the ethics of nonviolence a form of eudaimonism.) The word *ahiṃsā* appears in the *Bhagavad-gītā* only four times, listed among the cardinal virtues, and what is most curious is that it does not rank as supreme or ultimate. One might say that this should not be surprising given the fact that the setting of the work is a brutal fratricidal war that resulted in horrendous casualties. Furthermore, the *Mahābhārata* describes battles that did not at all follow the Hindu rules for a just war. Appealing to these laws, Kuru Karna, for example, begs Arjuna to allow him to pull his chariot out of the mud. Kṛṣṇa, however, commands him to attack before Karna can do so. Given the fact that the *Gītā* was Gandhi's favorite scripture, this raises important issues about his interpretation of this famous text.

Gandhi's View of the *Bhagavad-gītā*

For some time there has been a growing consensus that the traditional Advaitin reading of the *Gītā* is not well supported. Instead, the *Gītā* is the continuation of a strong tradition of personal theism that began with the Vedas, continued in the Upaniṣads, and culminated in the Epics and the Purāṇas. Anyone who has visited India realizes very quickly that no Indian worships a qualityless Brahman, just as no Greek or Thomist ever prayed to Aristotle's unmoved mover. Returning from their university offices every day, even most Hindu philosophers pay their respects at their local temples and family shrines, following in the footsteps of their Vaiṣṇava or Śaivite forefathers. Gandhi was no exception to this venerable Indian tradition and it is well known that Rāma was the personal name of God by which he communed with the ultimate.

Many of the Upaniṣads begin with invocations to the major deities, including a prayer to Viṣṇu in the *Māndūkhya,* the only Upaniṣad with the famous word *advaita* in it. Most commentators have now rejected Śaṇkara's reading of the crucial word *prasada* as a yogic "calming of the senses" in favor of the self receiving the "grace of the Ordainer" in the *Katha* and *Muṇdaka* Upaniṣads. In addition to a doctrine of grace in these texts there is also a doctrine of election: "By Him alone can He be won whom He elects."[29] The personal term *puruṣa* is used to name the highest reality, even beyond Brahman itself, something the *Gītā* does consistently. In the *Śvetāśvatāra* we find a "Blessed Lord" (identified as Śiva) higher than Brahman: "I know that mighty Person...beyond Him is nothing whatsoever, no other thing...the One, the Person, this whole universe full filling!"[30]

It is in Kṛṣṇa, however, that the ultimate expression of the *puruṣa* motif is conceived. Kṛṣṇa makes explicit his connection with the Vedic tradition: "Through all the Vedas it is I that should be known, for the Maker of the Veda's end am I...."; and "so am I extolled in Vedic speech as...the 'Person All-Sublime.' "[31] Kṛṣṇa declares himself "God of gods" and the "beginning of the gods"; and he transcends them so much that they are not allowed to see Kṛṣṇa's unmanifest form.[32] Kṛṣṇa also reiterates the subordination of Brahman to the Puruṣa, which we have already seen in the Upaniṣads: "Great Brahman is to Me a womb, in it I plant the seed: from this derives the origin of all contingent beings"; and "I am the base supporting Brahman...."[33] (Note not only the subordination of Brahman but also its feminization.) R. C. Zaehner states that Kṛṣṇa "transcends the immortal Brahman as much as He transcends the phenomenal world."[34] Both Zaehner and Robert Minor are determined to reject a nondualistic interpretation which would dissolve all selves into the one divine self.[35] What we have then is a relation of Kṛṣṇa to individual selves much like, with the major exception of *bhakti* intimacy, the relation of the Lord Īśvara and autonomous *puruṣas* of Sāṃkhya-Yoga.

The foregoing reading of the *Gītā* serves Gandhi very well in terms of embracing personal theism and preserving the integrity of the individual self. But what is most controversial about Gandhi's *Gītā* is his allegorical interpretation of the battle itself. One of the strongest supports for Gandhi's approach is the unrealistic juxtaposition of battlefield and philosophical discussion, a tension that can be resolved nicely by saying that the human soul is the actual focus of the battle. The key to reading Gandhi's *Gītā* lies in Kṛṣṇa's speech at the end of chapter 2. Gandhi plays the original Sāṃkhya dualism of these passages for all their allegorical worth. (When Gandhi says that Duryodhana and his men "stand for the Satanic impulses in us" or the "*Gītā* distinguishes between the powers of light and darkness and demonstrates their incompatibility,"[36] Gandhi has gone beyond dualism to Manicheanism.) Gandhi contends that Kṛṣṇa exhorts us to kill the passions in order to have peace of mind rather than killing our brothers for military victory. The sixty-first verse must have especially inspired Gandhi: "Then let him sit, curbing them all, integrated and intent on Me: for firm established is the man's wisdom whose sense are subdued." Given this clear spiritual psychology, it is impossible to read the *Gītā* as recommending violence. As Gandhi states, "Violence is simply not possible unless one is driven by anger, by ignorant love and by hatred. The *Gītā*, on the other hand, wants us to be incapable of anger...."[37] The destructive effects of anger is the one of the most fundamental aspects of Buddhist psychology.

A closer reading of Gandhi's interpretation of the *Gītā* shows that he also allows a literal reading of the text. Gandhi paraphrases Kṛṣṇa's advise to Arjuna in this way: "You have already committed violence. By talking now like a wise man, you will not learn nonviolence. Having started on this course, you must finish the job." Gandhi then uses the example of a person committing himself to a train trip, deciding midway not to continue, and then foolishly jumping off the train. Gandhi then reiterates one of his basic principles, that it is worse to be a coward than to commit violence. True Hindu *dharma* "does not under any circumstances countenance running away in fear. In this world that baffles our reason, violence there will then always be."[38] Gandhi is essentially conceding the point that the *Gītā* may indeed be an account of a battle in which Arjuna's duty is to fight his cousins or be condemned as a coward.

One does not have to accept Gandhi's allegorical approach in order to agree with his basic ethical theses about the *Gītā,* which are actually rather noncontroversial. Arjuna's *karma yoga* consists in not a renunciation of action but only the rejection of the fruits of action. What Gandhi draws from the *Gītā* is a basic philosophy of active nonattachment. Gandhi states that the "unmistakable teaching of the *Gītā*" is that "he who gives up action falls. He who gives up only the reward rises."[39] Furthermore, Gandhi maintains that the *Gītā*'s *karma yoga* is committed to this-worldly human welfare as well as spiritual liberation. He believes that the text is firm on this point: "So, unattached, should the wise man do, longing to bring about the welfare of the world."[40] What emerges from this short analysis is significant for the purposes of this book. What we have in the *Gītā* is the Hindu equivalent of the Buddha's Middle Way, between the extremes of active attachment and craving and passive nonattachment. (Some scholars are in fact convinced that the writers of the *Gītā* had Buddhism clearly in mind.)

Although he seriously considered embracing another religious tradition, Gandhi remained within his own Hindu faith and decided to tie his ethics to the *Gītā* as the essence of this tradition. We have seen, however, that Gandhi's view of nonviolence is not at all relative in the Hindu sense as we have defined it above. He agreed with the Jains that the vow of *ahiṃsā* is absolute, but he disagreed with them in that the exigencies of daily life force us to break that vow much more often than the Jains would ever allow. As we shall see in chapter 4, Gandhi is much closer to Buddhist pragmatism on these issues. We have, therefore, set the stage for a Buddhist interpretation of Gandhi's ethics of nonviolence. Before we continue that work in chapter 4, we must discuss the Vedāntist Gandhi in the next chapter.

Chapter 3

Vedānta, *Ātman*, and Gandhi

> *I believe in the rock-bottom doctrine of Advaita and my interpretation of Advaita excludes totally any idea of superiority at any state whatsoever. I believe implicitly that all men are born equal. All...have the same soul as any other.*
>
> —M. K. Gandhi

> *Individuality is and is not even as each drop in the ocean is an individual and is not. It is not because apart from the ocean it has no existence. It is because the ocean has no existence if the drop has not, i.e., has no individuality. They are beautifully interdependent. And if this is true of the physical law, how much more so of the spiritual world!*
>
> —M. K. Gandhi

> *Gandhi had no truck with the* māyā *doctrine. ... We are not called to a higher state of consciousness where the mesh of* māyā *will disappear.*
>
> —Margaret Chatterjee

Gandhi's commitment to individual autonomy was so strong that he unfortunately resisted the relational and social self he found in Hegel and Marx, a view shared by Confucius and the Buddha and confirmed and reformulated by twentieth-century thinkers as diverse as George Herbert Mead, Martin Heidegger, Maurice Merleau-Ponty, and Martin Buber. It is truly ironic that the loss of individual freedom that Gandhi feared in Hegel is immeasurably greater in Vedānta and especially the Advaita Vedānta with which major commentators associate him. In this chapter I discuss two of those thinkers—Bhikhu Parekh and Ramashray Roy—and critique their positions in the first two sections. In the last section I analyze Gandhi's "drop in the ocean" analogy, and I propose that an organic analogy would better support his belief in a reformed caste system and his view that individual self-realization is prior to the salvation of the whole.

Bhikhu Parekh's Advaitin Gandhi

It is common to interpret Gandhi in terms of Vedāntist philosophy, especially the dominant school of Advaita Vedānta. Gandhi's several references to a qualityless absolute and two equivocal affirmations of the principle of *advaita* offer some support for this view.[1] The Advaitin interpretation offers a solution to the basic puzzle about Gandhi's self-suffering. The principle of nondualism allows Gandhi to see the sin of the other as his own sin, because in reality there is no distinction between him and others, between the I and the Thou.

Gandhi declares allegiance to Advaita Vedānta, but he interprets it to mean simply the unity of God and humans: "I believe in the rock-bottom doctrine of Advaita and my interpretation of Advaita excludes totally any idea of superiority at any state whatsoever. I believe implicitly that all men are born equal. All...have the same soul as any other."[2] Gandhi extends this unity to "all that lives,"[3] which is a general Indian philosophical truth, not just an Advaitin doctrine. For all forms of Vedānta everything in the universe contains *ātman,* and "*ahiṃsā* is the very nature of *ātman,*" so Gandhian nonviolence is not only ecological, but also cosmic in scope. Gandhi's pantheism, rejecting as it does the concept of *māyā* as illusion, resacralizes the world, while Śaṅkara's transcendental monism (or more correctly a dualism, as we shall see) desacralizes it.

The best evidence for the Advaitin reading of Gandhi is the following passage: "I believe in [the] absolute oneness of God and therefore also of humanity. ... We have but one soul. The rays of the sun are many through refraction. But they have the same source. I cannot detach myself from the wickedest soul (nor may I be denied identity with the most virtuous). ... I must involve in my experience the whole of my kind."[4] I contend that we must qualify the implications of this passage both in terms of its moral implications and in terms of a coherent interpretation of Gandhi's philosophy. The Advaitin solution completely undermines the basic moral implications of the law of karma. If there is truly just one soul, one Ātman identical to Brahman, then individual moral responsibility is rendered unintelligible. Gandhi once stated that he supports the motto *brahma satyam jaganmithya*

("Brahman is real [and] this world is unreal"[5]) but this again is not consistent with his political activism and his general neo-Vedāntist commitment to the reality of the world.

Instead of the Advaitin model of total undifferentiated unity, I suggest that these passages be interpreted in terms of organic analogies. Organic holism has the distinct advantage over absolute monism in that it maintains the reality of the individual (on the analogue of the integral living cell) while at the some time making collective responsibility intelligible as well. In the last section I have reformulated Gandhi's refraction analogy so that it gives the equal weight to the unity and individuality that we find in Gandhi's writings. Although he supports the Advaitin reading, Serendra Verma realizes where Gandhi's real position lies: "Judged from the canons of nondualistic philosophy it may not seem to be logical, but Gandhi for all practical purposes observes a distinction between the individual soul and God to respect the religious need of the human heart which, it appears, proves stronger for him than the logical reasoning of philosophy."[6] As opposed to Verma's nondualism, I maintain that both logic and experience firmly support Gandhi's commitment to integral selfhood.

The problems of consistently maintaining an Advaitin Gandhi manifest themselves most clearly in Bhikhu Parekh's otherwise excellent book *Gandhi's Political Philosophy*. After summarizing basic Indian philosophy he claims that Gandhi, just as Śaṅkara, envisioned a two-tiered religion of a personal theism focusing on Śiva, Viṣṇu, Devī, and an impersonal monism of Ātman-Brahman. People in the second tier would recognize the illusion of individual self and consciousness, would eventually put the phenomenal world behind them, and would move from the worship of individual deities to experience the total unity of Ātman-Brahman. Gandhi must object already at this point, because he wavered between personal theism and impersonal monism and never claimed that one was superior to the other. And he certainly did not believe that individual consciousness was an illusion.

More problems arise with Parekh's interpretation, especially with regard to Gandhi's political activism and the dynamic and engaged individualism that such a view requires. There is indeed a tension in Gandhi between the ascetic and mystic Gandhi, who, as Parekh shows,[7] has difficulty justifying, from an Advaitin standpoint, the feeling of, let alone need for love, and the activist Gandhi, who is committed to moral autonomy, love, compassion, and justice. But nowhere in Gandhi's voluminous works does he indicate that the individual self is an illusion. Gandhi's thoughts range from the self's complete autonomy, where he has come under the powerful influences that he admits the Euro-American tradition had on him, to a relational, social self that has an organic relation with society and the cosmos as a whole.

Parekh cannot support both an Advaitin Gandhi and the Gandhi who exhorts individuals to conform to their own historical-cultural truths. Recall from chapter 1 the "distinctively human powers" that Parekh sees as a requirement for Gandhi's political philosophy. In addition to conforming to personal truth, three of the five—self-determination, autonomy, and self-knowledge—can have no reality in Advaita Vedānta.

Ramashray Roy's Nondual Gandhi

In his book *Self and Society: A Study in Gandhian Thought*, Ramashray Roy uses the Catholic philosopher Jacques Maritain to elucidate Gandhi's concept of self. Roy's exposition is clear and insightful and he introduces the concept of the relational self very effectively. Here is a sample of Roy's summary of Maritain's view: "[Maritain] considers freedom as self-activity, autonomy and transcendence of objective determination in which the conception of community happens to be an integral part of the human psyche and therefore individuality and sociality become mutually supportive."[8] Roy also interprets Gandhi as an Advaitin, so it is problematic for him to say that "Gandhi's conception of the self is no different from Maritain's concept of person."[9] Gandhi's position should have been more like Maritain's, but most texts reveal a radical individualism at odds with Maritain or a pantheism that swallows up the individual.

As we have seen, Gandhi does not have a consistent view of the self. It ranges from a strict individualism, perhaps inspired by Socrates and Thoreau, to a Vedāntist pantheism in which individual autonomy is not very well supported. I believe that it best to situate Gandhi somewhere in between and I call this position "organic holism." Roy correctly maintains that Gandhi preserves the "primacy of the individual."[10] (Gandhi's statement that "corporate growth is therefore entirely dependent upon individual growth" is one of the best texts for this point.)[11] This means that no commentator can succeed in any attempt to interpret Gandhi as an Advaitin, the Vedāntist school that deemphasizes the individual the most.

In an earlier book, *Gandhi: Soundings in Political Philosophy,* Roy correctly describes Gandhi's philosophy as an "organismic vision" that involves "the necessity of harmonizing oneself with an ever-enlarging network of relationships.... Thus this extended self becomes the ground for sociality. Society then turns out to be a network of extended selves rather than a mechanical aggregate of enclosed selves or an all-consuming totality of a fictional abstraction."[12] This is an eloquent and precise account of what I mean by the "relational self," and it most closely resembles the Confucian self, a connection that we shall pursue in chapter 7.

The Vedāntist Gandhi is a pantheist concerning the relationship of God and the world. The Advaitin, as John White has reminded us,[13] is not a pantheist, but a transcendental monist. For a pantheist God and the world are identical, but an Advaitin believes that Brahman completely transcends a fully derivative and separate world. Like a good pantheist, Gandhi constantly identifies God, the world, and life, and he does not believe that the world is unreal. He instinctively realized how incompatible such a view would be for his activist philosophy of nonviolence. If the world of constant change and social engagement is ultimately an illusion, Gandhi's dynamic *ahiṃsā* cannot find support in Advaita Vedānta. Some commentators have used term *māyā* to describe the illusion of the social distinctions that Gandhi wanted to dissolve,[14] but the Advaitin of course insists that all metaphysical plurality, distinctions that Gandhi never rejected, is an illusion.

Commentators on Indian philosophy are not always clear in distinguishing between the organic holism of the Upaniṣads and the absolute monism of Śaṅkara. There is a significant contrast between seeing the cosmos as a dream-like appearance (Śaṅkara) and the cosmos as the very body of the Godhead (Rāmānuja). Lance Nelson contends that Advaita Vedānta achieves its non-duality "exclusively not inclusively" such that disunity rather than unity with the world is the result. Citing Śaṅkara's writings directly, Nelson shows that the Advaitin imputes no value whatsoever to the natural world and by implication to the social world as well.[15] This is the only logical conclusion of a view that holds that our perception of the rich web of existence is the result of *avidyā.* Organic holism recognizes the reality of individuals and their complex relations while the Advaitin rejects it as at most only derivative.

Roy's chapter "Ātman versus the Self" contains a long, technical discussion of Advaita Vedānta, but he fails to connect it in any meaningful way to Gandhi, who rarely if ever employed these terms. Gandhi used the term *advaita* very loosely to mean the unity of humanity and reality and used the term *dvaita* to affirm the real plurality of individuals. It is puzzling that Roy does not respond to those scholars, such as Glyn Richards, who have correctly placed Gandhi among the neo-Vedāntists, not the Advaitins.[16] Margaret Chatterjee puts Gandhi's differences with Advaita Vedānta in bold relief: "Gandhi had no truck with the *māyā* doctrine.... We are not called to a higher state of consciousness where the mesh of *māyā* will disappear."[17] The translator of Gandhi's commentary on the *Gītā,* whose strong personal theism, as we have seen, has never been conducive to an Advaitin reading, renders *māyā* as "divine power," not as "illusion," and other translators of Hindu scriptures such as R. C. Zaehner also agree that the word "illusion" is misleading.[18]

Roy's proposed solution to the fragmentation of modern selfhood is a return to *ātman* as the proper ground for human agency. As our divine center, *ātman* is the principle that enables us to discipline the passions and center our lives on the things that really matter. The fact that Roy does some very instructive comparative analysis with Plato should remind any student of philosophy that there are standard, and many say persuasive, arguments against this concept of self. For instance, if *ātman* is the same in literally every thing, how can it be the basis for individual agency?

In response Roy claims that universal *ātman* is particularised as individual *ātmans,* just as the neo-Platonic world soul is instantiated as many *psychēs*. How is this possible and how does one make this intelligible? How do these spiritual selves interact with the nonspiritual? How can a pure soul carry karmic debt from one life to another? How, if Śaṅkara is correct, can the world exist for the ignorant ones, but at the very same time not exist for saints who experience the total unity of Ātman-Brahman? Following Śaṅkara's logic further, is the liberated one a spiritual Titan, that is, actually greater than Īśvara the Creator? Īśvara is inextricably linked to the phenomenal world as long as ignorance exists, so many saints will be enjoying total bliss long before God himself.[19] To my knowledge no one has ever given satisfactory answers to these questions. Saying that there is no world, no karma, no individual agency, and so forth does not count as an acceptable answer. Personal agency is, after all, what we are trying to explain.

In a very insightful analysis, D. K. Bedekar suggests that Gandhi attempted to escape the "the unbreakable spell" of Vedānta and he points out subtle nuances in the Gujarati text of his autobiography that show that Gandhi was very much committed to salvaging individual agency, engagement, and uniquely personal truths.[20] He argues that Gandhi deliberately avoids the word *ātman,* and instead uses *antarātman* for his authoritative inner self. Bedekar offers his own translation from Gandhi's autobiography: "But so long as I have not directly experienced this truth, till then that which my inner self *(antarātman)* counts as true, that which is only conceived by me as true, will be counted by me as my support, my beacon, as the foundation for the course of my life."[21] This passage, besides confirming conscience as the highest authority, also reveals a corollary maxim: as absolute truth is not available to humans, we must act on the finite truth we find in ourselves. It also supports the contextual pragmatism that will be central to the constructive postmodern ethics of this book. Therefore, Vedāntist metaphysics cannot possibly serve as an adequate foundation for Gandhi's philosophy. As an alternative, chapter 5 will demonstrate that Gandhi's empirical search for truth is very similar to the Buddha's search for Dharma.

Roy proposes that it is a mistake to conceive of *ātman* as a substance, and that is presumably why he prefers to refer to it as a principle and sometimes as a potential. In both Asian and European philosophy, substances are defined as those things that are self-existent, self-contained, independent, eternal, and immutable. Aristotle's prime matter, Plato's forms, the Christian

God, the Jain *jīva,* Vedānta's Ātman-Brahman, Mahāyāna's Dharmakāya, and Śāṃkhya's *puruṣa* and *prakṛti* are all substances according to this standard definition. I believe that Roy is wrong in claiming that *ātman* is simply a principle or only a potential. Aristotle's prime matter is actualized by form, but Ātman-Brahman is always complete, actual, and perfect reality. To claim that it is less than that simply does not do justice to either the Upaniṣads or general Vedāntist tradition.

Roy states that Gandhi's commitment to Advaita Vedānta allows him to have "a sense of relatedness with other determinate beings...which, in turn, manifests itself in compassion, the ability to be affected by the suffering of others."[22] The problem with this statement is that Śaṅkara believed that relations and determinations are ultimately unreal, which means that suffering is also illusory. Most forms of pantheism, especially the personalistic panentheism of Rāmānuja and process philosophy, do affirm real differences within a unitary cosmos. Given Gandhi's love for the *Bhagavad-gītā,* and the fact that it does support the plurality of souls and embodies a strong personal theism, he should have preferred this view over Advaita Vedānta.

The concept of a permanent self underlying the phenomenal self is one idea that Gandhi does sometimes appropriate from the Upaniṣadic tradition. ("Everything is transient, except the *ātman.*")[23] Roy supports this view of self in his retelling, from the *Panchatantra,* of the parable of the tiger cub.[24] One day a tiger, while planning an attack on a herd of goats, sees a tiger cub among them. The tiger takes the cub to a pond so that he can see in his own reflection that he is not a goat. After some adjustment the tiger cub eventually realizes his true predatory nature. Even though brought into the greatest dramatic relief by this story, Roy does not seem to realize the negative implications of the permanent self for the practice of *ahiṃsā.* He should have used recent experiments that have shown that aggressive monkeys, raised from birth with pacifist monkeys, learn the nonviolent behavior of their adopted parents and siblings.[25]

After explaining this story in terms of the unchanging *ātman,* Roy inexplicably turns to Gandhi's view that, although we have an animal nature, we can tap our spiritual natures and learn to become nonviolent. Interestingly enough, Gandhi uses the same story (substituting a lion for the tiger and sheep for goats), but he clearly distinguishes animals from humans, created in the image of God, who are free and obligated to change their animal natures.[26] Ironically, the tiger cub story is not compatible with any of the Indian selves, because the spiritually pure and empty *ātman, jīva,* and *puruṣa* are, strictly speaking, neither predatory nor nonpredatory. In a response, Roy chides me for being unable to distinguish between analogy and metaphor.[27] The relation of the cub's unchanging nature to his violent actions is obviously not analogous to our changing nature's capacity to turn away from violence. If the story is a metaphor for realizing our own unchanging natures, then it fails to convey Gandhi's point about our ability to change. If the story is simply a metaphor for self-realization, then the point is very weak indeed.

One of the most momentous discoveries in modern social thought—beginning with Marx, culminating in Sartre, and confirmed in studies of feral children—is that human beings have no "nature." (This is "no nature" in the sense of nonsubstantiality and potentiality, not in the sense of a fully actualized but empty spiritual substance.) In their concepts of no-self *(anātma)* and no-substance *(anitya),* Buddhists anticipated this revolutionary insight. Studies of feral children have shown that the so-called human essence is so malleable and so vulnerable that children raised without the benefit of parents and normal socialization are reduced to a state, sadly enough, lower than most animals. All things being equal, weaned puppies and kittens grow up to be well functioning cats and dogs, but a weaned child left completely to its own devices descends into an abyss of sensory deprivation and debilitating dysfunction. Such evidence supports a dynamic view of the self found primarily in Buddhism and process philosophy.

Metaphors of Self and World

Gandhi elucidated his pantheism with a beautifully expressed "drop in the ocean" analogy that introduces this chapter. Let us look at a similar passage before assessing the merits of this analogy for the self-world problem: "The ocean is composed of drops of water; each drop is an entity and yet it is a part of the whole; 'the one and the many.' In this ocean of life, we are little drops. My doctrine means that I must identify myself with life...that I must share the majesty of life in the presence of God. The sum-total of this life is God."[28] This last sentence identifying God and life, something that Śaṅkara never did, is the most succinct statement of Gandhian pantheism. Gandhi is certainly not the first to use water analogies to explain pantheism, so the criticism that follows is not solely directed at him.

The positive element of Gandhi's analogy is that he attempts to uphold individuation. Gandhi instinctively knew that political activism without individual agency is simply not possible. It is also true that any body of water is made of individual, but interdependent, molecules of water that offer a rough analogue of a community of persons. The problem is that individual water molecules are not perceptible, so the individual is still hidden in the whole. Except for rain storms and turbulent seas, separate individuation of the sort that persons experience in society is not found in water drops. Finally, if the analogue of the ideal state is a perfectly calm sea, there would be no significant differentiation at all. This analogy ultimately fails, for it does not present enough differentiation or qualitative difference. Gandhi is certainly correct to say that "the drop also has the essence of the ocean, so it is no small thing,"[29] but the content of the water is a "small thing" compared to the rich diversity of life both in and out of the ocean itself.

Spinning thread from a mass of cotton is yet another analogy of the self-world relation to which Gandhi alluded and actually practiced every day. He was fond of quoting a saying from Akha, a medieval Gujarati saint: "Even as the thread spins out so be your life. Do what you may and receive the grace of Hari." This analogy is better than the water drop image. The individual thread is clearly separate from its origin, and its connection to that origin (for Akha it is Viṣṇu) is equally clear. (We may think of the individual threads taking on various colors to symbolize qualitative differences.) Bedekar sums up the implications of this metaphor: "[T]he image evokes in Gandhi's modern mind a life-project of unrepressed and continuous activity leading one to an awareness of one's own being."[30] Again the analogy has its problems: thread is woven into cloth, and it, just like the water drop, is lost in the whole.

Gandhi's statement that "corporate growth is therefore entirely dependent upon individual growth"[31] implies two concessions: (1) that his adoption of Advaita Vedānta was ill advised; and (2) that the drop and thread analogies do not support such a crucial role for the individual. This passage suggests another analogy for the self-society relation: the living organism. Individuals are like bodily organs, each with their own identity and function and each contributing to the life of the whole. This model also keeps the Socratic Gandhi from falling into the fallacy of social atomism—person/organs separating themselves, by radical acts of conscience and protest, from the body politic.

The principal objection to this analogy is that it is hierarchical and authoritarian—giving, for example, more value and authority to the brain than to the lowly gall bladder or feet, the loss of which a person can survive. Gandhi, comparing organs of the body to the four castes, disagrees: "Is the head superior to the arms, the belly and the feet, or the feet superior to the other three? What will happen to the body if these members quarrel about rank?"[32] One might well answer "Yes" to the first question and strongly advise the lower parts to obey the brain. If the brain does not outrank the rest of the organs, occasionally suppressing the actions of errant members, then Gandhi's *ahiṃsā* would never be possible.

If we go from the level of organs to the level of cells, then we may have found the organic model that we are seeking. Gandhi's ideal of an egalitarian body politic is the ashram, where, as I personally witnessed in the Aurobindo ashram in Pondicherry, people, for no salary, were happily doing everything from washing dishes to speculating on Aurobindo's philosophy. Perhaps this is the way in which we ought to look at Gandhi's controversial support for a reformed caste system. "Caste" he explains, "does not connote superiority or inferiority. It simply recognizes different outlooks and corresponding modes of life."[33] But if Gandhi means something more rigid—something like the tiger cub locked into his role—then his defense of *varna* as true to the "laws of Nature" is more problematic.[34] The following passage is typical of this more conservative view: "Some people are born to teach and some to defend, and some to engage in trade and agriculture and some to manual labor, so much so that these occupations become hereditary. The Law of Varna is nothing but the Law of Conservation of Energy. Why should my son not be a scavenger if I am one?"[35] Gandhi's view here is completely consonant with the hierarchical body analogy, but it is also here where most of us want to break with it. I was told that the philosophers in Pondicherry sometimes wash dishes to clear their heads. In the human body, however, the liver or other organs have no such liberty or flexibility—nor presumably does Gandhi's scavenger who might want to become a philosopher.

One might conceive of both society and the universe as one living organism in which the parts are individual cells. The health of the organism depends on the harmonious interaction of the cells. One diseased cell will affect the whole being for the worse, just as the purification of one might start the healing of the body organism. This organic view of the cosmos is integral to contemporary process theology, a constructive postmodern view that has been aptly described in the following terms: "Our cells are...localized units of feeling with some measure of autonomy. We cannot willfully control their actions in most cases, and they cannot willfully control our actions. But the whole and the parts do interact and influence one another. As the localized cells of my body are injured and suffer, I suffer, and I [also] enjoy their well-being. ... We are all members of the body of God, autonomous parts of that divine whole in whom we live and move and have our being."[36] Gandhi would have embraced this view enthusiastically because of his total rejection of the social atomism of classical liberalism, in which individual selves, just like physical atoms, are self-contained and self-sufficient autonomous agents. Like the physical atom the social atom bounces around in the empty space of society, now just an abstract entity viewed as the simple sum of its individual parts. Whereas the lines of personal responsibility are very clean in social atomism, they are considerably more diffuse in the organic view. The organic view allows us to see that we do indeed have collective obligations and duties in addition to the individual ones of classical liberalism. This view supports Gandhi's egalitarian concerns very well and could very well explain his insistence on doing penance for another's wrong doing.

The more Roy expounds on the ideal relationship of the self and society, the more it becomes clear that his preference, Advaita Vedānta, is not the correct ontological base. Śaṅkara's philosophy does not allow us, as Roy rightly proposes, to extend "individuality in a way that all such extensions, while preserving the uniqueness, autonomy and reality of individuality, converge in a way that produces a viable social order subserving the good of all."[37] After such a cogent description of plural but relational selves, it is disheartening to find Roy lapsing back into absolute monism: "[T]he prior existence of a centre and all particulars are thought to be its manifestation. This centre manifests in the particulars which, in turn, are seen to be reflecting in it.... And it is this commonality that constitutes the ground for the self to treat others as distinct but not different. It is this shareability in a commonality that constitutes the foundation of sociality."[38] In Advaita Vedānta, individuals are, strictly speaking, neither distinct nor different. Roy's statement is closer to a holographic analogy, anticipated beautifully in the story of Indra's pearls. Each holograph is indeed a distinct piece, but it is not different from the whole. This produces, however, a rather bland view of sociality—almost like the drops in the ocean—each individual person, by analogy, essentially no different from the other.

Roy introduces George Herbert Mead's view that our evolving selves are constituted in dialogue with "significant others." Roy complains that the most we can get from Mead's dialectical model is a partial sociality, "which divides the world into the near and dear ones, and those who either do not count, or count only marginally."[39] Roy contends that only the universal egalitarianism of Advaita Vedānta can overcome these divisions. But what if Śaṅkara was wrong, as I believe he was, about the illusory nature of qualitative differences and the ultimate unreality of selves in society?

Roy's use of the Confucian model (which is not compatible with Vedānta as he implies) offers him a way out of Mead's dilemma. The extension from "near and dear" to the "far and alien" is made by sages and leaders such as Confucius, the Buddha, Aśoka, and Gandhi. Roy does not seem to appreciate the emphasis that Gandhi placed on human finitude and its limitations. It is certainly not un-Gandhian to conclude that the best that the rest of us can hope for is to emulate the sages through a process of intensive moral education focusing on the ideals of compassion and nonviolence.

An effective way of conceiving absolute monism is the prism analogy. If Brahman is white light, and the color spectrum is the phenomenal world, then the prism that refracts the light stands for ignorance. If one eliminates ignorance, then one can see that everything is just an undifferentiated one. Due to ignorance, the world and its qualitative differences have a derivative reality only. Realizing the identity of Ātman and Brahman is like waking up from a dream and discovering that those images were only fleeting agitations of the mind.

In the article cited above, John White has offered a criticism of Advaita Vedānta that goes very nicely with the prism analogy. If Śaṅkara assumes that some people are enlightened, while many others remain in ignorance (which he must obviously hold), then clearly Śaṅkara's transcendental monism is untenable. The world will continue to exist for the unenlightened, but somehow it has ceased to exist for the liberated ones. (As White points out, the only way that the Advaitin can answer his argument is to deny the validity of the law of contradiction.) The result is that Śaṅkara's alleged non-dualism is, at least until the liberation of all souls, a transcendental dualism, roughly similar to Christian orthodoxy. Furthermore, it means that, if some selves are liberated and some are not, there must also be a real plurality of souls—that is, many different soul prisms refracting their own perspectives of the world.

If the equality and integrity of all souls is our goal, then, returning to analogies of the self-world relationship, a revised prism analogy is the best alternative. In contrast to Advaita Vedānta, the prism no longer stands for an ignorance that must be removed, but our own window on reality that refracts our own perceptions of the world. Following Rāmānuja, this aperture of the soul remains for all incarnations and after liberation as well. Finally, the revised analogy still confirms the validity of mystical experiences: through spiritual exercise soul-prisms are able to make themselves, momentarily, transparent to the One. The revised prism analogy ties in nicely with the egalitarian cell analogy that we have discussed previously.

Growing numbers of twentieth-century Euro-American philosophers, sociologists, and psychologists have finally rediscovered what many ancient thinkers (and even common sense) already knew: namely, individual identities are just as much constituted by others as they are by themselves. This means that persons are not social atoms, analogous to the physical atom, moving accidentally through social space. The organic view that Gandhi and the thinkers above propose likens society to a living whole rather than to the simple sum of separate parts. This view is essential for understanding Gandhi's revision of the caste system and also his concept of villages as the real organs of a truly living society. It is also crucial in this study's attempt to move Gandhi from the Vedāntist school to a new Buddhist intellectual home. If *ātman* is immutable and not an actor, then how can Vedāntist philosophy render intelligible a real self that turns from being attached to nonattached? In the next chapter I will argue that Buddhism can better support the ethics of the *Gītā* and a general ethics of nonviolence.

Chapter 4

The Buddha and Pragmatic Nonviolence

I felt I was in the presence of a noble soul...a true disciple of Lord Buddha and a true believer in peace and harmony among all men.

—The Dalai Lama

[Gandhi is] the greatest Indian since Gautama Buddha and the greatest man since Jesus Christ.

—J. H. Holmes

...The effect of Buddha's nonviolent action persists and is likely to grow with age.

—M.K. Gandhi

Gandhi once said that the Buddha was the greatest teacher of *ahiṃsā* and that he "taught us to defy appearances and trust in the final triumph of Truth and Love."[1] Albert Schweitzer once said that "Gandhi continues what the Buddha began. In the Buddha the spirit of love sets itself the task of creating different spiritual conditions in the world; in Gandhi it undertakes to transform *all* worldly conditions."[2] Raghavan Iyer concurs: "Gandhi was, in fact, following in the footsteps of the Buddha in showing the connection between the service of suffering humanity and the process of self-purification"; and even more emphatically he speaks of "Gandhi's profound reinterpretation of Hindu values in the light of the message of the Buddha."[3] Observing that Gandhi establishes a middle path between Jain individualism and the Vedāntist dissolution of the individual, Margaret Chatterjee maintains that Gandhi's position most closely resembles Mahāyāna Buddhism. Chatterjee claims that one of Gandhi's prayers has Buddhist overtones: "The goal of the devotee is seen as the relief of suffering humanity, not as personal release from bondage. The mood expressed is much closer to the Bodhisattva than to the arhat ideal."[4]

This chapter covers several topics related to Gandhi and Buddhism. The first section discusses nonviolence in Buddhism and how it differs from Jainism and how it is compatible with Gandhi's view. The second section addresses the problems regarding Gandhi's misconceptions about Buddhism. The third section explores the issue of self-suffering in the Buddha and in Gandhi. The fourth section discusses the issue of the Bodhisattva ideal and Gandhi's status as the Mahātma. The fifth section offers a positive view of the Buddhist self in order to counteract the pervasive negative view that one generally encounters. The final section lays out a Gandhian and Buddhist humanism based on a view of the Buddhist self as a robust, personal agent.

Nonviolence in Buddhism

As in Jainism, *ahiṃsā* is preeminent in Buddhist ethics. Not killing is the first of the Five Precepts, and this prohibition includes all sentient beings from insects to humans. Buddhists (except some Tantric sects) firmly reject the ritual sacrifice of animals, although many allow the eating of meat as long as Buddhists are not the butchers. (Jains criticize Buddhists for being complicit in this violence against animals.) Both Buddhist and Jain farmers can eliminate pests that are destroying crops, but Buddhists perform atoning rites afterwards. While pacifism is the ideal, Buddhists and lay Jains may kill in self-defense. Unlike Jain ascetics, Buddhist monks have not only served as soldiers, but have raised and led armies, especially in Japan, Korea, and Tibet. Finally, in some Mahāyāna schools Bodhisattvas may kill persons who will, if not stopped, murder others in the future. Appealing to consequentialist arguments, Buddhists defend such preemptive strikes: Bodhisattvas accrue merit that they then can bequeath to others, and the would-be murderers are saved from the horrors of Hell.[5] Needless to say, Jains are scandalized by what they see as a crass rationalization of violence.

Many scholars have observed that the word *ahiṃsā* occurs only rarely in Buddhist scripture and commentary. Compared to the Jains, the Buddhists conceive of *ahiṃsā* as a positive virtue or, more precisely, an enabling virtue for higher virtues. (Enabling virtues are defined in chapter 9.) As a result Buddhists usually speak of these other virtues rather than *ahiṃsā* itself. In S. Tachibana's *The Ethics of Buddhism* the word is used only once, and then only as one of seven Sanskrit words meaning benevolence or compassion. Nonviolence, however, comes out very clearly in Tachibana's formulation of the Buddhist categorical imperative: "We ought not to hurt mentally and physically our fellow creatures as well as our fellow men, but to love and protect them."[6] The Jain formulation of *ahiṃsā* is almost always negative, while the Buddhist expression is almost exclusively positive.

One Jain scholar sums up the contributions of the two religions by suggesting that Jainism gave us *ahiṃsā* but Buddhism offered us *maitri* (friendliness) and *karuṇā* (compassion).[7] One *sūtra* describes a monk as "pervading one direction of universe...with his mind accompanied by *maitri,* with vast, great, undivided, unlimited and universal freedom from hatred, rivalry, narrow-mindedness and harmfulness."[8] In another story the Buddha tamed serpents by rays of *maitri* emanating directly from his body. (While Gandhi conceded that it might be necessary to kill poisonous snakes that threaten human life, the Buddha, in response to a monk's being killed by a snake, commanded *maitri* towards all snakes.[9]) While *maitri* is sometimes interpreted as compassion, it was Mahāyāna Buddhism that made compassion the highest virtue, along with generosity, good conduct, patience, courage, concentration, and wisdom.

While they were contemporaries in India, Buddhists criticized Jain monks for their extreme self-mortification, claiming that this constituted a form of self-violence. Jains and Buddhists also disagreed on the issue of suicide, the latter holding it to be the ultimate violence to self. Jains believe that it can be, as a fast unto death *(sallekhanā),* the highest form of spiritual sacrifice, whereas Buddhists usually condemn any form of suicide. (Buddhist monks immolating themselves to protest the Vietnam war was a dramatic exception.) It appears that extreme austerities and autonomous selfhood are conceptually linked. Spiritual suicide would constitute the ultimate release and isolation of the Jain *jīva* from the corrupting influences of matter. On the other hand, a Buddhist, because of a nonsubstantial view of the self, would recognize that a spiritual self free from matter is an illusion, and she would be more concerned about the karmic effects of suicide as the ultimate violence to the self.

Gandhi actually allowed many exceptions to *ahiṃsā,* based on very realistic and pragmatic considerations, exceptions that scandalized many Hindus and Jains. His view is summed up in the surprising qualification that "all killing is not *hiṃsā,*"[10] and his equally provocative imperative that it is better to fight an aggressor than to be a coward. In contrast to the Jain position, Gandhi's *ahiṃsā* is reactive and flexible, not passive and absolute. Throughout October 1928, Gandhi carried on a lively debate with various respondents in *Young India.* He defended his decision to euthanize an incurable calf, and even went on to list the conditions for human euthanasia that do not violate *ahiṃsā.* He also thought that tigers, snakes, and rabid dogs might have to be killed if they threaten human life. In a letter to man who is trying to occupy land "haunted by wild beasts," he advises him to kill them, because "*ahiṃsā* is not a mechanical matter, it is personal to everyone."[11] (Only a perfect yogi could pacify dangerous animals.) This comment is strong evidence that the ethics of nonviolence cannot be rule based; rather, it must be based on the development of virtues that are formed within the context of the person, his spiritual stature, his vocation, and the various situations in which he finds himself. Human life is a constant "experiment in truth" in which we all act out of distinctively personal behaviorial styles that do not lend themselves to the mechanical application of rules.

Some of Gandhi's exceptions to *ahiṃsā* would appear extreme and unacceptable even to contemporary proponents of euthanasia. He proposed that a dying man must euthanize his handicapped child if he thought that no one would care for the child. If his own son were suffering from rabies and there was no cure, then he should be euthanized.[12] In both cases it is more important to relieve pain and preserve personal dignity than to follow lockstep the rule of nonviolence. This means that in many cases passive *ahiṃsā* is actually *hiṃsā*. If a man runs amuck and threatens to kill others, Gandhi insists that he must killed; furthermore, the killer should "be regarded a benevolent man."[13] Gandhi once told a Jain friend that *ahiṃsā* was not absolute and that one should always be "capable of sacrificing nonviolence for the sake of truth."[14] If one cannot be true to oneself without defending oneself and others, then violence may be necessary.

Gandhi's Misconceptions about Buddhism

It was not until he reached England that Gandhi discovered the great religious classics of his own Indian tradition. He first read the *Bhagavad-gītā* in Sir Edwin Arnold's translation, and read with "even greater interest" Arnold's verse rendition of the Buddha's life and thought.[15] Ghandhi wrote to a Burmese friend in 1919, Gandhi, "[W]hen in 1890 or 1891, I became acquainted with the teaching of the Buddha, my eyes were opened to the limitless possibilities of nonviolence."[16] Gandhi declared that he was proud of the accusation (lodged by his own son) that he was a closet Buddhist, and he claimed that Buddhism was to Hinduism as Protestantism was to Roman Catholicism, "only in a much stronger light, in a much greater degree."[17] This comment represents a slight against Roman Catholicism, which currently has the most compassionate and most understanding Christian mission in Asia. It also reveals Gandhi's mistaken belief that Buddhism and Jainism are simply reform movements within Hinduism.

During November 1927 Gandhi was on tour in Sri Lanka, and he naturally had occasion to present his views on Buddhism.[18] He maintained that the Buddha's extreme austerities during the time before his enlightenment were done as penance for the sins of corrupt brahmin priests. Using the time-honored practice of *tapasyā,* the Buddha, according to Gandhi, had only one principal goal: to convince Hindus to give up animal sacrifice. With remarkable candor Gandhi told his Buddhist audience that he was shocked that they could justify eating the flesh of animals that they themselves had not killed. He claimed that vegetarian Hindus were more consistent in their adherence to *ahiṃsā* and were thereby the true heirs of the Buddha's gospel of nonviolence. Reminding them of the Buddha's principle of dependent origination, Gandhi told his audience that any meat eater is causally linked to the violence of the one who butchers the animal. His judgment against Burmese Buddhists in 1929 was equally harsh, and there he speculated that their meat eating was the reason why Burma had a higher crime rate than India.

In his first speech in Sri Lanka Gandhi said that the Buddha only meant to reform Hinduism and not start a new religion of his own. It was his disciples, not the Buddha, who established a religion separate from Hinduism. According to Gandhi, the Buddha never rejected Hinduism; rather, he "broadened its base. He gave it new life and a new interpretation." And, most incredibly, Gandhi claims that any element of Buddhism not assimilated by Hinduism "was not an essential part of the Buddha's life and teaching."[19] Unfortunately, Gandhi's effusive praise of Buddhism is rather backhanded, because he unwittingly eliminates the separate identity that it rightly deserves: "It can be said that, in India at any rate, Hinduism and Buddhism were but one, and that even today the fundamental principles of both are identical."[20]

Gandhi was not always a very good scholar, and his passionate belief in the basic unity of all religions made him distort what we know to be the Buddha's intentions. There is no question that Siddhartha Gautama envisioned a clean break with the Hindu tradition. The Buddha preserved the time-honored techniques of yogic meditation, but his Middle Way contained a strong critique of India's ascetic traditions. He also broke with orthodox Hindus on other major issues, such as the nature of reality and the self and its relationship to the gods. In addition, the Buddha totally rejected the caste system, which Gandhi wanted to preserve in a revised form. My view is that Gandhi should have broken with his Hindu tradition on all of these points except perhaps for his views on the deity. Most importantly, we will find that Gandhi often speaks of the self, God, and reality in dynamic and relational ways that are Buddhist in their implication. A process theologian, for example, would be thrilled to read that for Gandhi God "is ceaseless activity.... God is continuously in action without resting for a single moment."[21]

Gandhi's persistence in believing that the Buddha was a theist is yet another instance in which his own religious views clouded his understanding.

His argument that "the Law (dharma) was God Himself"[22] is true only in Mahāyāna Buddhism, where the cosmic Buddha is called the *dharmakāya,* literally, the Body of the Law. (Surendra Verma's suggestion that Gandhi's idea that God is Law, as it is not a Hindu or Jain idea, must have come from Buddhism is certainly worth serious consideration.)[23] The Buddha himself, however, did not claim any transcendental or cosmic nature, and the deification of the Buddha came after his death. Furthermore, Gandhi's insistence on the Buddha's theism is ironic given the fact that he constantly wavered between personal theism and an impersonal pantheism, or even an impersonal "truthism." After all, Gandhi is most famous for his proposition that "Truth [not a supreme person] is God," a strategy partially designed to attract atheists to his cause. In any case, the Buddha adopted the Jain-Sāṃkhya-Yoga view of the relationship between humans and gods. This view is neither theistic nor atheistic: the gods do indeed exist, but they, like all other nonhuman beings, have to have human incarnations in order to reach Nirvāṇa. Finally, although I personally embrace Gandhi's theism, if the ethics of nonviolence is to have the most comprehensive acceptance, a nontheistic form would obviously be more preferable.

To his credit Gandhi did have the correct view of Nirvāṇa, and he is to be commended for his clear understanding of it. He said that "Nirvāṇa is utter extinction of all that is base in us, all that is vicious in us, all that is corrupt and corruptible in us. Nirvāṇa is not like the black, dead peace of the grave, but the living peace, the living happiness of [the] soul...."[24] This is a perfect response to perennial charges of Buddhist nihilism. Nirvāṇa is, in a word, freedom—freedom not only from hate and greed, but freedom from craving, the unquenchable desire for those things that we can never attain. One significant assumption of the Buddha's position is that ordinary desires, even for the Enlightened One, are acceptable. This is the clearest mode of understanding the Buddha's Middle Way between extreme asceticism on the one hand and sensualism on the other. It is also a good way to see Buddhism as a religious humanism accessible to all people. Finally, if Nirvāṇa is "the living happiness of the soul," then we have a firm basis for the Buddhist and Gandhian eudaimonism that is the goal of this book.

A Hungarian convert to Buddhism once asked Gandhi whether God could change because of human prayer. Sensing that his questioner was not sympathetic to the idea of petitionary prayer, Gandhi answered that God was of course immutable, so "I beg it of myself, of my Higher Self, the Real Self with which I have not yet achieved complete identification."[25] This answer may well have satisfied the Buddhist interlocutor if he were a Mahāyānist, but not so in the case of a Theravadin. The latter has a belief closer to the Buddha's own: that there is no higher self at all. It is clear that Gandhi is much more in line with the Mahāyānists with regard to his concept of self. (There is good reason to believe that the Mahāyānist higher self is a philosophical import from Hinduism, although Mahāyānist doctrines of *śūnyatā* and total interrelatedness mean that this self is very different from the Hindu *ātman*.) This issue aside, it was never reported that the Buddha petitioned either a god (except in legends) or a higher self for any favor. So Gandhi was wrong when he insisted that the Buddha "found illumination through prayer and could not possibly live without it."[26]

Gandhi and Buddhists definitely find common ground if Gandhi really means that prayer is chanting or meditation, which is, in fact, what he suggests in his conversation with the Hungarian. "You may, therefore, describe it as a continual longing to lose oneself in the Divinity which comprises all."[27] In this regard it is instructive to note Gandhi's observation that a Japanese monk chanting at his Sevagram ashram was engaged in Buddhist prayer.[28] Mahadev Dasei, Gandhi's faithful secretary, gives us more information about this person, who was obviously a follower of Nichiren Daishonin: "There is among us a Japanese monk who works like a horse and lives like a hermit, doing all the hard chores of the ashram and going about merrily beating his drum early every morning and evening, filling the air with his chanting of *Om Namyo Hom Renge Kyom*. ... I do not believe there is one iota of truth in the charge some people have leveled at him of being a...spy. If he is a spy, spies must be the most amiable specimens of humanity and I should like to be one. To my mind he lives up to the gospel of *ahiṃsā* better than any one of us not excluding Gandhiji."[29] Unfortunately, the Japanese monk's practice of *ahiṃsā* did not stop the Indian police from arresting him and removing him from the ashram.

Gandhi, Self-Suffering, and the Buddha

A typical Gandhian response to the misdeeds of others was to shame them completely by doing their penance for them. This proved to be very effective not only against the British but with his own family and followers as well. It is most intriguing to see how Gandhi has imposed his own principle of self-suffering on the life of the Buddha. Although not used by the Buddha or his immediate disciples, civil protest through acts of self-immolation has been common in ancient as well as modern Asia. (Buddhist monks burning themselves to death during the Vietnam War and Falun Gong suicides in China are the most recent examples.) Gandhi was of course aware of this tradition of self-immolation,[30] but he still believed that his own particular adaptation of yogic *tapas* was new with him and that his practice of it had not yet been perfected.[31] Presumably he would have seen protests through self-immolation as still too passive as compared to the engaged and dynamic nature of his own *satyāgrahas*. (The Vietnamese monks, as far as I can remember, were not actively engaged in dialogue with the American officials.) Some commentators contend that there are instructive parallels between Gandhi's self-suffering and the suffering of the Bodhisattva, and we shall assess this claim in the next section.

If Gandhi does conceive of self-suffering as doing penance for others, then he has gone far beyond the traditional view of *tapas*. Indeed, it may even be at odds with the law of karma, which holds that karma is always individual, not collective. (This means that only individuals can work off their karmic debt.) Gandhi, however, appears to believe in collective guilt: "If we are all sons of the same God and partake of the same divine essence, we must partake of the sin of every person."[32] He once observed that the "impurity of my associates is but the manifestation of the hidden wrong in me,"[33] so this does appear to focus on individual karma, but his position is still equivocal and problematic. Margaret Chatterjee finds Gandhi's position very implausible, for, in the two cases she mentions, it is very difficult to see any "strict causal line[s]" between the actions of others and any implication of guilt on Gandhi's part.[34]

By seeing *tapasyā* as a process of self-purification rather than doing penance for other people, one can make better sense of Gandhi's actions. In this light Gandhi would have said that he could not demand perfection in others as long as he found imperfection in himself. During his fast against the violence at Chauri Chaura in 1922, Gandhi announced, "I must undergo personal cleansing. I must become a fitter instrument able to register the slightest variation in the moral atmosphere about me."[35] (Gandhi explains Buddhist mindfulness in this statement just as well as any Buddhist.) This interpretation is most consistent with his expanded concept of *brahmacharya* as self-control in all actions and his commitment to spiritual purity for himself and his followers. The concept of collective karma might be made intelligible on the basis of the organic analogy discussed in the last chapter.

The Mahātma and the Bodhisattva

A critic might say that the most significant difference between the Buddha and Gandhi was that the Buddha was a world-denying ascetic and that Gandhi was not. The following passage sums up this view very nicely: "Outwardly it would be hard to conceive of two individuals more different. On the one hand is the tranquil Buddha who walks serenely and calmly across the pages of history, or traditionally sits peacefully on a lotus with a gentle smile of infinitive compassion. ... On the other hand is the Mahātma, speed and energy in every movement, laughing and sorrowing in his ceaseless endeavour to help mankind with the problems of human life. ..."[36] Gandhi must have heard similar comments, because he formulated this own firm response: "The Buddha fearlessly carried the war into the adversary's camp and brought down on its knees an arrogant priesthood. [He was] for intensely direct action."[37] Who is correct? The truth as usual lies somewhere in between. Although he did frequently confront brahmin priests (the scriptures report that they were almost always converted), it can hardly be said that the Buddha destroyed the Vedic priesthood. (It continues to have great power even today.) Furthermore, although Buddhism and Jainism can take much credit for the reduction of animal sacrifice, it still continues today as an integral part of Goddess worship in Northeast India and Nepal. And even Gandhi admits that because of India's own weaknesses, the Buddha's, as well as the Jains', message of universal tolerance and nonviolence failed miserably. (Much blame, according to Gandhi, must be laid at the feet of Śaṅkara for his "unspeakable cruelty in banishing Buddhism out of India."[38]) Finally, Gandhi is making the Buddha more of a political activist than he ever was. Gandhi should take sole credit for his own brilliant synthesis of religion and political action. As one commentator has said, "One cannot picture the Buddha training his disciples to face lathi charges as did the Mahātma."[39]

A growing scholarly consensus now recognizes that the Buddha was less ascetic and less world denying than his disciples and the early schools that followed him. For example, as opposed to most Indian philosophy, the Buddha recognized the body as a necessary constituent of human identity, rather than something to be negated in the spiritual life.[40] (Gandhi appears to join other traditions—Cartesian and as well as Jain and Vedāntist—which maintain that the body has nothing to do with true personal identity.) It was his disciples who kept asking for more behavioral restrictions, and this difference is summed aptly in the Buddha's observation that sometimes he ate a full bowl of food while his monks only ate only half a bowl.[41] Despite Buddhism's somatic selfhood and a later doctrine of universal Buddha-essence, its strong ascetic traditions did not allow Buddhist practice to be as body or world affirming as it could have been. The influence of Chinese naturalism (especially on Zen Buddhism) and the Buddhist-Christian dialogue have turned contemporary Buddhism much more in this direction.

The spiritual transformation of the entire world is the goal of most schools of Mahāyāna Buddhism. As opposed to the ascetic ideal of early Buddhism, where the emphasis was on personal liberation, the focus in Mahāyāna schools is on universal salvation. The vow of the Bodhisattva should be well known to those who know Buddhism: the Bodhisattva, even though free of karmic debt, vows not to enter Nirvāṇa until all sentient beings have entered. (The Bodhisattva's extra sacrifice caused some perceptive Buddhists to ask whether that made Bodhisattvas superior to the Buddha himself, who of course did not wait for the others.) The Bodhisattva ideal and the comprehensive range of universal salvation make it relevant to contemporary debates about animal rights and the protection of the environment.

Gandhi constantly emphasized that his focus was universal this-worldly salvation and not individual spiritual liberation: "I have no use for them [love and nonviolence] as a means of individual liberation."[42] As with Latin American liberation theology, Gandhi's soteriology maintained that God assumes a preferred option for the poor and the oppressed; indeed, Gandhi sometimes speaks of God existing in suffering humanity and not in heaven: "God is found more often in the lowliest of His creatures than in the high and mighty."[43] Does this, then, make Gandhi "the Bodhisattva of the twentieth century," as Ramjee Singh has so boldly suggested?[44] The answer must be negative if we insist on early formulations of the Bodhisattva concept. Using the innovative idea of Nichiren Buddhism that all of us become Bodhisattvas by virtue of our service to humanity, Singh's claim is closer to the mark.

On the face of it Gandhi's self-suffering does appear to be similar to Śāntideva's view of the Passion of the Bodhisattva: "By my own self all the mass of others' pain has been assumed: ... I have the courage in all misfortunes belonging to all worlds to experience every abode of pain. ... I resolve to abide in each single state of misfortune through numberless future ages... for the salvation of all creatures. ... I for the good of all creatures would experience all the mass of pain and unhappiness in ... my own body. ..."[45] Gandhi does claim to have suffered—his fasts were long and many—for the good of all *(sarvōdaya),* and he did declare that in his next life he wanted to be reborn an untouchable,[46] but this still does not constitute anything like the soteriology that we find in Buddhism and Christianity. Gandhi obviously did not claim to have taken away the sins of the world as Buddhist and Christians claim their saviors do.

Following the idea of penance as self-purification, Gandhi may be more like the Bodhisattva, who, although sinless, nonetheless "think[s] of [him]self as a sinner [and] of others as oceans of virtue."[47] But just as we cannot believe Gandhi guilty of the crises for which he fasted, we certainly cannot believe, nor of course could he, that he was sinless. Not even his most ardent followers have claimed that Gandhi had the redemptive powers of a savior. Revealing his strong Vaiṣṇava background, Gandhi once declared that he wanted to tear open his heart for the poor just as the monkey god Hanuman did to show his devotion to Rāma, but he said that he did not have the power to perfect such absolute loyalty.[48] Finally, it must be observed that Gandhi practiced self-suffering in order to change other people's behavior, whereas the Passion of Christ and the Bodhisattva are conceived of as totally unconditional, expecting nothing in return for their grace and compassion. Gandhi realized the danger in making his self-suffering conditional on the actions of others: it might very well violate the principle that he had learned so well from the *Bhagavad-gītā*, namely, that we must not act with regard to the fruit of our actions.[49]

We must again place all aspects of Gandhian religion in its proper political context. (The more appropriate comparison would be Gandhi and Emperor Aśoka, who through political means attempted to establish a nonviolent society in third-century-B.C.E. India.) Gandhi called his fasting a "fiery weapon" and said that we must fight the "fire" of violence with the "fire" of our own self-sacrifice.[50] "It was," as Madan Gandhi says, "a potent weapon to convert the evil doer, i.e., to make him conscious of the spiritual kinship with the victim."[51] It was, as I said above, an effective means of shaming Gandhi's opponents into mending their ways. Joan Bondurant describes it as the "willingness to suffer in oneself to win the respect of an opponent."[52] For Gandhi himself it had the effect of establishing his absolute seriousness, sincerity, and fearlessness. For those close to him, especially his wife and his sons, it was a test of love—"tough love" as it is now called. "The only way love punishes," as Gandhi once said, "is by [self]-suffering."[53] (The coercive effect of Gandhi's fasts has been widely discussed and accepted by many scholars.)[54] We are now quite distant from the Suffering Servants of Christianity and Mahāyāna Buddhism.

The Buddhist Self as Functional

Siddhartha Gautama's response to the axial discovery of the self was strikingly unique: he proposed the doctrine of no-self *(anatman)*. This conceptual innovation was so provocative that it was bound to invite misinterpretation, and unfounded charges of Buddhist nihilism continue even to this day. Gautama anticipated Hume's view that the self is the ensemble of feelings, perceptions, dispositions, and awareness that is the center for agency and moral responsibility.[55] The Buddha's view, however, is superior to Hume's, primarily because Gautama supported real causal efficacy among internally related phenomena. While Hume deconstructed any theory of causality, the Buddha reconstructed causal relations with his theory of interdependent coorigination.

Gautama rejected the soul-as-spiritual-substance view of the Upaniṣads, Jainism, and Sāṃkhya-Yoga, and he deconstructed the "spectator" self of these philosophies 2,500 years before recent thinkers dismantled the Cartesian self. As opposed to strict deconstruction, for example, Buddhists hold that selves, though neither the same nor different throughout their lives, are nevertheless responsible for their actions. These selves are also real in the sense that they are constituted by relations with their bodies, other selves, and all other entities. This is why the Buddhist self should be viewed in relational or process terms rather than through the negative implications of the no-self doctrine. The Buddhist self is relational primarily in the sense of its dependence on the five *skandhas* and the internal relations this dependence entails. The Confucian and Hebrew self is primarily relational in the social sense, that is, the literal meaning of the Confucian *ren** (human relatedness) is "two peopleness."[56] While Buddhism's relational ontology certainly implies social relationality, the Buddhist self is definitely more individualistic than either the Hebrew or Confucian view. By contrast Zhuangzi's fully relational ontology does not lead to a commitment on his part to any social relations at all. This is why the phrase "relational and social" is not redundant for our comparative purposes.

Another positive way to express nonsubstantiality is to describe the Buddhist self as "functional." In fact, each of the *skandhas* should be seen as functions rather than entities. On this point, Kalupahana makes good use of William James (a far better Euro-American counterpart than Hume), who, while denying a soul substance, maintained that consciousness is a function. As Kalupahana states, "*Rūpa* or material form accounts for the function of identification; *vedanā* or feeling and *saṃjñā* or perception represent the function of experience, emotive as well as cognitive; *saṃskāra* or disposition stands for the function of individuation; *vijñāna* or consciousness explains the function of continuity in experience."[57] Both Kalupahana and Peter Harvey describe the Buddhist self in the positive terms of psychophysical unity, process, and interrelation. According to Harvey, the Buddha never rejected the existence of a life-principle *(jīva),* which "is not a separate *part* of a person, but is a process which occurs when certain conditions are present...."[58]

From this analysis we can clearly see that the Buddhist self is a robust personal agent fully capable of maintaining its personal integrity and taking full responsibility for its actions. This view of the self is also fully somatic, giving full value to the body and the emotions. At the same time it is embedded in a social and organic nexus of cosmic relations. Surendra Verma is unduly puzzled when he asks how it was possible for the Buddha to be filled with thoughts and emotions and "at the same time preaching *annattavada,* the theory of the nonexistence of the soul."[59] Like many other commentators, Verma simply does not understand the meaning of the Buddha's Middle Way, in this case the mean between annihilationism (no self at all—substantial or otherwise) on the one hand and eternalism (substantial self) on the other. What appears not only puzzling but impossible is for the Vedāntist *ātman* to have any relation at all with the finite world, let alone the emotions and the body.

Turning now to Gandhi, he explicitly connects "the capacity of nonviolence" with a rejection of "the theory of the permanent inelasticity of human nature."[60] If this statement is interpreted metaphysically, Gandhi seems to have joined the Buddha in his critique of the *ātman* of the Upaniṣads and all other Indian views of an eternal, immutable self. Although Mahāyāna Buddhists reinstate an eternal soul, in most schools this self, like early Buddhist views, still enters into relations and is responsive to change. When Gandhi states that "to endure suffering in one's own person is the nature of *ātman*,"[61] the logical implication is that the self actually undergoes change.

Mahāyāna Buddhists tend to be more supportive of real diversity within unity, and especially helpful is the Mahāyānists' suggestion that nonduality be expressed as "two but not two" so as to avoid the implication of the total nondifferentiation that we find in Advaita Vedānta.[62] Thich Nhat Hanh has his own playful way of phrasing this profound point: "Non-duality means 'not two,' but 'not two' also means 'not one.' That is why we say 'non-dual' instead of 'one.' "[63] Zen Buddhists as well as many other Mahāyānists also reject the mind-body dualism that even infects some of Gandhi's writings. These observations allow us to see the possibility of both a Buddhist naturalism and a Buddhist humanism, that is, a view that affirms both the reality of nature and individual personal identity.[64]

Gandhian and Buddhist Humanism

In an unpublished paper entitled "Buddhism and Chinese Humanism," David Kalupahana contends that it is Buddhism (and I would say Confucianism, too) that should be promoted as the true humanism of Asia. He claims that Gautama's rejection of transcendental knowledge, his declaration of moral freedom in the midst of karmic determinants, and his refusal to go beyond immediate experience all converge nicely with major elements of European humanism. Based on knowledge gained from experience and induction, a Buddhist, says Kalupahana, can use an evaluative knowledge called *anumana,* a mode of moral reflection which allows one to complete the eight-fold path and become an *uttamapurisa,* an "ultimate" person. This ideal person is one who acts with a clear goal in view and harms neither herself nor others. Although Kalupahana translates *uttamapurisa* as "superman," this obviously does not represent a Buddhist Titan, as it may have in Hinduism or as it does in the later Buddhist *Mahāvastu.* The *uttamapurisa* simply acts "with a clear goal in view and does not waver when faced with obstacles. He is one who has attained freedom from the suffering and unhappiness in the world. ...Such a person...is not only happy by himself, but also makes other people happy by being pleasant and helpful to them."[65] This Buddhist saint sounds very much like a Confucian sage rather than a spiritual Titan.

Kalupahana sums up his view of Buddhist humanism in this way: "The philosophy of early Buddhism...undoubtedly represents one of the most comprehensive and systematic forms of humanism. It is based on naturalistic metaphysics, with causal dependence as its central theme. Rejecting any form of transcendentalism, determinism, or fatalism, it emphasizes its ultimate faith in man and recognizes his power or potentiality in solving his problems through reliance primarily upon empirical knowledge, reason and scientific method applied with courage and vision. It believes in the freedom of man, not in a transcendental sphere, but here and now. The highest goal it offers is not other-worldly but this-worldly."[66] Kalupahana concedes that European humanists would not be sympathetic to the Buddhist belief in transmigration, but he counters that the Buddhist version of reincarnation does not undermine human freedom in the way that he believes that Hindu or Jain views do.

Two other objections to Kalupahana's thesis should be mentioned. First, Buddhist monks claim that the capacity of retrocognition, clairvoyance, and telepathy aids them in apprehending the twelve-fold chain of causal dependence. Contemporary Euro-American humanists, especially those associated with the leading humanist journal *Free Inquiry,* have consistently rejected claims of ESP and other claims of paranormal experience. Second, these same critics might also respond negatively to Buddhism's "soft" determinism, claiming that true humanism must be based on a theory of genuine self-determination. If freedom of this sort is a requirement for humanistic philosophy, then none of the classical Asian philosophies qualifies as such. Ironically, contemporary Euro-American humanists cannot consistently hold to this criterion of freedom either. The Humanist Pantheon, comprised of historical humanists chosen by the editors of *Free Inquiry,* is filled with determinists such as Lucretius, Epictetus, Spinoza, Hume, Mill, and Freud.[67] Their Academy of Humanism also contains sociobiologist Edward O. Wilson and other prominent scientists who subscribe to the theory of universal determinism. It is clear that ancient and contemporary humanists support moral and social freedom, but do not agree on the issue of free will and an internal self-determining agent.

Spiritual goals are present in both Buddhism and Confucianism, so again we must reject the proposals of those who insist that true humanism must be thoroughly secular. Although it is more anthropocentric than Confucianism, early Buddhist humanism never exaggerates the human position as much as Sāṃkhya and Jainism or the technological Titanism of Europe, America, and Japan. Without falling into Titanism, Buddhists agree with the Jains that human beings can achieve liberation under their own power and with their own efforts—without divine aid, prayer, or sacrifice. With all these qualifications in mind, Kalupahana's thesis that early Buddhism contains an "enlightened form of humanism"[68] is well supported.

Japan's Soka Gakkai is one contemporary Mahāyāna school that continues the tradition of Buddhist humanism. Its leader Daisaku Ikeda has written a very fine biography of the Buddha that strongly emphasizes his humanity,[69] and thus avoids the Docetism that characterizes many other Mahāyāna schools. Ikeda also paraphrases the medieval monk Nichiren Daishonin as saying, "The Buddha is an ordinary human being; ordinary human beings are the Buddha."[70] There are two interpretations of the second phrase depending upon whether one follows Pāli texts or the Mahāyāna sūtras. From the standpoint of Pāli Buddhism to say that we are all Buddhas simply means that all of us have the potential to understand the Four Noble Truths and to overcome craving in our lives. The Mahāyānist interpretation would be that we all possess a Buddha-nature metaphysically equivalent to the Dharmakāya, the cosmic "body" of the Buddha. The monism of this position—namely, the implication that all individuals are essentially one—undermines a central tenet of humanism: the individual integrity of each human being. The individualism of humanism has been seen as its greatest flaw, and it certainly is if the individual is conceived as a social atom externally related to other isolated selves. But if the individual is interpreted as the relational and social self of Buddhism and Confucianism, then we have an idea of self that avoids the two extremes of monistic dissolution and social atomism.

Given his commitment to a general Vedāntist concept of soul, Gandhi would have felt very comfortable with the Mahāyānist position, particularly the Soka Gakkei position that respects diversity within unity and supports a dynamic and engaged concept of self. It is also clear that Gandhi's individualism is balanced by a social view of the self and a general organic holism, a position that he should have chosen rather than Vedāntist monism. Gandhi's political activism simply cannot be supported by any view that effaces the self in a divine unity. Furthermore, except for some passages, Gandhi maintains a balance between divine power and individual autonomy in the same way that many Christian humanists do. I therefore propose that Buddhist humanism—a humanism of nonviolence and compassion—may be the very best way to take Gandhi's philosophy into the twenty-first century.

Chapter 5

Experiments with Truth

Therefore, we ought to pay as much attention to the sayings and opinions, undemonstrated though they are, of wise and experienced older people as we do to demonstrated truths. For experience has given such people an eye (nous) *with which they can see correctly.*

—Aristotle

As long as I have not realized this Absolute Truth, so long must I hold by relative truth, as I have conceived it. The relative truth must meanwhile be my beacon, my shield, my buckler.

—M. K. Gandhi

The Buddhist solution to the problem of civilization is for each individual to live self-correctively. ...

—Nolan Pliny Jacobson

In this chapter practical reason as it functions in Aristotle, Confucius, and the Buddha will be used as a key to understanding Gandhi's famous "experiments with truth." The first section is a discussion about Aristotle's intellectual virtues and distinction among *nous, sophia,* and *phronēsis.* Using Aristotle's own language, I conclude that *sophia* gives us universal truths while *phronēsis* produces distinctively personal truths. The second section demonstrates how the Confucian concept of *yi* performs roughly the same function as *phronēsis* in Aristotle. *Yi* allows people to make a personal appropriation of societal norms *(li)* to become true human beings *(ren*)*. The third section analyses the Buddha's motto, "Those who know causation know the

Dharma," and concludes that he agrees with Aristotle and Confucius on the operation of practical reason. The fourth section discusses the Buddha's eight-fold path, and the concluding section offers Confucian and Buddhist experiments with truth. Pliny Jacobson said that two of the most profound examples of philosophies of self-correction have been modern science and Buddhism, but now we must add Gandhi to this honor roll of thinkers who sought to promote "searching, flexible, and receptive habits of thinking."[1]

Before proceeding we should mention some basic differences between Aristotle and the Buddha and Confucius. Both of the latter would have requested at least three changes in Greek virtue ethics. First, neither the Buddha nor Confucius would have accepted Aristotle's claim that the intellect (*nous*) defines what it is to be human. Second, the two Asians thought that pride is a vice, so the humble soul is to be preferred over Aristotle's "great soul" *(megalopsychia)*. Third, neither the Buddha nor Confucius would have accepted Aristotle's elitism. (Universal brotherhood is far more dominant in Confucian texts than the occasional allusion to class distinctions.) For Aristotle only a certain class of people (namely, free-born Greek males) could establish the virtues and attain the good life. (Greek eudaimonism has been called "an ethics of the fortunate.")[2] In stark contrast, the Dharmakāya contains all people, including the poor, the outcast, and women. The Buddha and Confucius would have been more sympathetic to Plato's ideal of balance among the parts of the soul rather than self-loving *megalopsychia*. An Asian definition of virtue ethics might well be "the art of making the soul balanced and harmonious," the virtue aesthetics discussed in the next chapter. It is quite clear that Gandhi would have agreed with the Confucians and the Buddhist on all these basic issues.

Aristotle on Practical Reason

In this section we will discuss three of Aristotle's intellectual virtues: *nous, sophia,* and *phronēsis*. I am personally not happy with any of the standard translations of *sophia* and *phronēsis*, especially "prudence" for latter. ("Prudence" is particularly inapt if it is viewed as moral virtue, which *phronēsis* is not, with a mean between impulsiveness and overcautiousness.) Wisdom does not work for either *sophia* or *phronēsis,* and I would rather render them as "theoretical reason" and "practical reason" respectively. (The principal disadvantage with this choice is that it obscures the fact that Aristotle believes that both are virtues and not faculties, a concept alien to the Greek mind.) We should agree with Aristotle that there are many experts in the theoretical sciences who should not be trusted to rule other people's lives, let alone their own, so it is particularly unsuitable to use the word "wisdom" for the *sophia* these people display. Aristotle also allows the possibility that some animals display practical reason, so it is also inadvisable to call "wise" those who simply use but have not mastered *phronēsis*. These people Aristotle called *enkratēs,* those literally "having the will" to overcome temptation and develop the virtues as opposed to the *akratēs,* those "having no will" to live in the mean and therefore very likely to develop the vices. The truly wise person is the *sōphrōn,* one who is at ease with one's virtue and knows one's true purposes and the means to attain them.

Nous is that human faculty that apprehends fundamental principles, both theoretical and practical. *Nous* apprehends these truths directly and without demonstration or inference, which is the job of theoretical reason *(sophia).* The importance that Aristotle gives to *nous* is seen in this definition of human nature: "Intelligence *(nous),* above all else, is man."[3] *Nous* is also used to refer to practical reasoning, and in one passage he states that we love *nous* in this practical sense more than any other human faculty.[4] Aristotle follows Plato in using the metaphor of *nous* as the "eye of the soul,"[5] the mind's eye or the "third eye" that "looks" inward at rational things rather than outward towards sensible objects. One could call it a form of nonsensuous perception.

Sophia is a combination of knowledge of fundamental principles *(nous)* and knowledge of what follows from those principles *(theōria). Sophia* is science, "in its consummation...the science of the things that are valued most highly."[6] Aristotle observes that practical reasoning could even be discerned in some animal behavior, but theoretical reasoning is unique to humans and the gods and that is presumably why we should value it more. Aristotle, however, is not consistent on this essential point. While he praises Anaxagoras and Thales for their theoretical achievements, he charges that "their knowledge [was] useless because the good they are seeking is not human."[7] Even more troublesome is Aristotle's statement that *sophia* will not "make a man happy,"[8] and another where it does indeed produce *eudaimonia* after all,[9] but only as a formal, not an efficient cause, which of course is *phronēsis.* The solution to this problem is to preserve Aristotle's distinction between the intellectual and moral virtues; maintain the essential role of practical reason in their formation; insist, contrary to some indications in Book Ten, that the moral virtues are a necessary condition for *eudaimonia;* and conclude that *sophia* alone cannot make humans happy, although it will be an essential virtue for the good life.

Phronēsis differs from science *(theōria)* in that the objects of the latter do not change, whereas *phronēsis* deliberates about things that can be other than they are. *Sophia* seeks, as John Kekes phrases it, "knowledge and truth *sub specie aeternitatis,* while practical reason does so *sub specie humanitatis.*"[10] *Phronēsis* differs from art *(technē)* because it deals with actions rather than products. ("For production has an end other than itself, but action does not: good action is itself an end.")[11] *Phronēsis* gives us the ability to develop virtues that are means "relative to us"; and enables us to determine the right amount, the right means, the right goal, the right time, the right situation, the right person, and so forth. I would like to call this Aristotle's "contextual pragmatism": "what is suitable is...relative to the person, the circumstances, and the object."[12] We will find the same contextual pragmatism in the Buddha, Confucius, and Gandhi.

Aristotle's distinction between theoretical and practical reason represents a decisive break with Plato, who, at least in the Socrates of the early dialogues, equated theoretical knowledge and virtue. In stark contrast Aristotle observes that while young people gain theoretical wisdom by studying geometry and math, "they apparently do not attain *phronēsis*. The reason is that practical wisdom is concerned with particulars as well (as with universals), and knowledge of particulars comes from experience."[13] Later on Aristotle phrases his point with an odd, but effective locution, fusing the particular with the universal (or a *telos*, to be more precise): *phronēsis* "is concerned with ultimate particulars, since the actions to be performed are ultimate particulars."[14] Aristotle adds that there is a nonsensory perception of these ultimate particulars but there is no *theōria,* presumably because it would be relative and particular to each individual. Later on Aristotle will call this nonsensory perception the "eye of with which [we] can see correctly."[15] As we have already seen this is the eye of *nous,* which obviously has taken on a practical function here.

Let us now summarize how practical reason functions in the moral life. First, *phronēsis* allows us to discover the reasons why we must be virtuous. This knowledge then gives the proper motivation for virtue so that it is not a mindless emulation of others' behavior. In this way the virtues are fully internalized and made truly our own. Second, since any idea of the good life is always going to be rather general, *phronēsis* allows us to determine the proper means to the specific ends of our own lives. (Nancy Sherman argues that in Aristotle's view of the law *phronēsis* allows us to apply the law to specific cases.)[16] Third, *phronēsis,* as opposed to other intellectual virtues, is attuned to context and aids us in finding our own personal mean between deficient and excessive behavior.

Yi and *Phronēsis*

In this section I wish to demonstrate that the Confucian concept of *yi* is the functional equivalent of Aristotle's *phronēsis*. The *Analects* state that *junzi* "are neither bent on nor against anything; rather, they go with what is appropriate *(yi).*"[17] Roger Ames and Henry Rosemont have given the most intelligible reading of this passage so that the personalism and contextualism of *yi* comes forth. Just as *phronēsis* is Aristotle's guide to a personal mean, so is *yi* for the Confucian Dao. Confucius says that he acts on his "sense of what is appropriate *(yi)* to extend [his] way *(dao).*"[18] Confucius says that the *junzi* gives *yi* "first priority," and then goes on to argue that one achieves only semblances of the virtues without *yi.*[19] One could, for example, be physically brave but lack true courage, or one could be clever without being very wise. This corresponds to the first function of *phronēsis* mentioned above.

Confucius also claims that *yi* is our "basic disposition" that allows us to put *li* into practice.[20] Without *yi* Confucian morality would a mere moralism based on strict conformity to social norms *(li). Li* is best translated as "propriety" because the Latin *proprius* integrates the meaning of *yi* as "making one's own," as in acquiring property. This makes *li*, as Ames and Rosemont contend, "profoundly different from law or rule [because it] is this process of making the tradition one's own."[21] Therefore, for a contemporary virtue ethics one could formalize the Confucian position as *ren* + *yi* + *li* = *ren**. To expand the parallel to Aristotle we can propose an equivalence between *li* and *ethos* as social custom, and with the aid of *phronēsis*, this *ethos* becomes particularized as unique character traits (ēthos) and the moral virtues. The corresponding Aristotelian formula would then be *anthropos* + *phronēsis* + *ethos* = *ethikē aretē*.

JiyuanYu rejects the connection between *yi* and *phronēsis* primarily because Confucius's idea of *li* does not allow for any variation or personal appropriation. The best argument that Yu gives for this position is that while Aristotle believes one could be a good citizen without being a good person, Confucius would reject this disjunction outright. Civic and personal virtue are both grounded in conformity to *li,* whereas *phronēsis* would allow a person such as Socrates to critique the state. In this same vein Yu also believes that *yi* always refers to the judgment of the many rather than any personal moral discernment.

We, however, can still speak of *yi* as personal appropriation without allowing a single variation in *li.* For example, even though judges interpret the same set of laws, their judicial decisions will have a very distinct personal style and character. Similarly, even though violin virtuosos are reading the same musical score, each them will give the piece a unique interpretation. We should assume that the dances the Confucians performed had a set choreography, but we could easily imagine each having particular styles as varied as all classical ballerinas do. These examples obviously support the idea of personal judgment rather than a group decision.

As we have seen, Nancy Sherman argues that Aristotle's concept of equity, the ability to apply the law to particular cases, is also one of the functions of practical reason. If she is correct, Yu's rejection of the *phronēsis-yi* parallel is especially curious because he says that *yi* "is something like the principle of justice or what action one should follow or conform to."[22] Furthermore, Yu admits that *yi* as "natural character" (Ames and Rosemont's "basic disposition") is contrasted with cultural refinement,[23] so Confucian *yi* could serve as a basis for a sense of personal justice and hence cultural and political criticism. Indeed, the principal message of the *Analects* is that current social and political arrangements are clearly not acceptable. It is evident from the negative reception that Confucius generally received from the rulers of his day that his ideas were no more tolerated than Socrates's were. Furthermore, Confucius never insisted on a strict interpretation of *li:* for example, he was willing to embrace a man without relatives and to include him in a universal human family.[24]

Yi as the capacity to adapt to context is clearly seen in the *junzi*'s freedom from invariable norms and permission to ignore the small rules and concentrate on the good.[25] In fact, at the age of seventy Confucius claims that he had reached the point where he could do anything that he pleased without "overstepping the boundaries."[26] Furthermore, *yi* enables the *junzi,* just as *phronēsis* does for Greek gentlemen, to distinguish real virtue from its semblances. An inferior man may seem brave, but without *yi,* his rashness may turn him into an outlaw.[27] The example of courage is an especially instructive one to answer Yu's specific point: no other person or group could possibly determine the very personal judgments that are required in the development of courage.

Tu Weiming is very helpful in demonstrating that *yi*, like *phronēsis,* allows us to apply the universal to the particular: "Explicitly defined as fitness and appropriateness, *yi* mediates between the universal principle of humanity and the particular situations in which the principle is concretely manifested. ... *Yi* is the human path *(renlu)* through which one's inner morality becomes properly realized in society. This involves a practical judgment based upon the holistic evaluation of objective conditions."[28] "Right" rather than the traditional "righteousness" is a much better translation of *yi,* as long as we realize that this would always mean what is right for us or right for our conditions. (Righteousness as being right with God is particularly inapt because *yi* involves a being right with oneself and others.) For example, in Mencius's time it was generally not right to touch your sister-in-law, but you certainly must do so if she is drowning and only your hand can save her. *Yi* is acting appropriately given one's own personal history and situation. The meaning of one's life is a creative fusion of external *li* and internal *yi*. Interestingly enough, Michel Foucault finds the same dialectic in Hellenistic ethics, namely, "codes of behavior" *(li)* coupled with "forms of subjectivation" *(yi)*.[29] Speaking of Greco-Roman ethics, Foucault also maintains that moral practices are "not something that the individual invents by himself. They are patterns that he finds in his culture."[30] Ancient virtue ethics is therefore personal, contextual, and normative.

Sherman has observed a dual function in *phronēsis,* an ability not only to discern what is appropriate for the agent but also an equally important perception about the needs of others and corresponding responsibilities.[31] I suggest that there is a Confucian parallel in the difference Hall and Ames find between *yi* as "self-assertive and meaning bestowing" and its homophone *yi** as "self-sacrificing and meaning-deriving." They state: "Whereas *yi* denotes appropriateness to one's own person, *yi** refers to appropriateness to one's context."[32] Using the language of Merleau-Ponty, Confucian sages involve themselves in a process of personal *Sinngebung,* a centrifugal process of meaning giving *(yi)* to the centripetal influx of social patterns *(yi* + li)*. For both Merleau-Ponty and the Confucians, human freedom and creativity happen right at the intersection of this internal-external dynamic. Merleau-Ponty, Wittgenstein, process philosophers, and the pragmatists all join most ancients in their fusion of the inner and the outer, refusing to dichotomize subject and object. In the next section we will see that such a perspective might solve the notorious conundrum of the Is and the Ought.

Thinking of *yi* as a capacity for premoral discrimination is particularity helpful in understanding why the *ren** person, who presumably uses *yi,* is "capable of liking or disliking other men."[33] It also might explain the passage where Confucius believes something is terribly wrong when either everyone hates or likes something.[34] Morally inferior people may either be indifferent and indiscriminately like anything; or alternatively, they may easily be swayed to hate those whom the group hates. What is appropriate, according to Confucius, is that people love virtue and the virtuous person and hate the lack thereof.[35] (In a note to his translation Wing-tsit Chan clarifies that "hate" in this passage "means dislike, without any connotation of ill will.")[36] *Yi* as premoral discrimination appears to play the same role as feeling *(vedanā)* in Buddhism, which H. V. Guethner describes as "a kind of judging, although it does not establish an intellectual connection but merely sets up a subjective criterion of acceptance, rejection, or indifference."[37] Finally, the distinction between likes and dislikes fits nicely with a virtue aesthetics and Robert C. Roberts's proposal that the virtuous person be seen as an "artifact— a configuration of his cares and uncares."[38]

Mencius verifies the connection between *yi* and personal preference that I am proposing. In his discourse on the four beginnings, Mencius proposes that *yi* originates in the sentiments of "disdain and dislike."[39] Confucius's observation that if a person is still disliked at forty, he will be always be disliked not only shows how lack of discernment becomes habitual, but also how this prevents such a person from enjoying the joys of a full social life.[40] Some people continually misjudge how to act and relate to others. For Aristotle this would demonstrate a serious failure in practical reasoning and ultimately an inability to establish lasting friendships.

Phronēsis is sometimes translated as "practical wisdom," so it is important that we look at the connection between *yi* and the Confucian virtue of wisdom *(zhi)*.[41] Confucian ethics does not distinguish between intellectual and moral virtues, so Confucian wisdom represents a fusion of practice and theory by an integrated heart-mind *(xin)*. With regard to the relation between *yi* and *zhi*, Confucius states, "To devote yourself to what is appropriate *(yi)* for the people, and to show respect for ghosts and spirits while keeping them at a distance can be called wisdom (*zhi*)."[42] Confucius then connects *zhi* and *ren**: "If your wisdom can grasp it, but your *ren** is incapable of maintaining it, even though you have grasped it, you will certainly lose it."[43] Tu's position that *ren** is the one comprehensive virtue that perfects the others is supported here. Even though we may perceive what is proper for us to do, we will not be able to follow through consistently without being *ren**. (Indeed, virtually all who do wrong know what the right is.) The common people may follow the Dao and may grasp it in a personal way *(yi)*, but they do not necessarily realize *(zhi)* it.[44]

Mencius describes the relationship between *yi* and *zhi* in a way that supports the present analysis. For him *zhi* is a skill and it is like Aristotle's practical wisdom, because its origins lie in feelings of right and wrong, whereas *yi* is a more general capacity of discrimination arising in likes and dislikes.[45] One could say that *yi* provides the initial preference for acting, while *zhi* would give us the skill necessary for carrying it out. This point is confirmed even in the *Analects*: "When faced with what is right *(yi)*, to leave it undone shows a lack of courage."[46] True courage, we will recall, requires the presence of *ren**. Mencius insists on the strict alliance between *ren** and *yi* in achieving *zhi*: "The actuality of *ren** consists in serving one's parents. The actuality of *yi* consists in obeying one's elder brother. The actuality of wisdom consists in knowing these two things and not departing from them."[47] Although the Confucians never affirm the unity of the virtues in the way that Aristotle does, they both share a functional holism in which the virtues must always work together in harmony with one another.

Dharma and the Middle Way

By proposing a Buddhist eudaimonism, David J. Kalupahana was one the first scholars to suggest parallels between the Buddha and Aristotle, but in his later work he mistakenly identifies Buddhist ethics as primarily utilitarian.[48] Damien Keown critiques Kalupahana and others on this point,[49] and proposes a full-fledged Buddhist virtue ethics with a brilliant detailed comparison between the Buddha and Aristotle. (While neither the Buddha nor Gandhi are utilitarians, in chapter 9 we will side with P. J. Ivanhoe over Keown by supporting a "character" consequentialism.) Keown should also be commended for rejecting an intellectualist reading of Buddhist ethics, one that holds that insight *(prajñā)* alone, just like *sophia,* can leads us to *nirvāna/eudaimonia.* Keown states that *prajñā* "is the cognitive realization of [no-self] while śilā (virtue) is the affective realization," and cites Croom Robertson to strengthen the point: "[W]isdom...is a term of practical import; it is not mere insight, but conduct guided by insight. Good conduct is wise; wise conduct is good."[50] Confucius does not make a distinction between moral and intellectual virtues, so this issue is moot for Confucian ethics. Confucian wisdom *(zhi)* is the realization of excellence *(de = aretē)* in all the virtues. Both these Buddhist and Confucian notions of wisdom match how I choose to interpret Aristotle in the first section. All three thinkers also use craft analogies to show how important it is to create a harmonious ensemble of virtues for the good life.[51]

I would now like to supplement Keown's excellent work by proposing that one can discern the operation of practical reason in the Buddha's eightfold path and also in one of his most famous sayings: "They who know causation *(pratītyasumutpāda)* know the Dharma."[52] Let us unpack the meaning of this pithy proposition. First, a better translation of the Sanskrit phrase *pratītyasumutpāda* is "interdependent coorigination." Second, the word "Dharma" can be translated as "truth," "moral law," or "righteousness." The word fuses the worlds of facts and values. Sometimes the term is used to describe basic moments of reality, an anticipation of the quanta of energy of contemporary physics. Dharmas in this sense are not substantial things but events and processes. Whereas the elements of Hume's field of experience are externally related and brought together by custom and habit, the Buddha's field of experience is dominated by internal relations, that is, relations of interdependence. To put it in other terms, Hume was captured by a mechanistic worldview of inert atoms bouncing around in empty space, but the Buddha embraced what is best called an organic, holistic, interdependent world, one that has been reaffirmed in many disciplines, including contemporary physics. The Buddhist virtue of compassion *(karuṇā)* is based on the interrelatedness of all life, and this was the fundamental moral discovery of the Buddha's Enlightenment. The Buddha realized that compassion and sympathy can have no meaning if Sāṃkhya *puruṣa,* Jain *jīva,* or Vedāntist *ātman* are, as these schools hold, independent substances.

We are now ready for an interpretation of this powerful phrase: Those who know their own causal web of existence know the truth (that is, the true facts of their lives) and they will know what to do. As Kalupahana states, "Thus, for the Buddha, truth values are not distinguishable from moral values or ethical values; both are values that participate in nature"; and this means that Dharma consists in moral and physical principles derived "from the functioning of all *dharma*," as basic constituents of existence.[53] The truths we discover by means of this formula will be very personal truths, moral and spiritual truths that are, as Aristotle says of moral virtues, "relative to us." As we will see in chapter 8, Aquinas preserves Aristotle's relativism (the virtues are skills that "suit us [personally] for life generally")[54] and he also reaffirms the basic identity of truth and being. Thomistic *prudentia,* as Gilbert Meilaender phrases it, is "a fundamental openness" that "enables us to perceive the truth of things." *Prudentia* is the ability to get past how we would wish things to be to what is "really there."[55]

This motto can also be interpreted in terms of the Buddhist idea of mindfulness. (It is also significant that Nancy McCagney translates *śūnyatā* as "openness.")[56] Those who are mindful of what is going on inside of themselves as well as what is going on in the world about them will know what to do. (For all the ancients this meant breaking through the veil of disordered desire to the truth of the situation.) This is not simply a cognitive knowing of everything but a practical grasp of what is appropriate and what is fitting for us and our surroundings. (Like *phronēsis* it is primarily nonsensuous correct perception.) The famous "mirror of Dharma" is not a common one that we all look into together, as some later Buddhists believed, but it is actually a myriad of mirrors reflecting individual histories.

Both Aristotle and the Buddha thought it was always wrong to eat too much, but each person will find his/her own relative mean between eating too much and eating too little. A virtue ethics of moderation is still normative, because the principal determinants in finding a workable mean for eating are objective, not subjective. If people ignore these objective factors—for example, temperament, body size, metabolism, and other physiological factors—then their bodies, sooner or later, will tell them that they are out of their respective means. From their standpoint in Confucian philosophy, Ames and Rosemont claim that Dharma signifies "what we can do and be, if we realize *[zhi]* the most from our personal qualities and careers as contextualized members of a specific community. ...[*de* is] becoming one's own person."[57]

The Buddha's famous motto, "Those who know causation know the Dharma," sometimes has a provocative addition: "Those who know the Dharma know me."[58] This conclusion appears to undermine the thesis that we are essentially our own standard for determining the Dharma. In Māhāyana schools that deify the Buddha one is faced with the possibility that the Buddha becomes the absolute standard for value in the same way that God is in Christian ethics. The fact that this additional phrase appears in Pāli texts as well as later Sanskrit texts indicates that there may be an alternative reading to "knowing me." It would not necessarily be an act of hubris for the Buddha to claim, especially in the context of the Indian acceptance of knowledge of past lives, that he knows the Dharma better than anyone heretofore. One need only compare the moral knowledge that mindful people learn from trial and error in one life to a vastly expanded font of moral lessons one could learn from thousands of past lives. Therefore, we can see the Buddha as a paragon of virtue without at all deifying him, and "knowing me" could be interpreted as an invitation for us to find our own middle way in the same way that Confucius offered the ancient sage kings as models of virtue. I therefore reject Keown's claim that the Buddha's choice "determines where virtue lies."[59] I do not think this is compatible with Buddhist personalism and contextualism.

One might object that this motto has confused facts and values and therefore it illicitly derives the Ought from the Is. These well honored distinctions are the result of the dichotomizing tendency of modern European philosophy. Here subjects were distinguished from objects; the inner was carefully demarcated from the outer; and percepts were strictly separated from concepts. Drawing on his radical empiricism, the Buddha's response to these dichotomies would be that they are not found in experience but are abstracted from it. As he states, "What one feels, one perceives; what one perceives one reasons about."[60] The Buddha's process philosophy and his rejection of absolute existence—either material, mental, or spiritual—also undermines any firm distinction between the physical and the psychological. Kalupahana maintains that the moral Ought is no longer "an absolute command or necessity, but a pragmatic call to recognize...the empirical existence and adopt solutions to whatever problems are associated with it."[61] Here indeed is a beautiful description of Buddhist experiments with truth.

The Eight-Fold Path

Turning now to the Buddha's eight-fold path, one could argue that the traditional translation of these moral imperatives is misleading. Translating the Sanskrit stem *samyak* that appears in each of the words as the "right" thing to do makes them sound like eight commands of duty ethics. Instead of eight universal rules for living, most of them should be seen as virtues, that is, dispositions to act in certain ways under certain conditions. A translation of *samyak* more appropriate to Buddhist pragmatism would be "suitable," "fitting," or the "appropriate action" of Confucian *yi*. So we would have suitable view, fitting conception, appropriate speech, suitable action, appropriate livelihood, suitable effort, appropriate mindfulness, and suitable concentration. It is only fitting, for example, that a warrior eat more and more often than a monk, or it is suitable that the warrior express courage in a different way than a nonwarrior would. Both are equally virtuous, because they have personally chosen the virtues as means, means relative to them. Right livelihood proves to be an particularly telling example. Under a universalist reading of "right," one might derive the absurd conclusion that we must all choose the same vocation, rather than one suitable to our talents and circumstances.

A. J. Bahm's more literal translation of *samyak* as "middle-wayed" view, "middle-wayed" conception, and so forth brings out the parallel with Aristotle's doctrine of the mean even better. The Buddha made it clear that the Fourth Noble Truth required determining a mean: "What Brethren is this Middle Path...? It is this Noble Eightfold Path."[62] Bahm observes that the Buddha's mean "is not a mere, narrow, or exclusive middle [limited by strict rules or an arithmetic mean], but a broad, ambiguous, inclusive middle."[63] Therefore, the virtues of the eight-fold path are seen as dispositions developed over a long time, and they are constantly adjusted with a view to changing conditions and different extremes. Bahm acknowledges that the translation of "right" is acceptable if, as it is in both Buddhist and Greek ethics, it means "that which is intended to result in the best. ...However, right, in Western thought, tends to be rigorously opposed to wrong, and rectitude has a stiff-backed, resolute, insistent quality about it; right and wrong too often are conceived as divided by the law of excluded middle. But in *samyak* the principle of excluded middle is, if not entirely missing, subordinated to the principle of the middle way."[64] Neither the Buddha nor Aristotle give up objective moral values. It is also impossible to find a mean between being faithful and committing adultery or killing and refraining from doing so. But even with this commitment to moral objectivity, we must always be aware that the search for absolute rightness and wrongness involves craving and attachment. Besides, the cultivation of distinctively personal virtues would make such a search misdirected and unnecessary.

Before concluding with some examples of experiments with truth, I wish to summarize Keown's analysis of the Buddha and Aristotle so as to complete the comparative picture. According to Keown, there is no Buddhist equivalent for *phronēsis,* but he believes that there is a very good match between *prohairesis* and *cetana. Prohairesis* is the act of moral choice that occurs after *phronēsis* has judged an action to be correct. Keown rejects the interpretation that the Buddhist *cetana* is purely intellectual. He maintains that it integrates both intellectual and emotional aspects of the soul; like *prohairesis* it is both deliberative thought and deliberative desire. It organizes the entire personality to focus on the task at hand, like a supervisor in the field of workers. *Cetana* comes closest to *phronēsis* in this image of the foreman who organizes all premoral and moral labor. In a brilliant fusion of the inner and the outer, *cetana* joins both intention and action, such that the virtue generosity *(dana)* is both something given as well as the intention to give. Keown states that "*cetana* is morally determinative, and therefore action without *cetana* is not ethically charged."[65] This fundamental intentionism constitutes a crucial blow to any utilitarian interpretation of Pāli Buddhism. It also means that lusting in one's heart is a complete and culpable immoral action, just as blameworthy as Augustine's sinning while dreaming.

Experiments with Truth

Let us look at some issues regarding "right" speech. The Buddha explained that right speech is the expression of both right views and right conception. Right view must be both as comprehensive and attuned to individual variations as possible. (The latter qualification joins right mindfulness to the total vision of right view.) It requires attaining a mean between absolute certainty and absolute doubt. Right view also means a fusion of the subjective and the objective. All truths are basically intersubjective truths. A comprehensive view has to be both objective and subjective—that is, everything that is an object had some subject in it; and everything that is a subject had some object in it. This follows because of interdependent coorigination.

Specifically, suitable speech means not to lie or slander, but this is not to be taken as an absolute prohibition. Obsession with lying in Judeo-Christian ethics culminated in Kant's moral absolutism, in which even white lies were not allowed. The concept of right speech as "suitable" speech is found in Confucian ethics as well as in Buddhism. Confucius once told his servant to get rid of an especially irritating visitor by saying that he was not home. In Māhāyana Buddhism the idea of fitting or appropriate speech is found in the doctrine of "expedient means." The loving father in the *Lotus Sūtra* found that he had to lie to his children in order to get them to leave a burning house, symbolic of the fire of craving. Suitability in Buddhist ethics parallels quite closely Aristotle's view that what is "suitable is...relative to the person, the circumstances, and the object."[66]

Those who insist on an absolute prohibition against lying are those who are secretly craving that the world should be different from what it is. As Bahm states, "Unwillingness to accept things as they are is the basis of lying, and any expression of that unwillingness is wrong speech."[67] This is one of the subtlest forms of self-deception—lying to oneself about the nature of the world—which is obviously a deeper and more profound lie than the father's white lie in the *Lotus Sūtra*. Acceptance of the world as it is and not craving that it can be radically changed is fundamental for the realism and pragmatism found in Buddhist ethics. This is one way of understanding the Māhāyanist's provocative claim that Saṃsāra is Nirvāṇa and Nirvāṇa is Saṃsāra. Nirvāṇa is not simply personal extinction at the end of life, but full commitment to this world as the focus of the spiritual life. Reaching Nirvāṇa while in the body does not entitle the aspirant to ignore worldly concerns; on the contrary, it means that this person is supposed to be even more committed to the moral and spiritual welfare of all living beings.

Although Confucius claimed that he was not an innovator, he did add something new to the Zhou traditions that he embraced. His concept of *ren**, best translated as "being truly humane," is his own unique contribution. It can be defined as the one comprehensive virtue in which all others are perfected. Commentators as well as his own disciples bemoan the fact that the Master never defined *ren** very well. The answer to this puzzle is that Confucius was simply being honest about how context-dependent the virtues actually are. Therefore, what was *ren** to one person may not be *ren** to another. Ames and Rosemont explain it well: "Confucius based his specific response to the question on the specific perspective—lived, learned, experienced—from which he thought the disciple asked it."[68] Confucius advised the disciple Zilu to wait before he acted on what he had learned, whereas he urged Ranyou to act. When asked the reason for the contrary advice, Confucius said, "Ranyou is diffident, and so I urged him on. But Zilu has the energy of two, and so I sought to rein him in."[69] What we see here is Confucius's own method of specific experiments with truth and how he wants his disciples to test their actions according to their temperaments and circumstances.

Although Gandhi expressed faith in eternal Truth, he always reminded himself and his followers that finite beings could only know finite truths. D. K. Bedekar is the one Gandhi scholar who sees the implications of this most clearly:

> He unmistakably refers to the finite truth which can be grasped by a finite mind, and boldly asserts that we, as finite human beings, must chart our voyage with this compass, as our only guide. Here Gandhi appears a humble seeker of human truth, as distinguished from eternal Truth sought by ancient seeks of Moksha, Nirvana or the eternal Bliss of Brahma-jnana. …
>
> It appears to me that Gandhi bypasses metaphysical clarity, and he wants to confront issues directly. He wants to experiment with truth and *ahiṃsā;* in other words, he has no use for definitions and concepts, but wants to live out, or try out, certain tentatively held beliefs or instinctively felt urges.[70]

If Bedekar is correct, and I believe that he is, then Gandhi cannot appeal to his "Higher Self," as he sometimes calls Ātman, for particular ethical guidance. Ātman is a universal self and can only give universal answers. (If it is truly undifferentiated it may not be able to do even that.) Therefore, Vedāntist or Jain philosophy cannot possibly be the guide for Gandhi's experiments with truth. Thus I conclude that the best way to conceive of these experiments is by means of the personal practical reason discussed in this chapter, and that is why I have offered a Buddhist interpretation of Gandhi's ethics of nonviolence.

Chapter 6

The Aesthetics of Virtue

Elegant is the junzi; *he is as if cut, as if filed; as if chiseled; as if polished; how freshly bright; how refined. ...*

—*The Book of Odes*

The good, of course, is always beautiful.

—Plato

The function of reason is to promote the art of life.

—Alfred North Whitehead

Logic concentrates attention upon high abstraction, and aesthetics keeps as close to the concrete as the necessities of finite understanding permit.

—Alfred North Whitehead

This chapter will propose that the best way to refound virtue ethics is to return to the Greek concept of *technē tou biou,* literally "craft of life." The ancients did not distinguish between craft and fine arts and the meaning of *technē,* even in its Latin form of *ars,* still retains the meaning of skillful crafting and discipline. In Greco-Roman culture these techniques were very specific, covering dietetics, economics, and erotics. In ancient China moral cultivation was intimately connected to the arts, from the art of archery to poetry, music, and dance such that virtually every activity would have both a moral and an aesthetic meaning. In a recent discussion of saints and virtues this process has been described as "making persons into classics."[1] The Christian appropriation of this was the medieval *imitatio Christi* in which the Christian exemplar expresses the original beauty of Adam as it was restored in Christ.

A Chinese poet of the *Book of Odes* conceives of moral development as similar to the manufacture of a precious stone. At birth we are like uncut gems, and we have an obligation to carve and polish our potential in the most unique and beautiful ways possible. Using R. D. Collingwood's distinction between craft and fine art, I will propose that the fine arts, particularly the performing arts of music and dance, can serve as a model for virtue ethics in our times. I will also demonstrate that Confucian philosophy has much to contribute to this project, although I want to emphasize that I am making a contemporary appropriation of an ancient view that did not recognize the full range of individual creativity that the fine art model allows. Furthermore, I will argue that a contemporary virtue aesthetics need not assume an ethical naturalism whose identity goodness and beauty raises the issue of the conundrum of the evil artist.

The first section will use Michel Foucault's insightful study of Greco-Roman ethics and compare it to Confucian philosophy. The second section will demonstrate that *phronēsis* is a form of synthetic reason, which is then related to the distinction between rational and aesthetic order. The third section is a summary discussion of virtue aesthetics in Confucian philosophy, which will be compared to Gandhi's views in the next chapter. The fourth and final section will return to Aristotle and argue that the fine art model for virtue ethics essentially undermines Aristotle's distinction between artistic making *(poēsis)* and moral practice (*praxis*).

A Confucian Critique of Greco-Roman Ethics

Michel Foucault has translated the Greek *technē tou biou* as the "aesthetics of existence" and, drawing on Greco-Roman ideas of care of the self, he urges us "to create ourselves as a work of art."[2] Such an ethics, claims Foucault, would satisfy our "desires for rules [and] form" and would give us "a very strong structure of existence...with a disciplinary structure,...without any relation with the juridical per se."[3] In his study of Hellenistic culture Foucault found a powerful synthesis of ascetic and aesthetic practices. During this time many people took very seriously Socrates's admonition about not allowing reason to be dragged around like a slave by the passions. Following strict discipline they subjected the passions to the rule of master reason. Foucault is especially fond of this exhortation from Plutarch: "You must have learned principles so firmly that when your desires, your appetites, or your fears awaken like barking dogs, the *logos* will speak with the voice of a master who silences the dogs by a single command."[4] With such a regime in place people would, according to Foucault, be able to achieve a "stylization of conduct" that would give their "existence the most graceful and accomplished form possible."[5]

A very striking and philosophically significant difference stands between Confucian and European philosophy. (American process and pragmatic philosophy are instructive exceptions on this point.) The latter generally followed Aristotle in his claim that reason is the essence of being human, but instead of this the Confucians offered a marvelous pun: *ren ren**. The character *ren** is a combination of *ren* meaning person and the number two, so the concept of relationality is at the origins of this character. *Ren** is variously translated as "humanity," "benevolence," "human heartedness," "love," and "compassion"; and, according to Tu Weiming, it is the comprehensive virtue that allows the perfection of all the others.[6] At the heart of Confucian ethics is virtuous relationality rather than rational autonomy. Reasoning was of course important for ancient Chinese—their logical canons are impressive even without the syllogism—but reason was never granted the pride of place that relationality was. This means that self-mastery through reason plays no role in Confucian ethics, and that a male reason/female passions duality was not a conceptual weapon for Chinese males in the way it was for European patriarchy.

Aristotle defines human beings as social as well as rational animals, but this dual definition leads to an unresolved dichotomy in Aristotle's moral philosophy. In the early books of the *Nicomachean Ethics* the conditions for human happiness *(eudaimonia)* are thoroughly social and include material goods, friends, a good looking wife, and handsome children. In the tenth book, however, war and politics are declared "unleisurely" and happiness is equated with isolated contemplation. The moral virtues, which unified reason and the passions and were essential to the success of the *polis*, now give way to a life of intellectual virtue. As reason is that which is most divine in us, we should emulate the gods in their freedom from society, the emotions, and nature. There is also a corresponding change in the pleasure that we experience in the virtues. The pleasure of the moral virtues involves the nonrational parts of the soul, whereas the contemplation of Book 10 produces pure intellectual joy. When the Confucians speak of the joy of virtue they are definitely referring to the embodied pleasure of the moral virtues.

Aristotle is therefore faced with an irreconcilable inconsistency between rational autonomy and social relationality. Jiyuan Yu argues that Aristotle's clear preference for the former over the latter appears in Aristotle's claim that friendship is primarily based on self-love. Yu states that "a good person will perform actions in other people's interests, but that is for the perfection of one's own character. If so, when there is a conflict with other agents in pursing the development of their own characters, it is rational for a moral agent to develop his own, rather than curtailing it."[7] There is no ambivalence at all in the Confucian view that social relations constitute human nature, and Yu argues that if we conceive of *ren** as filial love, then the expansion of this basic virtue to others gives a secure foundation for graded altruism and a truly other-regarding view of friendship. A virtue ethics based on aesthetic self-cultivation might well fail to encourage the other-regarding virtues of love and compassion, but the thoroughly social self of Confucianism gives the proper psychological foundation for care for others. In chapter 8 we shall see that Thomas Aquinas agrees with the Confucians that *prudentia* must be guided by love.

The Chinese character *xin*—translated as "mind" or "heart" but best rendered "heart-mind"—represents the "ruler" of the Confucian self. Reason and the passions are united in *xin* so the dichotomy that has plagued European thought is simply nonexistent. Assuming a thoroughly somatic soul, the Confucius of the *Analects* does not even oppose heart-mind to the senses and appetites, although this dichotomy does appear later in Mencius and Xunzi. Even so Mencius believes that the body is nevertheless constitutive of personal identity, because the virtues of the good person, while "rooted in his heart," manifest themselves "in his face, giving it a sleek appearance. It also shows in his back and extends to his limbs...."[8] The authors of *The Great Learning* make the same point: "For other people see him as if they see his very heart. This is what is meant by saying that what is true in a man's heart will be shown in his outward appearance. ...[W]ealth makes a house shining and virtue makes a person shining. When one's mind is broad and his heart generous, his body becomes big and is at ease."[9] The evil person thinks that he can do what he wants in private, but the virtuous person can read him like a book.

This means that sages literally image the virtues in their bodies and make even more evident the fusion of the good, the elegant, and the beautiful. Learning *li* is essentially a "discipline of the body" and the literal meaning of teaching by example *(shenjiao),* which is to be preferred over teaching by words *(yanjiao),* means "body teaching."[10] Learning *li* begins with physical exercises such as archery and charioteering and extends to the choreographing of every single bodily movement. This matches Foucault's view that the *bios* of the human body should be the "material" from which we fashion our own virtuous "piece[s] of art."[11]

In many instances Greco-Roman "care of the self" tended to narcissism as self-indulgent ascetic-aesthetes poured their energies into their own body building and soul crafting. While definitely not narcissistic, Seneca, Epictetus, and Marcus Aurelius certainly encouraged long periods of solitude and retreat from the world. Nevertheless, Foucault's conclusion is that the best of Hellenistic moral self-cultivation was "not an exercise in solitude, but a true social practice; ...the care of the self...appears...as an intensification of social relations."[12] The evidence that Foucault adduces for this conclusion is the solicitude that the masters show for their pupils and how reflection in solitude resulted in fuller relations with others.

As we have seen, Confucian self-cultivation has a strong social dimension, but I contend that this rests on firmer psychological and philosophical grounds than Hellenistic counterparts. When Epictetus, for example, reflects about the nature of the self he discovers the true Self, one that never sleeps and is never compromised by the passions. This is the spiritual self that we share with all human beings and that is the basis of our common humanity. The phrase "self-examination" *(shen du)* appears often in Confucian texts, but what Confucians find in their solitude is not a spiritual substance of Stoic or Cartesian variety, neither a dissolution into a universal self nor a solipsism and the egocentric predicament. Confucian self-examination reveals a self that has its own individual integrity and is united with its desires and emotions. Confucians also discover a self that is a process rather than a static substance, and they see for themselves the single thread of which Confucius spoke: the constitution of the self *(zhong)* is related to the constitution of others *(shu)*.[13]

Tu Weiming has phrased this Confucian fusion of the inner and the outer in the following way: "The more one penetrates into one's inner self, the more one will be capable of realizing the true nature of one's human-relatedness. ... The profound person *[junzi]* does not practice self-watchfulness *[shen du]* for the intrinsic value of being alone. In fact, he sees little significance in solitariness, unless it is totally integrated into the structure of social relations."[14] In short, the Confucians have a concept of self that gives full meaning to Foucault's claim that retreat into the soul is the ground for true social practice. No substantialist or essentialist view of the self, which assumes that it is basically atemporal, unchanging, asocial, disembodied, and non-plural, is able to do this. Furthermore, the Confucian view does not require us to put care of the self before care of others. Because of the full relationality of self and others, Confucians would find the Greek priority of self over others as unnecessary. As Foucault observes, "One must not have the care for others precede the care for self. The care for self takes moral precedence in the measure that the relationship to self takes ontological precedence."[15] Again we see rational autonomy overwhelming social relations and any secure foundations for the other-regarding virtues. This is simply another expression of Aristotle's belief that friendship is based on self-love. If this is correct, then this mitigates significantly Foucault's claim that Hellenistic ethics was as truly social as he claims it to be.

Let us now summarize the advantages of Confucian over Greco-Roman ethics. First, the absence of any major conflict between reason and the passions allows Confucians to integrate the affective parts of the self without any difficulty. We have also argued that the Confucian view of the self supports the moral imperative of concern for others without sacrificing individual integrity. Confucian morality aims at an ideal of the coincidence of self-interest and other-interest. On the other hand, a substantialist view of a universal Self in Hinduism, Mahayana Buddhism, and Christianity appears to promote a more self-sacrificial ethic, arguably because this Self is always to preferred over the ego self, namely, "Not I but Christ" or "Not I *(jīva)* but Ātman." The fact that process theologian John Cobb is committed to preserve self-interest within the performance of other-regarding Christian virtues may reveal significant shared assumptions between American and Confucian process views of the self.[16] For years Cobb has worked diligently on the Buddhist-Christian dialogue and we should not be surprised that he found the same common ground.

With regard to common ground between Confucius and Aristotle, we have seen that ancient virtue ethics can preserve normative morality within a very dynamic personalist and contextualist framework. The idea that virtue ethics is a voyage of personal discovery dovetails nicely with the idea of self-creation, so that a capacity such as *yi* or *phronēsis* must be central to a contemporary aesthetics of virtue. In the last section we will see that the performance arts will allow us to overcome the distinction Aristotle established between artistic making and moral practice. Despite this distinction both Plato and Aristotle still assumed the unity of goodness and beauty, and Flint Shier sums up the Greek view aptly: "A good man is a perfectly functioning hierarchy of goals in which his projects cooperate harmoniously under the direction of more general, overarching goods.... Analogously, the plot of a good tragedy is thus a formal emblem of the well-planned life. Work and life are noble to the extent that they manifest the handiwork of a virtuous practical intelligence."[17] It should be obvious that the Confucians agree with Aristotle in his perfectionism and functional holism.

Rational versus Aesthetic Order

Before turning to the Confucian texts to establish a connection between the good and the beautiful, let us work more generally with the concepts of rational and aesthetic order. Our word *reason* goes back to the Greek verb *lego,* the verbal noun of which is the famous word *logos*, which was translated into Latin as *ratio*. *Lego* has two principal meanings: "to say" (hence the Word of John's *logos*) and "to put together." The most general definition of rationality that we could draw from this etymology is the following: "Rational beings are those beings who are able to put their world together so that it makes sense to them." We could then say that in addition to analytic reason, one that is prescriptive and insists on universal laws of thinking, there is also synthetic reason, which is descriptive and does not bind us to the laws of logic.[18] We could also propose that synthetic reason has generally been passive in the sense that most people have accepted the way religious and cultural institutions have put their world together for them. Traditional religions, then, are constantly involved in *relego,* faithfully repeating the words *(logoi)* and ritually putting the world together again and again according to accepted ways. Synthetic reason, however, can also be active, creative, and even anarchic, defying the old rules and proposing new ways of looking at the world. Cézanne, for example, rejected the laws of perspective and ushered in a whole new way of doing art. Scientists working on the cutting edge go with their intuitions, putting together the most elegant and sometimes daring new theories. Only afterward are they tested by analytic reason, whereas both artists and virtuous persons rightly resist such testing.

I will now relate synthetic reason to the distinction between rational and aesthetic order.[19] By abstracting from the particular, rational order is ultimately indifferent to concrete individuals because it generates the rule of complete substitutability. For example, *p* and *q* can stand for any word in any natural language, just as in classical physics one atom can take the place of any other atom without changing the whole. Morally this idea of substitution finds its ultimate expression in the interchangeability of the sovereign in Kant's Kingdom of Ends. An equivalent uniformity is obtained in the modern bureaucratic state where individuals are leveled and made abstract by social rules and regulations. Even libertarians who criticize the welfare state for these indignities share the same axiom of social atomism with their social utilitarian opponents. Regardless of context and circumstance the social atom of classical economic theory can take the place of any other agent.

Confucius says that the *junzi* "seek harmony not sameness; petty persons, then, are the opposite."[20] Hall and Ames propose a contrast between the rational order of liberal democracy in the sameness of consensus making and the *junzi*'s attempt to harmonize among real differences.[21] They refer to a culinary analogy in a commentary on *Analects* 13.23 on which I would like expand. The recipe could be seen as an explicit formula for the rational ordering of the ingredients. But just as in the case of following the rule of not overeating, a tasty dish is not guaranteed by merely following the recipe. Rather, good cooks must judge the nature and condition of their ingredients and as the dish is near completion they must adjust the seasonings. Those who follow *li* in all their social roles must make the same personal judgments and appropriate adjustments. This is the making of aesthetic rather than rational order.

Aesthetic order focuses on the concrete particulars so thoroughly that there can be no substitution and no interchangeability. This applies to the work of art as much as the person of great virtue. This means that something aesthetic is ordered primarily in terms of internal relations, the basic elements being dependent on one another. By contrast physical or social atoms are externally related, independent of their environments, and for Kant's moral agents, immune to their emotions and bodies. Even though Aristotle is the origin of the idea of rational autonomy, this applies only to the intellectual virtues and only when Aristotle sees the highest good as pure contemplation. It is important to remember that he joins reason and the passions in the moral virtues and he holds that these virtues are the unique self-creations of practical reason.

Aristotle claims that theoretical reason *(nous)* would give us a universal law suitable only for the gods. For human action, however, the law is "deficient," a flaw corrected, as we have seen, by the ability of *phronēsis* to apply it to particular cases.[22] Theoretical reason would give us an arithmetic mean between excess and deficiency, thereby fulfilling the criterion of universalizability of deontological ethics. Moral agents will have exactly the same duties, so moral rationalism also conforms to analytic reason's rule of subsitutability. It should be clear, however, that such a theory cannot determine any individual action. For example, one might hold that it is always wrong to eat too much but only individuals themselves can find the mean that is right for them. (It is significant to note that this decision is not simply a subjective whim, but is governed primarily by objective factors such as body size, metabolism, and general physiology.) Aristotle and Confucius saw moral virtues as relative means derived not from a universal moral calculus but from a careful process of personal discovery. Aristotle's *phronēsis* and Confucius's *yi,* therefore, could be seen as the moral expression of synthetic reason, and its creative aspects further augment our case for an aesthetics of virtue.[23]

Analytic reason establishes rational order by reducing the whole to a simple sum of parts, while aesthetic order is synthesized from particulars in such a way that its unity is organic and immune to complete analysis. (Intimately paired subatomic particles also appear to make the universe far more organic than mechanical.) Rational order is ruled by universal laws—either physical or moral—while aesthetic order is created by imprecise rules of thumb, by emulating the virtuous person or master artist, or ideally self-creation by practical reason. Rational order can be articulated in clear language, but no one can tell us explicitly how to be a good person or a great artist. Rational order involves "knowing that" whereas aesthetic order is produced by "knowing how"; the former can be said and cognized, while the latter can only be shown in practice. Commentators and disciples alike bemoan the fact that Confucius never defined *ren**, but they should have realized that the Master, without ever thinking about the distinction between rational and aesthetic order, knew that it could not be done.

Applying the concept of aesthetic order Hall and Ames portray the Confucian sages as virtuoso performers who use their *yi* to create their own unique style of appropriating the social patterns of their community. This achievement is both moral and aesthetic because it results in the embodiment of the good *(li)* and the personal creation of an elegant, harmonious, and balanced soul. The beauty of such a creation is reflected in the person's demeanor as well as the face, limbs, and back, as Mencius told us above. Chinese sages are so unified with their instruments (for example, Butcher Ding's knife) and their bodies that their actions appear effortless and magical. The emperor sits with his back to the north star, does nothing, and all is right with the empire. It is in this meaning of *wu wei* ("effortless action") that both Confucianism and Daoism are united in an aesthetics of virtue.

A Confucian Aesthetics of Virtue

The earliest Confucians, not surprisingly, were not only teachers but musicians and dancers as well. Indeed, if Robert Eno's extensive linguistic analyses are correct, then the original meaning of *ru,* the Chinese character for "Confucian," is "ritual dancer."[24] Furthermore, Eno has traced the crucial word *wen,* translated as "pattern" or "culture" and taken by Confucians to mean Zhou culture, to a graph that stands for a dancer costumed as a bird. Eno finds it significant that the Mohists criticized the Confucians for their archaic speech and dress and also described them as dancing around making bird-like gestures.[25]

Even the casual reader of Confucian literature is struck by the many references to the *Book of Odes*. This poetry was not meant for silent reading and was usually accompanied by music and dance. Here is a passage from the *Liji:* "One must teach noble heirs and cadets according to the proper season. In spring and summer they learn dances of the shield and spear; in autumn and winter, dances of feather and flute."[26] The description of the proper acts of the *junzi* in chapter 10 of the *Analects* reminds one very much of the movements of a ritualized dance. This demonstrates the truth of Robert Neville's observation that "learning the rhythms of one's own movement is part of learning to perceive the being of others," thereby confirming our moral connection with them.[27]

Confucius was not only an expert on *li* but also a very accomplished zither player. In his conversations with the Grand Music Master of Lu it is clear that Confucius considered himself at least the master's equal.[28] Once Confucius was lost so deeply in a Shun melody that he did not have any taste for meat for three months.[29] He claimed to have the ability to read the character of composers by listening to their music. Along these lines it is said that Confucius, after his return from Wei to Lu, finally put the *Book of Odes* to music in the proper way, presumably based on a correlation between notes and virtues.[30] Confucius is definitely committed to the fusion of the moral and the aesthetic.[31] The beauty of the sage kings lies in their virtue; the beauty of any neighborhood is due to the goodness of its residents; a person without *ren** could not possibly appreciate music; and a society without *li* and music would not be just; indeed, *li* cannot be perfected without music.[32]

At the end of chapter 11 of the *Analects* four men are asked what they would do given their greatest wish. The first two answered that they would like to rule great and prosperous kingdoms. The first claimed that in three years' time his people would be courageous and follow directions. The second admitted that he would have to wait for the appearance of a *junzi* to introduce *li* and music. The third had lower ambitions: he said that he would like to be a junior official in charge of the rites. The fourth Zengxi was playing his zither and apologized to Confucius for having such modest hopes for himself. Zeng confessed that all that he wanted to do was to go out of doors in the late spring, bathe in the river, perform the rain dance, and "go home chanting poetry." Confucius replied that he was in agreement with Zeng's dream.

As we now turn to Mencius we see that he, too, continues the early Confucian fusion of the ethical and the aesthetic. The lost beauty of devastated Ox Mountain is a metaphor for moral depravity, and in a famous passage on the stages of human perfection the attribute of beauty stands higher than goodness.[33] Mencius also continues the detailed choreography of virtue when he says that the highest virtue requires that a person's every movement be in accordance with *li*.[34] The Confucians agree with Aristotle that we should take pleasure in the virtues, and Mencius believes that music best expresses the joy of mature virtue.[35] (Chinese aestheticians happily capitalize on the fact that music *[yue]* and joy *[le]* are represented by the same character.) For Mencius the joy of virtue is so infectious that when it arises one cannot stop it, "and when one cannot stop it, then one begins to dance with one's feet and wave one's arms without knowing it."[36] One cannot imagine Confucians ever reaching the frenzied state of a Dionysos or a Śiva, but this passage paints a far more dynamic picture of them than is ordinarily assumed.

In his eagerness to refute Gaozi's analogical arguments, Mencius misses an opportunity to use one of Gaozi's examples as way to express the aesthetic dimensions of moral self-cultivation. At the beginning of chapter 6a Gaozi proposes that we see the development of virtue as analogous to the making of cups and bowls from willow wood. As one who was presumably reluctant to use the dialectical methods of his day, Mencius is remarkably quick to show that Gaozi's argument implies an absurdity. The woodworker uses violent means to make his products, so that would imply that evil methods are used to produce the virtues. There is a double *reductio* in this response because these violent means would produce both vices and virtues.

Mencius could have responded much more constructively to this analogy. Woodworkers always look for certain features in the wood they select, sometimes choosing certain patterns in the wood's grain or even a knot around which there are sometimes beautiful swirls. On this alternative reading of Gaozi's analogy, the person of vice would be like the woodworker who works against the grain and destroys the beauty of the original forms. Virtuous people, on the other hand, work with the grain of their own nature, respecting its innate patterns, and make themselves into a thing of moral beauty. It is instructive to contrast Zhuangzi's view of crafting bowls of wood. He concedes that the bowl is beautiful and the shavings that are left are ugly, "yet they are both alike in having lost their inborn nature."[37] The Daoist goal is to leave all as it is, like an uncarved block *(pu)*, the significant exceptions being, as we shall see, Butcher Ding and Wheelwright Pian.

With his view of human nature Xunzi would be unmoved by Mencius's *reductio ad absurdum*. For him it is not absurd to admit that violence is necessary for moral development. Sometimes crooked wood must be made straight and dull metal must be put to the grindstone.[38] I also believe that Xunzi would embrace my alternative formulation of Gaozi's analogy. Xunzi's negative view of human nature does not in the least compromise his thoroughgoing humanism and his full commitment to moral self-cultivation. Nor does Xunzi break with earlier Confucians on the importance of music and dance. If anything, Xunzi makes the fusion of the arts and morality even more explicit and central. Xunzi declares that "music unites what is the same; rites distinguish that which is different; and through the combination of rites and music the human heart is governed."[39] Without the unifying power of the arts one could easily get lost in ritualistic minutia and lose sight of morality's proper purpose. The unity of physical movement, the order of heaven, musical harmony, and proper behavior are epitomized in the dance of the sage, who, as Xunzi describes it figuratively, "moves along with time; he bows or arches as the times change. [Fast or slow, curled or stretched], a thousand moves ten thousand changes: his Way is one."[40] The sage's *dao* is unified because his "spirit of the dance joins with the Way of Heaven. The drum is surely the lord of music, is it not? Hence, it resembles Heaven, while the bells resemble earth, the sounding stones resemble water, the mouth organs and lutes resemble the sun, and the scraper resembles the myriad beings of creation."[41] Edward Machle proposes that the cosmic dance is the central metaphor for Xunzi's concept of self-cultivation: "*Li* is correlative to dance; both are the embodiment of that order or harmony which in natural things follows *li* and in human affairs appears as *wen*."[42] (The second *li* is a character that means the natural principles in all things.)

Medieval Confucians preserved the early views that great music has correct notes because of the virtue of the composer, and that beautiful paintings contain great thoughts as "prints" of a harmonious heart-mind *(xin)*. They generally upheld the doctrine that the greater the virtue the greater the art.[43] Neo-Confucian philosopher Zhou Dunyi preserves the isomorphism of heavenly and musical harmonies and their importance for virtue. He complains, however, about people who have rejected ancient music in favor of contemporary sounds. The former "appeased the heart," while the latter "enhances desire."[44] Just as music is a vehicle of moral principles so is good literature. Zhou observes that many young people are mere aesthetes: they have not obeyed their parents and have not applied themselves to virtue, so when they create literary works "this is no more than art *(yi)*."[45] Zhou's statement that "literary style is a matter of art, whereas virtues *(daode)* are a matter of substance"[46] appears to move in the direction of European philosophy's tendency to separate matters of taste and things of true value.

A Fusion of Making and Doing

Mencius states that wisdom *(zhi)* "is like skill...while sageness is like strength,"[47] and he explains that the ability to hit the bull's-eye with a bow is not due to strength but to skill. Mencius joins both Plato and Aristotle in claiming that there are significant parallels between learning skills and learning virtues. In each we learn by doing and end up doing it either well or badly, and this value judgment is primarily aesthetic. Aristotle defines a skill or art *(technē)* as "a state *(hexis)* concerned with making things, which has a true account (*logos*)."[48] In each there is an apprehension of the principles involved, and therefore we can give a partial account of our actions. We cannot articulate the exact details of how to perform an action, so this account falls under practical-synthetic reason, not theoretical-analytic reason. In other words, one does not learn skills or virtues out of a book or by mere reflection; they are not open to complete analysis but holistic in form. It is clear that both *phronēsis* and *zhi* are still basically know-how and not purely intellectual virtues.

Both skills and virtues require a long apprenticeship before their respective ends can be achieved. The ingrained habits of both leads to a body knowledge that knows more than it can tell. Although skills involve a knowledge that cannot be completely formalized, they are amendable by critical reflection, including the ability to test options and change one's actions if better methods are discovered. Furthermore, the person who is mature in virtue acts on the knowledge of why the virtues are noble and why they must be practiced for their own sake. The person who seems virtuous by copying generous acts may have only the semblance of generosity, because a simple knowing how without proper motivation must be perfected by a knowing why. A carpenter can explain why it is wrong to go against the grain just as an adult can explain to a child why it is wrong to eat too much. Practice, however, in both instances will be required to confirm this and to perfect the skill. As Confucius states, "The common people can be induced to travel along the way, but they cannot be induced to realize *(zhi)* it."[49]

Even with all these similarities Aristotle concludes that a virtue is not a skill because it does not produce a product. A potter makes a pot separate from the potter's self and the excellence of the pot lies in it and not in the person or its production. By contrast bravery produces a brave action, not a separate product, and the value of bravery lies in the brave person and the action combined. For Aristotle this marks a clear difference between *poēsis* (making) and *praxis* (acting)—the third category of knowledge *(theōria)* being different from these two: "For production has an end other than itself, but action does not: the good action is itself an end."[50] Furthermore, Aristotle believes that virtue requires a much more specific knowledge than skill. In pottery making the end product and its universal are very clearly defined, whereas a virtue is a mean specific and relative to us, guided by *phronēsis*, subtly and finely tuned to our person and our unique situation. Finally, it follows that a potter can throw a good pot regardless of whether the potter is a good person, while virtue in the person and the action is a necessary unity.

The Stoics, however, defended virtue as a very special type of skill. They exploited the common intellectual component and used that as a way to further devalue the affective elements of virtue. The success of a skill depends on a finished product, whereas a mature virtue is always complete because, as Julia Annas explains, a "virtue can be said to succeed the whole time it is activated."[51] Indeed, Stoic virtue is complete even if it is not connected to happiness nor activated in social relations. We can use this Stoic insight about holistic virtue without embracing Stoic intellectualism or the Stoic rejection of the passions. For the Confucians mature virtue is whole not only because it is complete in its every expression but also because it represents a unity of body, heart, and mind. The Stoic view of virtue as skill also helps us bridge Aristotle's gap between making and doing if we think of moral cultivation as a form of self-creation. The skill of the dancer and the musician is also complete in the sense of the product already being finished in the first moment of performance. Like the Stoic view of virtue, musical and dancing skills "succeed the whole time [they are] activated." They are also whole in the sense of expressing a unity of body, heart, and mind.

Anthony Kenny's distinction between a performance and an activity can be put to good use here. For Kenny a performance is a whole action that must be completed, and an activity even though whole can be broken off.[52] A person is dancing during the whole time of a dance performance, just as one is walking the whole time one is taking a walk. The crucial difference is that the dancer has not performed the dance if it is broken off, but one has still taken a walk if one turns back home earlier than expected. The virtues are obviously more like performances than activities, but there are some instructive differences. Artistic performances and virtuous activities must be complete in their momentary yet continuous wholeness but also completed in the sense of having a specific end. Courage or compassion broken off in their expression are obviously not these virtues; indeed, one could say that in certain circumstances they become their corresponding vices.

It is clear, however, that an artistic performance succeeds in a way different from the virtues. When a dancer has completed the performance, the dancer's success or failure is determined solely by aesthetic criteria. The virtues, however, have good consequences and we discuss this issue in more detail when we come to character consequentialism in chapter 9. Furthermore, I propose that there is a significant analogy but not an identity between the arts and virtues, thereby answering the challenge of the evil artist. The single disanalogy of the evil artist does not undermine in any way the many fruitful analogues that we have drawn from the arts.

Let us use William Wallace of the movie *Braveheart* to explicate further the difference between virtuous and artistic performances. In his battles with the English, Wallace lost everything in the performance of his virtues, so it is clear that success in one's virtue projects is different in yet another significant sense from the artistic performer. While we have argued that we do and should use aesthetic criteria for judging the virtuous person, Wallace's failure has nothing to do with such standards; rather, they have everything to do with the exigencies of English history. (The Stoic might say that here is a virtuous life that does not lead to *eudaimonia* as Aristotle promised, but Aristotle would remind his critic of his important caveat: Wallace would probably have been very happy if great misfortune had not intervened and we would also expect that he would have still been a great person.) Courage is courage the whole time one is courageous; furthermore, it is still courage even if you lose every single battle. (It is inconceivable that artists could preserve their reputations in face of comparable failures.) You are courageous even if the aggressor defeats you, or if you fail to save a drowning person.

R. G. Collingwood observes that the while the craftsperson and the artist may share some of the same specific skills, the former has some specific end in sight while the latter does not.[53] The potter, for example, shapes a very fine coffee mug on the potter's wheel. Then a mold is made of the mug so that it can be reproduced and sold in the marketplace. The ceramic sculptor, on the other hand, proceeds very differently. Most of such work is not done on a wheel and, according to Collingwood, is not produced with any particular form in mind. If the sculptural work begins with a sketch, as is sometimes the case, then the artistic indeterminacy resides there primarily, although the execution of the sketch in clay may often require basic modifications because of differences in the media. The potter produces perhaps thousands of copies of the same fine mug, but the ceramic sculptor creates only one unique work.

The implications for the practice of virtue ethics are, I believe, quite instructive. In contrast to the father who tells his son, "Be just like me," following the craft analogy, a contemporary Confucian would say, "Be your own person" and develop a unique ensemble of character traits, moral dispositions, and behaviors. Confucius might have said, "Don't be just any old mug; be a gem!" Or a contemporary Confucian would say, "Don't be a chip off the old block, but carve your own creation from your own nature." It is significant to observe that we sometimes use the word gem to describe a person of good character. It is worth reiterating here Robert Roberts's thesis that the virtuous person is an artifact—a unique and aesthetic configuration of cares and uncares.[54]

The authors of the *Doctrine of the Mean* attribute a text to Confucius that discusses the topic of hewing an ax handle from a pattern, which is a metaphor for the *dao*.[55] He quotes this from the *Book of Odes:* "In hewing an axe handle, in hewing an ax handle, is the pattern not far off?" Confucius warns about the error of simply copying from existing ax handles and not realizing the real pattern is near at hand. To read this as an exhortation to make exact copies of a standard *dao* would ignore the principle of personal appropriation we have found in *yi*. To avoid reducing Confucian morality to a mere moralism, we must assume that each of us has our own *de,* which is the pattern for our own moral self-cultivation through *yi*. As we have seen, Confucius claims that he uses his *yi* in order "to extend [his] *dao*."[56] This would conform to the general *dao-de* ontology, with myriad *de* as particular instantiations of the *dao,* that Confucianism shares with Daoism.

Laozi's ideal of remaining an "uncarved block" *(pu)* and Zhuangzi's frequent preference for a faceless and undifferentiated *hundun* stand as major Chinese objections to the cultivation of virtue. Liezi, for example, returned "from the carved gem...to the unhewn block."[57] Butcher Ding and Wheelwright Bian, however, do not leave things as they are: neither the ox nor the wood is left uncarved. Furthermore, Ding and Bian have developed consummate skills. Using these masters rather than Liehzi as ideals diminishes significantly the antisocial implications of the Daoist sage. Eno is doubtless correct in observing that Confucian social skills are intersubjective and Daoist skills are intrasubjective.[58] Nevertheless, Ding teaches Lord Wenhui how to nurture life, presumably without rejecting society and his position in it. (Duke Han does not respond to the Bian's lecture, but one may assume an equally positive response.) Liezi, however, is not a man of any particular skill, "stand[ing] alone like a clod" and "remain[ing] sealed,"[59] and it is clear that no ruler would have taken notice of him. Therefore, Zhuangzi's knackmasters are more sympathetic allies for a Chinese virtue aesthetics.[60]

The Greeks did not operate according to a craft versus fine art distinction, which, in fact, appears to have originated in the Renaissance. In his search for the proper function of human beings, Aristotle claims that it is analogous to the functions of many types of people, and he made no distinction among flue players, sculptors, carpenters, or tanners. Furthermore, skilled work in ancient societies was centered in the crafts, so that it is not surprising that craft skills were used as an analogue for ancient moral philosophy. Julia Annas states that the "insistence on the common structure of skills and virtue was an insistence that being moral is like *working;* the virtuous person is importantly like the good worker."[61] Living as we do in not only a postcraft but a postindustrial society, Annas goes on to observe that we see the crafts as hobbies and curiosities at craft fairs, thereby further undermining our ability to appreciate the basis for ancient virtue ethics. The fine arts are still central and valuable to our contemporary lives, so this is why I propose that they become the model for virtue ethics.

One could continue the conversation with Annas in the following way. Does not going to craft fairs bring us in touch with what it must of been like to live like this, and do not many of us admire not only the excellence of good craft but also the virtues of the people who produce them? Aristotle is certainly correct in observing that an evil man can be a good artist, but this point tends to obscure the equally important fact that disciplined work is one of the best ways to develop an entire ensemble of virtues. We have already proposed a solution to the conundrum of the evil artist (goodness and beauty are analogous, not identical), and we have now shown that Aristotle has overdrawn his distinction between making and acting. Both Stoics and Confucians have helped us see the virtuous person as an ideal combination of making one's self and living by means of this moral-aesthetic creation. A commentator on Aquinas reiterates Aristotle's distinction between *poēsis* and *praxis*, but he then continues to speak of the "shaping" of a person's character such that the self becomes a "work" that "surpasses all preconceived "blueprints. ..."[62] An aesthetics of virtue would fuse, without identifying, making and doing.

In a recent article James D. Wallace contends that the craft analogy breaks down because we can specify quite nicely the skills needed and the end result of craft art, but no one has ever been able to give the comparable specifics, especially with regard to ends, about the art of human flourishing.[63] Wallace believes that the craft analogy can be saved by focusing on the analogous way in which skills are used to solve specific problems presented by craft materials and the moral life respectively. (This is essentially what Aristotle draws from the craft analogy.) What Wallace is essentially saying is that the craft analogy succeeds with regard to means but fails with regard to ends. I propose, however, that by using the fine arts as a model we can solve what Wallace calls the "fixed goal" problem. The objects of craft art are determinate, whereas the goals of both fine art and life itself are indeterminate. In *The French Lieutenant's Woman* John Fowles confesses that he cannot control the lives of his characters, so, despite the claims of earlier omnipotent novelists, fictional lives are just as indeterminate as real human lives.[64] Fowles strengthens Flint Shier's earlier comparison of a plot elegantly written and a life well lived.

To make the fine arts analogy really sing we would have to think of human life as one long musical improvisation, and for the swingers among us that would have to be a life long jazz session. The dance and dancer is an even better analogue, because here it is clear that both *poēsis* and *praxis*—producing and acting—are fused in one event. The beauty of this solution is that we can still retain Aristotle's principal point: craftpersons, artists, and moral agents use requisite skills for problem solving in each of their areas. There is yet another aspect of *phronēsis* that further reduces the difference between *poēsis* and *praxis*: practical reason gives us the ability to apply proper means to specific ends. Applying this insight to the fine arts we can see once again that practical reason is a form of synthetic reason, one that is able to create aesthetic order. This means that both artistic *poēsis* and moral *phronēsis* can achieve unique and creative ends.

In his article "Hume and the Aesthetics of Agency" Shier supports the Mencian view of the "physiognomic" perception of virtue. Most European philosophy has always held that since virtues are internal properties there can be no objective theory of the virtues. Both Confucius and Hume, however, reject the modernist distinction between inner and outer and offer the obvious examples of the clear perception of the shame of vice and the glow of virtue, especially in the saint or sage. (Even though Hume believes that virtues are secondary qualities, they are still just as visible as color and sound.) The fact that we do not always perceive this connection or sometimes make mistakes about it does not in any way discount the truth of the many instances in which we do get it right.

Shier's best insight, however, is his explanation of why we find endless fascination in Van Gough's *Peasant's Shoes* but nothing at all comparable in the same type of real shoes, even if expertly displayed in a folk museum. Shier claims that in the painting we perceive a unique "style of agency" that captures us in a profound way that the museum shoes do not. As he argues,

"The deposits of agency in action and creation must be aesthetically relevant, not only as determinants of what we are to appreciate (sonnet, painting, etc.), but as objects of aesthetic appreciation in their own right."[65] This argument serves to strengthen our distinction between the value of the fine arts and the art of moral self-creation as compared to the value of the craft arts of shoemaking, and so forth. In each we recognize a style of agency that is admirable on a different level than the manufacture of useful goods.

Conclusions

Several of our examples have suggested a difference in kind between art and craft, but it should be a difference in degree instead. This would establish a continuum with craft excellence at one end and free, normless creativity at the other end. This is a horizontal continuum to avoid the elitist implications of a hierarchy of fine art over craft art. Craft excellence would be found in the examples used earlier: a judge's interpretation of the law, a musician performing according to a standard score, and a ballet dancer following a fixed choreography. The examples serve as apt analogies for the person who follows Confucian *li:* the judge, the musician, the dancer, and the Confucian still preserve the concept of personal appropriation of norms. Note that none of these examples can be reduced to a mere subjectivism or personal whim. In each good objective reasons can be given for the respective interpretations; furthermore, we can say not only that a performance is bad form but that it is simply wrong.[66] We have, therefore, fulfilled the promise in the introduction: we have shown that virtue ethics can be normative as well as personal and contextual.

Ancient virtue ethics, therefore, involves craft excellence rather than an art of free creativity. There will be personal appropriation and a relative mean within the bounds of Confucian *li* and Greek *ethos*. Furthermore, as we have seen, a Confucian virtue ethics is role specific. Sovereigns can change places in Kant's Kingdom of Ends, but even Confucius could not change places with the emperor. One could even say that the fine arts of the Renaissance and later periods remained within the *ethos* of the times. Only in the nineteenth and twentieth centuries did some artists break completely with social standards. Here figures such as Friedrich Nietzsche and Oscar Wilde proposed an ethics of total self-creation without regard for norms or standards. The best musical analogy is jazz, where players, even though required to stay in the same key, can freely improvise on the melody, all can take their turn at playing it, and the musicians can even change instruments if they wish. It is interesting to note that the jazz example still assumes conformation to the laws of classical harmony. On this point Confucius would be almost in agreement with the jazz musicians: "[O]ne begins with playing in unison, and then goes on to improvise with purity of tone and distinctness and flow, thereby bringing all to completion."[67] In the next chapter I will argue that Gandhi and a contemporary Confucian can support an ethical pluralism in which all people experiment with truth using their own *yi* and improvising within their own distinctive *li*.

Let us now summarize some general points of our contemporary adaptation of a Confucian aesthetics of virtue. As opposed to a rule-based ethics, where the most that we can know is that we always fall short of the norm, virtue ethics is truly a voyage of personal discovery. Buddhist, Confucian, and Aristotelian ethics always aim at a personal mean that is a creative choice for each individual. Virtue ethics is emulative—using the sage as a model for virtue—whereas rule ethics is based on simple conformity and obedience. The emulative approach engages the imagination, personalizes, and thoroughly grounds individual moral action and responsibility. Such an ethics naturally lends itself to an aesthetics of virtue: the crafting of a good and beautiful soul, a unique individual gem among other gems.

Chapter 7

Gandhi, Confucius, and Virtue Aesthetics

I...find beauty in Truth and through Truth. All Truths, not merely true ideas, but truthful faces, truthful pictures, or songs are highly beautiful. People generally fail to see beauty in Truth, the ordinary man runs away from it and becomes blind to the beauty in it. Whenever men begin to see Beauty in Truth, then true Art will arise.

—M. K. Gandhi

Moral beauty is an exceptional and very striking phenomenon. He who has contemplated it but once never forgets its aspects. This form of beauty is far more impressive than the beauty of nature and of science. It gives those who possess its divine gift a strange and inexplicable power. ...It establishes peace among men. Much more than science, art and religious rites moral beauty is the basis of civilization.

—Alexis Carrel

The influence that emanated from [Gandhi's] personality was ineffable, like music, like beauty...[and we are] struck by the analogy of his character with that of the great masters, whose spiritual inspiration comprehends and yet, transcends all varied manifestations of humanity. ...

—Rabindranath Tagore

A chapter on Gandhi and Confucius initially appears to be a very unpromising exercise in comparative philosophy. Nevertheless, I proposed to show that even on the points on which they seem furthest apart—Gandhian asceticism and Confucian centralized political philosophy—they are closer than we initially think they are. I maintain that their views of human nature and the self-society-world relationship are instructively similar. Both of them also balance a belief in human dignity and integrity with a belief in divine providence. In chapter 5 we have seen that they both have their own method of experiments with truth. Although Confucius does not have an explicit ethics of nonviolence, he and Gandhi share the same idea of the pacifying effect of charismatic leaders. On the fundamental issue of the unity of truth, goodness, and beauty they are in profound agreement. On the basis of this fusion of fact and value I will propose that they both share an aesthetics of virtue that should be the model for ethical practice today. This chapter will be divided into an initial section discussing significant differences between Confucius and Gandhi, a middle section discussing instructive similarities, and a concluding section on virtue aesthetics.

Confucius versus Gandhi

When Buddhists first arrived in China the Chinese were baffled by their asceticism and monasticism. Even though fair-minded Chinese realized that the monks' severance of family ties did not mean that they necessarily lacked filial piety, they were nonetheless very much concerned about the advocacy of celibacy in a society built on the integrity of the family. As late as the Sixteenth century Wang Yangming was still reiterating the basic Confucian complaint that Buddhists were "afraid of the troubles" involved in five Confucian social relationships.[1] Asceticism of course was not unknown to the Chinese, because they had a long tradition of mountain hermits who rejected society and the family. But the prospect of thousands of monks living in and requesting alms from the general population was a completely new situation for them. To their eternal credit the Chinese, except for the persecutions of the Tang Dynasty, integrated Buddhism into their society without major conflict.

One of the most famous lines in the *Analects* is "the ruler must rule, the minister minister, the father father, and the son son."[2] It is clear, however, that Confucius allowed many exceptions to this social ideal. First, if any of these agents do not have the requisite virtue, then the moral or political imperative is null and void. Second, when a certain Sima Niu despairs because he has no brother, the Confucian answer is a declaration of universal brotherhood,[3] implying that having a family is just as much a moral concept as it is a biological one. (The lesson here is even more dramatic because we know that Sima Niu does indeed have a brother, but he has disowned him because he made a threat on Confucius's life.[4]) Third, Confucius himself paid far more attention to his disciples than to his own family. His wife is never mentioned and his critical relationship to his son is very similar to the conflict between Gandhi and his sons. Confucius rebukes his son Boyu for his moral laxity and showers much paternal affection on Yan Hui, his favorite disciple. On the occasion of Yan Hui's death Confucius was beside himself with grief and he performed the mourning rites as if Yan Hui were his own son. It is in these practices that the Chinese have their own austerities. Mourners were required to wear coarse clothes, give up music, eat thin gruel, and seclude themselves for three years in rustic huts near their parents' graves. Gandhi's principle of self-suffering and his commitment to complete spiritual purity is of course alien to the Confucian mind, although similar ideas have been integral to Chinese Buddhism.

The Confucian idea of a central government under the rule of the "Son of Heaven" stands in stark contrast to Gandhi's completely decentralized village republicanism. A few observations, however, mitigate the differences here and also reveal some ironies. With the demise of the Zhou dynasty, there was no central authority during Confucius's era, the so-called Warring States period. The Chinese were not fully organized again until the Han Empire and imperial Confucianism soon forgot many of the innovative elements of its founder. Although Confucius praised the ancient sage kings, there is no necessary connection between Confucian virtue ethics and a centralized state. Indeed, a fully personalized ethics of Confucius, drawn from the concepts of *ren** and *yi,* would be more compatible with small-scale political units. Confucius repeatedly denied that he was a sage and he knew of no others who qualified for the title, so he could only envision the continued existence of small states with the faint hope that they would adopt the rule of virtue rather than that of law and heredity. Later texts contain more utopian views but such optimism is not present in the *Analects*.

Before the advent of the British, India was also a loose collection of over five hundred princely states. Under their charismatic leadership, Gandhi, Nehru, and others managed to unify the disparate peoples of the Indian subcontinent under the banner of the Congress party. Even with the tragedy of partition this was a remarkable achievement and the continued unity of twenty-five states, fourteen major language groups, and six principal religions is nothing short of a political miracle. Even though lip service has been paid to village autonomy, Gandhi is today the uncrowned sage king of a huge central government in New Delhi.

Although we will find common ground between Confucius and Gandhi on the virtue of love, we do not find any strict Confucian prohibition against injury or retribution by the state. In fact, traditional accounts tell of

Confucius ordering the execution of a criminal with only the expedient hope of deterring future crimes. Gandhi would have of course condemned Confucius's relishing of roast meat, and would have also been appalled by the fact that animal sacrifices to the emperor, the gods, and even Confucius himself continued up until 1917. In the *Analects* we find the story of a disciple who wishes to spare the sheep at one of these sacrifices, but Confucius chides him for straying from the strict requirements of *li,* the proper code of ritual observance.[5]

It appears that Gandhi would have sided with Christians, Daoists, Mohists, and Buddhists with their common doctrine of unconditional love as opposed to the Confucian principle of "graded" love, the requirement that we love those closest to us more than those distant from us. The following passage from the *Analects* contains Confucius's answer to the Daoist version of unconditional love:

> Someone asked: "What do you think about the [Daoist] saying: 'Repay ill will with beneficence *(de)*'?"
> The Master replied: "Then how would one repay beneficence? Repay ill will by remaining true. Repay beneficence with gratitude *(de)*."[6]

This is the Confucian reply to the Daoist version of "love your enemy" and "turn the other cheek." This response to unconditional love contains at least two major arguments. First, loving the wrongdoer ignores the crucial question of justice. Confucius believes that it is essentially irrational for one to reward vice with virtue. Recall that in the case of Sima Niu, the demands of justice are so strong that he must suspend filial piety to his brother. Note, however, that Confucius does not recommend retribution or even personal judgment. Confucius would agree with Gandhi that violence to the thief does not in any way reform his character, but he would probably not agree with Gandhi's proposal to reduce one's possessions to a bare minimum and place them in the open for all would-be thieves to see. Second, it is only natural to love those closest to you more than those who are distant; loving everyone equally is not only impractical but unnatural. The "Self-Taught-Man," Jean Paul Sartre's character in *Nausea,* is a person who loves everyone but actually loves no one in particular. This Confucian insight might serve as a critique for Gandhi's view that one cannot love humanity if one loves a few people more than others.

The passage above has always been an obscure one for translators (Wing-tsit Chan offers "repay evil with uprightness" and Chichung Huang translates it as "requite enmity with impartiality"), but Confucius appears to recommend that we should remain firm in our virtue, presenting it as a model for the moral rehabilitation of the wrongdoer. Heaven remains steadfast, does not retaliate, and does not take sides. Emulating heaven we should remain true and impartial in the same way.

If we look at the way Gandhi responded to wrongdoing, we might conclude that he is actually much closer to Confucius's position. A typical Gandhian response to the misdeeds of others was to shame them completely by doing their penance for them. This proved to be very effective not only against the British but with his own family and followers as well. These actions cannot be described as a passive turning of the cheek, but as an active attempt at the moral transformation of others. Gandhi's fasts forced the British and his fellow Indians to look inside themselves and reassess their attitudes and actions. Gandhi responded by remaining true to himself and to his principles. He replaced the motto of the Indian nationalists who espoused violent *jaise ko taisa* ("tit for tat") or *satham prati shatayam* ("be wicked with the wicked") with *shatham pratiyap satyam* ("be true even with the wicked"). In order to make sense of doing penance for acts that he had not committed, Gandhi could say that he could not demand moral purity in others if he was not completely pure himself. Even though Gandhi had more austere ideas about moral purity, he also, in his own way, "repaid evil with uprightness."

Nevertheless, the doctrine of graded love drives a wedge between law and filial piety that most ancients and moderns would find unacceptable. Readers of Plato's *Euthyphro* are always surprised to find that Socrates chides Euthyphro for prosecuting his father and most think that Socrates must be playing the fool in not praising him for his moral courage in applying the law equally to all. There is, however, no irony in Confucius's strong position that the son should always protect a guilty father just as Mencius retells the story of Shun, the sage king who goes to great lengths to protect his murderous father. Although Gandhi obviously supports the virtues of filial piety, he declared, "I must apply the same rule to the wrong-doer who is my enemy or a stranger to me, as I would my wrong-doing father or son."[7]

Gandhi and Confucius diverge significantly on the issue of the relation of mind and body. As we have already seen, Gandhi believes in a strict dualism between soul and body, and he speaks constantly of a Manichean battle between our spiritual natures and our animal natures. Gandhi's Vedāntist monism mitigates somewhat the negative effects of this dualism, but it still remains the most problematic aspect of his moral philosophy. In stark contrast we have seen that the Confucians never split the self into warring factions and embrace a fully somatic and social concept of the self. Giving Gandhi a Buddhist concept of self, as we have done in chapter 4, narrows this gap between him and Confucius significantly.

Instructive Similarities

There are instructive similarities in Gandhi's and Confucius's view of God or heaven *(tian)*. They even share the same ambivalence between personal theism and impersonal Providence. The worship of Rāma, which was the Gandhi family religion, was always part of his spiritual practice. At several crucial passages in the *Analects* Confucius appeals to heaven in a very intimate way. When his favorite disciple died, Confucius strongly implied that heaven had forsaken him,[8] and when his disciples criticized him for visiting the notorious Madam Nan he called on heaven as his personal witness.[9] Other than these examples, however, heaven as impersonal Providence completely dominates Confucian philosophy. When pressed to reconcile the tension between personal and impersonal theism, Gandhi was usually quick to explain that he definitely did not mean Rāma, the historical incarnation of Viṣṇu and King of Ayodhya; rather, Rama was simply a way to name the impersonal Godhead.

The most innovative way that Gandhi named ultimate reality was to call God "Truth," and it is at this point that Gandhian and Confucian theology converge very nicely. The regularities of heaven and earth were basic guidelines for the ancient Chinese. When the Confucians attribute sincerity *(cheng)* to heaven, which to all of them is essentially impersonal Providence, they mean that heaven will always be true to itself. (As one of my students has pointed out, this is not committing the pathetic fallacy because it is the sincerity of heaven, not human sincerity, that is the model.) Social custom *(li)*, the proper way to do things, is modeled on heaven because it is always constant and predictable. The sincerity of the sage kings also meant that they would be true to themselves and could always be counted on to guide the people properly. This government would operate by moral example and not by law and order: "Lead the people with administrative injunctions and keep them orderly with penal law, and they will avoid punishments but will be without a sense of shame. Lead with excellence *(de)* and keep them orderly through observing ritual propriety *(li)* and they will develop a sense of shame, and moreover, will order themselves."[10] Gandhi's village republicanism most definitely requires the rule of virtuous men and women. Turning finally to family government, Gandhi's revised caste system suggests some instructive Confucian parallels. His proposal that the son should follow the vocation of the father (unless the work violated fundamental ethics[11]) can been seen as a strong example of filial piety. Confucius and Gandhi agree that one's station in life is something that is determined by karma or heaven, and therefore free choice is not a relevant issue on this point. Finally, both thinkers firmly agree that our obligations to social roles are canceled if the people to whom we are obligated are immoral.

Although Confucius presents no explicit or even consistent ethics of nonviolence, his virtue ethics could be interpreted as such. The pacifying power of virtue can be seen in this text from the Zhou dynasty:

> The marquis declared: "Fighting with these multitudes, who can withstand me? What city could sustain their attack?"
> The reply was, " If you, my king, were to pacify the feudal lords through the power of virtue *(de)*, who would dare not to submit?"[12]

Both Confucians and Daoists proposed that any person, not just royalty, could develop the power of their virtue. Mencius states that "if people can fill out the heart that does not desire to harm others, their benevolence *(ren*)* will be inexhaustible."[13]

P. J. Ivanhoe explains that the concept of *de* gradually changed from having a special relationship with powerful spirits to having "something like moral charisma: the natural attraction one feels toward morally great individuals, the same kind of feeling that people claim to have experienced in the presence of Mahātma Gandhi or Martin Luther King, Jr."[14] Reiterating the heaven-moral individual correlation, the Confucian texts claim that the virtuous leader draws in and regulates the behavior of the masses in the same way that the North Star controls the heavenly bodies orbiting it. Yet another instructive parallel to Gandhi is the Confucian doctrine that the leader who puts himself at risk for his people is the one whose *de* increases, a view that is found as early as the Shang dynasty.[15] (This is opposite to most Daoists who celebrated the hermit who withdrew to mountain refuges, preserved his *de*, and avoided the cities of the plains.) A final parallel to Gandhi is the problematic concept of leaders accepting blame for the wrongdoing of their people. In the *Analects* King Wu states that "where the people go astray, let the blame rest with me alone," and King Tang expands the extent of blame dramatically: "If any of the many states do wrong, the guilt lies with me personally."[16] In chapter 4, I proposed that the most intelligible way to understand Gandhi doing penance for other people's sins was the idea that his own virtue was not yet perfected. Although Gandhian and Confucian concepts of spiritual purification are quite different, the basic principle is the same: the common people can thrive morally only with moral paragons as examples.

Throughout the *Analects* Confucius rejects not only the title sage but also the attainment of *junzi* and even of *ren**. (In contrast his favorite disciple, Yan Hui, was able to remain in the *ren** state for up to three months at a time.) In another passage, however, Confucius implies that he is a *junzi*.[17] Confucius is contemplating a trip to a foreign province and his disciples object that their rude manners would compromise his virtue. Confucius's answer is that there could be no rudeness if a *junzi* were among the barbarians. Gandhi's disciples were equally worried about Gandhi's plans to visit the infamous Pathan warriors of the Panjab. His trip was a great success: he persuaded a great number of them to disarm and to commit to his policy of noncooperation and nonviolence. Apparently they found persuasive his argument that true courage required them to face their enemies unarmed. Their leader Abduhl Ghaffar Khan became famous as the "Frontier Gandhi." Here is yet another powerful example of the power of the Chinese *de* in the charismatic leader. In chapter 10 I will argue that abundant *de*, not moral perfection, is what the saint or sage possesses.

In China the child has the fullest amount of *de* (hence the overwhelming charm of any infant) and the goal of most Confucians is to expand their childlike hearts. In another work I have used the Three Metamorphoses of Nietzsche's *Thus Spake Zarathustra* as a heuristic for explaining the power of constructive postmodern thought. Graham Parkes proposes that we conceive of the Three Metamorphoses as a dialectical triad of "immersion, detachment, and reintegration."[18] A person of the first stage is immersed in society and nature without any clear delineation of self and other. People at this stage typically take on the values that are given them, hence Nietzsche's image of a camel carrying the burdens of a herd morality. Persons in the second stage (the lion) develop fully self-conscious egos and separate themselves from society/nature through either active protest and rebellion or ascetic withdrawal. (This is the point at which "spiritual Titanism" is possible, and my book of that title examines this stage in both the Asian and European traditions.[19]) Parkes describes the third stage (the child) as a "return to participation, but now reflective and self-conscious. The self reengages with the world without being totally taken in by it."[20] The child is the true *Übermensch* and conventional wisdom has simply been wrong in claiming that the Titanistic lion is Nietzsche's ideal person. In chapter 10, I will propose that this third stage represents the true sage or saint and is also comparable to Charles Taylor's "strong evaluator."

It is clear that we are dealing with metaphors in the Three Metamorphoses and that the reintegrated person will be *like* a child in her spontaneity, her acceptance of things, and her love of body and the earth. Unlike the literal child, the Overperson will have refined raw instincts into a harmonized life of impulse and reflection. Reinterpreting Wordsworth somewhat, Nietzsche's child will be "Father to the Man," a new humanity beyond the camel and the lion. This is the Confucian or Daoist sage (each with its distinctive emphases), the Zen Buddhist pilgrim at the end of the Ten Oxherding Pictures, and those Hindu saints, such as Ramakrishna, who have avoided spiritual Titanism. For the most part Gandhi moves towards this childlike ideal, especially in his relationship to women. When he once spoke about his experiments with truth, Gandhi admitted that he did not "have an elaborate scheme to apply my eternal principles"; rather, "like a child I did whatever occurred to me on the spur of the moment during the course of events."[21] At the age of seventy, Confucius declared that he could do anything that his heart desired without "overstepping the boundaries."[22]

Gandhi's controversial experiments with *brahmacharya* are an instructive example of how he put aside traditional rules and found his own way, dictated solely by his own experience, his own dispositions, and his very unique way of purifying himself of sexual desire. He made it perfectly clear to his followers that no one should imitate the quasi-Tantric methods he used. This was his own personal mean between the excess of sexual indulgence and the deficiency of complete withdrawal from women. (He thought yogis who did the latter were cowards.) He once declared that "Brahmacharya is not a virtue that can be cultivated by outward restraints. ... The true Brahmachāri will shun false restraints. He must create his own fences according to his limitations, breaking them down if he feels that they are unnecessary."[23] John S. Hawley has pointed out that Hindu saints practice what might be called a "morality beyond morality."[24] In this view the yogis are not moral paradigms; rather, they perform spiritual theater in which charismatic power is displayed, not normative ethics.

For Gandhi virtues are developed from the exigencies of one's own person, history, and environment. Sleeping with his grandniece was right for him, and Manu claimed that it was as innocent as sleeping with her mother, whom she claimed Gandhi had replaced. Thakkar Bapu, convinced that Gandhi had corrupted himself and had ruined his entire political program, visited Gandhi and expected the worst. Gandhi's sleeping area was open for all to see, and he found Manu and him sleeping peacefully and innocently. Gandhi's visitor was completely disarmed in his criticism. Abduhl Ghaffar Khan, the leader of the fierce Pathan fighters Gandhi had won over to his cause, also came to check out the sleeping couple. Geoffrey Ashe vividly describes his reponse: "The ancient wonder-worker [Gandhi] had invented a new human relationship. The intimacy that ought to have been repellent was not."[25] One could say that Gandhi's achievement here represents the third stage of Nietzsche's Metamorphoses. Gandhi appears to preserve a childlike innocence in spite of full sexual knowledge and experience. At the end of chapter 10 we will raise the sticky issue of Manu not being at the same stage of maturation as Gandhi. The "right-handed" Tantrism that Gandhi's experiments resemble (he was aware of the works on Tantrism[26]) would have required fully equal partners.

One might choose Confucius's encounter with Madam Nan as a comparable test in Confucius's life. Madam Nan, the notorious concubine of the Duke Ling of Wei, invited Confucius to her inner apartments and his disciples advised him not to accept her invitation. Presumably caught between the wrong of declining hospitality and the vice of indiscretion, Confucius decided to visit her. All the laconic *Analects* report is that afterwards Confucius swore an oath: "For whatever I have done to offend, may heaven abandon me! May heaven abandon me!"[27] One implication is that, in contrast to Gandhi's experiment with his grandniece, Confucius somehow failed or thought that others would perceive that he had failed. One could conclude that Confucius's failure was a lack of courage either to decline the invitation or to see the visit through without embarrassment. Gandhi's bedroom was open for inspection whereas Madam Nan's boudoir was not. The least we can say is that Gandhi appeared much more confident that he had done no wrong than Confucius was. Indeed, Gandhi proposed that he sleep with thousands of women in order to prove his point and his innocence.

This particular incident notwithstanding, we can say that Confucius generally exhibited as much courage as Gandhi. Confucius's campaign of political reform throughout the Warring States period was filled with danger and intrigue and this took as much courage as Gandhi's programs in India. Both of them also carefully distinguished between mere bravery and true courage, a virtue possible only in a person of *ren** or Gandhi's spiritually pure *satyāgrāhi*. (Both appeared to agree with Aristotle's concept of the unity of the virtues: if one truly has one virtue then one must have them all.) The courage of Confucius and Gandhi is the unswerving commitment to be true to oneself and to be true to others.

Confucius's disciple Zilu is called "bold" but Confucius reminded him that a truly virtuous person puts *yi* first, because it is the faculty that can bring any particular virtue into its proper mean.[28] The bold person without *yi* will become "unruly." Earlier Confucius had praised Zilu because he thought that Zilu would be the first disciple to join him on a dangerous journey, but he was also uncertain whether Zilu had sufficient personal resources to survive the trip.[29] Although they do not put it as strongly as Gandhi, the Confucians, especially Mencius, also agree with him that courage is the key virtue for the good life. As Gandhi wrote in 1930, "Fearlessness is a sine qua non for the growth of the other noble qualities."[30] Again we see a holistic view of the unity of the virtues.

A Gandhian Aesthetics of Virtue

Although the Buddha and Gandhi were not at all as active in the arts as Confucius, they were committed to the same ancient trinity of truth, goodness, and beauty. It is Japanese Buddhism that is most aware of the aesthetic dimension of being moral, and Tsunesaburo Makiguchi, the founder of the

Soka Gakkai, is a good example. Even though Makiguchi substituted benefit for truth in his trinity of benefit, goodness, and beauty, he still agreed with the Greeks that good deeds are performed by beautiful souls.[31] Gandhi also made the same connections among truth, goodness, and beauty. The identity of reality and truth is clear in his adoption of the intimately related ideas of *sat* and *satyā*. Gandhi is following Hindu philosophy very closely in his identification of God, truth, beauty, and goodness.

Gandhi, however, appears more committed to prioritizing truth: "Truth is the first thing to be sought for, and Beauty and Goodness will then be added unto you."[32] Gandhi's focus was also more on the inner beauty of the pure heart rather than natural or artistic beauty. In praising the life of the deceased Pandit Khare, who taught music in his ashram, Gandhi said, "Purity of life is the highest and truest art.... The art of producing good music from a cultivated voice can be achieved by many, but the art of producing that music from the harmony of a pure life is achieved very rarely."[33] Confucius would certainly agreed with this statement. Gandhi rejected the concept of art for art's sake and its amoral aestheticism, and there is no question that Confucius would have agreed with the proposition that art must be an ally of the good life or it loses its value. While in England Gandhi experienced the controversy surrounding Oscar Wilde and he joined Wilde's critics with the charge that he was guilty of "beautifying immorality."[34]

From the standpoint of heaven the Confucians would have agreed with Gandhi that its truth [*cheng*, "sincerity"] is most important, and its beauty and goodness follow second and third. Gandhi may have subordinated beauty to both truth and goodness so as to forestall any philosophy of life that would place the acquisition of artworks before basic needs of the people. He believed that for the masses to appreciate beauty it must come through truth: "Show them Truth first and they will see beauty afterwards. Whatever can be useful to those starving millions is beautiful to my mind. Let us give today the vital things of life and the graces and ornaments of life will follow."[35] In this passage Gandhi's passion for justice appears to have led him to reduce beauty to utility. He may, however, have had a more sophisticated aesthetics in mind, one in which form follows function, one that is manifested in the exquisitely beautiful and simple Shaker furniture. This is how Gandhi relates asceticism to aesthetics: "Asceticism is the highest art. For what is art, but beauty in simplicity and what is asceticism if not the loftiest manifestation of simple beauty in daily life, shorn of artificialities and make-believe? That is why I always say that the true ascetic not only practises art but lives it."[36] In a personal conversation I had with Gandhi's grandson Ramachandra, a creative writer and philosopher in his own right, he described the way that Gandhi led his daily prayer services as a form of minimalist art.

Gandhi once asked a disciple, is a "woman with fair features necessarily beautiful?" The initial affirmative answer was quickly withdrawn when Gandhi followed with "[E]ven if she may be of an ugly character?" For Gandhi beauty is always "an index of the soul within."[37] He also observed that although they say that Socrates was not a handsome man, "to my mind he was beautiful because all his life was striving after Truth. ..."[38] M. Kirti Singh has remarked that Gandhi was perhaps as ugly as Socrates, "yet there was a rare spiritual beauty that shone in his face."[39] This is a moral beauty that comes from the courage of being true to one's self and being true to others. Gandhi's virtue aesthetics is best summed up in this passage: "Life must immensely excel all the parts put together. To me the greatest artist is surely he who lives the finest life."[40]

Moral aesthetes may be tempted to judge those who are not well formed in body or in action as morally unfit and not suitable for human interaction. For example, the beggars on the streets of large Indian cities are not a pretty sight, and an aesthetics of virtue might lead one to be less compassionate towards them. Both Confucius and Gandhi remind us, however, that moral beauty is primarily an inner quality. (Zhuangzi's story of the ugly man of Wei whose virtue was "whole" and who was chosen by the Duke to be prime minister is a good Daoist example for this point.[41]) The external beauty of some aesthetes may blind us to the fact that they may be too glib and too self-conscious about the gems they have created. Natural moral beauty is never showy and ostentatious; if it is, it is false and only a semblance of virtue. (As Chinese Queen Man of Deng said, "He steps proudly [but] his heart is not firm."[42]) In answer to the conundrum of the evil artist, Gandhi's answer is as good as that of any professional philosopher I know: "That only means that Truth and Untruth often coexist: good and evil are often found together. In an artist [sometimes] the right perception of things and the wrong coexist."[43] Recall that earlier we proposed that we conceive of an analogy between the arts and goodness, and not an identity.

Along the same lines one might test the unity of truth, goodness, and beauty with this thought experiment: two people have exactly the same virtuous dispositions, but the one is outwardly beautiful and the other is ugly. One might be tempted to conclude that the former is more admirable than the latter. But moral beauty is not simply a sum of inner and outer qualities, and Gandhi and the Chinese will insist that the inner qualities will always trump any external features. Furthermore, one can imagine even the most crippled and deformed presenting themselves with elegance and dignity. The literary examples of the monster in *Beauty and the Beast* and *The Elephant Man* make this point dramatically. The final line of the former is "To judge by appearance is to miss the beauty of our inner souls." In the ballet version the Beast's movements become increasingly elegant as he realizes his true nature as a prince.

In real life President Jimmy Carter's Veteran Affairs Administrator Max Cleland, a Vietnam War survivor with only one arm and no legs, was remarkably elegant on the basketball court. His experience had given him a moral beauty that was an inspiration for not only other disabled veterans but for people with disabilities everywhere. These examples prove Gandhi's thesis that beauty always begins from the inside and is produced by a pure spirit: "The outward forms have value only in so far as they are the expression of the inner spirit of man."[44] In answer to the question of natural beauty, the experience of which he preferred to art, Gandhi not surprisingly said that it comes from God, the purest spirit of all. Mencius reminds us that if the most beautiful woman in the land "is covered with filth, the people will hold their noses when they pass her. But should an ugly man fast and cleanse himself, he would be fit to offer sacrifices to God."[45] This passage makes the point semantically as well by playing on the fact that the Chinese character *e* for "ugly" also means "evil," thereby breaking provocatively the standard parallelism of virtue/beauty and vice/ugly.

Not only did Jawaharlal Nehru see Gandhi's inner beauty, but he also observed a external aesthetic as well: "According to the teachings of the *Gītā*, he laboured dispassionately without attachment to results, and so results came to him. During his long life, full of hard work and activity... there is hardly any jarring note anywhere. All his manifold activities became progressively a symphony and every word he spoke and every gesture that he made fitted into this, and so unconsciously he became the perfect artist, for he learnt the art of living. ... It became apparent that the pursuit of truth and goodness leads among other things to this artistry in life."[46] Robert Payne adds his own elegant version of this point: "He acted many roles and never wearied of his performances. Since he played these changing roles so well, he was sometimes accused of being a virtuoso performer with extraordinary powers of improvisation. In fact, he was the author of the play, the stage manager and most of the players."[47]

The test of a true Chinese sage was to act in such a way that things came spontaneously and effortlessly. This is what P. J. Ivanhoe has called a "performance" mysticism, joining nicely with our view that virtues are like artistic performances. This is where Daoism and Confucianism meet: the sage king simply sits facing south and all is right with his realm.[48] The virtuous person never looks to profit but simply to the joy of virtue itself. In the next two chapters we will address the many issues concerning the nature of the virtues, Gandhi's vows, and the virtue of nonviolence.

Chapter 8

Rules, Vows, and Virtues

A good rule is a good summary of wise particular choices and not a court of last resort.

—Martha Nussbaum

I would risk violence a thousand times than the emasculation of the whole race.

—M. K. Gandhi

Woman is the incarnation of ahiṃsā. …*I hope you have not missed the woman in me."*

—M. K. Gandhi

Mahātma Gandhi has been given the love of many women for his womanliness.

—Mrs. Polak

I have felt during the whole of my public life that what we need, what any nation needs, but we perhaps of all the nations of the world need just now, is nothing else and nothing less than character building.

—M. K. Gandhi

The initial task of the this chapter is to determine the relationship of the virtues to moral rules. The first section will defend the priority of virtues over moral laws, drawing on hackneyed phraseology to demonstrate that the virtues are ultimately blind without the abstract ideals embodied in moral rules, but these norms are empty without the particular work of the virtues.

The second section will discuss the traditional connection between virility and virtue, and, contrary to our first impressions, we will find that Gandhi completely subverts patriarchy's bias on this issue. Gandhi speaks more of vows than virtues, so the third section will analyze the distinction between vows and virtues. The fourth section will summarize Gandhi's vows and propose that they can be reinterpreted as enabling virtues, which are defined in chapter 9. The fifth section deals with the Gandhian virtues, interpreting the unity of the virtues by means of practical reason and focusing on truth, love, courage, *ahiṃsā*, and humility.

Rules and Virtues

Which came first—moral rules or virtues? The obvious answer, I contend, is that virtues came first. Moral imperatives are abstractions from thousands of years of observing loyal, honest, patient, just, and compassionate behavior, just as moral prohibitions have come from equally ancient experiences with the vices. There is good evidence that the expression of moral rules requires a spoken language and one could argue just as persuasively that virtues manifested themselves in prelinguistic human beings. For example, strong circumstantial evidence for compassion among the Neanderthals can be joined with the hypothesis that their very high larynx made it impossible for them to articulate the basic vowels.[1] Michael Spangle and Kent Menzel state that "spoken language transformed our species and was a major factor in forging the human world as we know it."[2] They also argue for the existence of an "acoustic trigger to conceptualization" that gestural language obviously lacks. While there is now a consensus that gestures are integral to all natural languages (remarkably, the blind gesture when they speak), it is generally agreed that they do not express abstractions very well.

It is even clearer that divine virtues precede divine law, because God's virtues would remain even if God chose not to create a world. The doctrine of the Trinity allows the possibility that the divine virtues are not exclusively self-regarding. The Pauline view that the Law was created only to manifest human sin further proves its contingency and confirms the idea of a lawless God before creation. For medieval nominalism the moral law characterizes what God has ordained *(potentia ordinata)* for a sinful world, and it is not part of God's absolute power *(potentia absoluta)*. Even though Aquinas maintains that there is practical as well as theoretical reason in God—specifically, God would know the rule that good always excludes evil—this argument is open to serious objections. (My bias for process theology is showing, but Aquinas, along with all other classical theologians, has real difficulty in relating God to the world.)[3] Furthermore, Gandhi speaks of God's laws frequently and if he believes those laws are part of the nature of God, then it would be difficult to argue for the priority of the virtues in Gandhian ethics.

Philosopher Leslie Stephen describes virtue ethics as follows: "Morality is internal. The moral law...has to be expressed in the form, 'be this,' not in the form 'do this.' ...The true moral law says 'hate not,' instead of 'kill not.' ... The only mode of stating the moral law must be as a rule of character."[4] In other words, people of good character and virtue require no reminder of what the rules are or what their duty is. For John Stuart Mill the application of internal sanctions has much more moral value than the imposition of external sanctions, those most often used by parents and societies to control human behavior. Mill's argument is persuasive: a society of mature virtues would require few police, judges, and prisons, thereby maximizing utility. Generally speaking, the sanctions for virtue ethics are internal and self-regulating, whereas the sanctions for rule ethics, especially in its popular religious form, are external. (Kant and contemporary Christian ethicists join virtue ethics in favoring internal sanctions.) For the Greeks, the Roman Stoics, Buddhists, and the Confucians, virtue is its own reward, but popular Christianity appears to have made the incentive for good deeds eternal life in heaven, with eternal damnation for those who do not follow the rules.

One of the problems with rule ethics is applying the rules to specific cases. The imperatives of virtue ethics—be patient, be kind, be generous, be compassionate, be courageous—better equip an individual to negotiate the obstacles of the moral life. The virtue ethics approach is not to follow a set of abstract rules, but to develop an ensemble of behaviors, dispositions, and qualities that lead to human excellence and the good life. Virtue ethics may not have pat answers to specific cases—no ethical theory could offer this—but it does prepare the moral agent for adaptation, innovation, and self-discovery. (Chapter 5 has covered this topic in depth.) As Martha Nussbaum states, "The good agent must therefore cultivate the ability to perceive and correctly describe his or her situation finely and truly, including in this perceptual grasp even those features of the situation that are not covered under the existing rule."[5]

Annette Baier's analysis of trust is a good example of the specific adaptability of the virtues.[6] Rule based ethics and its contractarian social and political arrangements give the false impression that the essence of the moral life consists of conforming to general rules. Obeying rules can be made specific in a legal contract, but it would of course be impossible to cover the exigencies of our lives with such formal arrangements. It is the virtue of trust that is basic to human interactions and only a few of the myriad promises necessary for the smooth running of human life could ever be spelled out in contractual form. It would be not only absurd but also a great insult to plumbers (Baier's hilarious example) to "have it in writing" that they promise not to plant explosives in the pipes of the houses they work in. Again it is the virtues that come first and they are the tools that do the work of the moral life. Without directly affirming the priority of the virtues, Gandhi makes a similar argument: "Life is governed by a multitude of forces. It would be smooth sailing if one could determine the course of one's actions only by one general principle whose application at a given moment was too obvious to need even a moment's reflection. But I cannot recall a single act that could be so easily determined."[7] Martha Nussbaum phrases the point even more aptly: "A good rule is a good summary of wise particular choices and not a court of last resort. Like rules in medicine and in navigation, ethical rules should be held open to modification in the light of new circumstances."[8]

Interestingly enough, some virtuous behavior is not always required in cases that might call for it, while conformation to rules demands no exceptions. For example, generous people do not lose their virtue if they do not give to all charities as a rule to give might command or what Peter Singer requires for maximum world-wide utility. Let us imagine a burning house where a hedonic calculator is indicating that it is too dangerous to go in and save the children inside. While all utilitarians would be bound by the calculus and all Kantians would be bound by the rule that it is always irrational to go beyond one's duty, virtue theory would allow people to act on their own personal mean between cowardice and foolhardiness. Turning to yet another virtue, it is clear that even justice always amounts to more than simply conforming to the strict letter of the law. The craft excellence of judicial review, as well as daily extralegal decisions, always lead to unique, distinctive, and noncompulsory results.

Another way to demonstrate the superiority of virtues over rules is to think of the life of the consummate couch potato. He is a man who essentially lives and works on his couch. His job is entering data via a modem attached to his computer. It does not take much thinking to enter the data, so he is able to view his favorite TV shows all the time. His refrigerator and microwave, of course, are handy for snacks, drinks, and frozen dinners. Our sofa slug is also a very religious person. He tunes into to his favorite TV preachers on Sunday morning and sends in his tithes by mail. Finally, let us say that this man has never broken a law or committed a major sin in his life.

According to Aristotle, the couch potato's life lacks virtually everything that counts as human excellence, and for Confucius, this man remains very much an uncut gem. Our couch potato obeys all moral laws, but he does not aspire to cultivate the virtues of the good life. According to rule ethics of popular Christianity, however, this man is fully moral, and, assuming divine favor, saved as well. Bernard Mayo clearly sees the implications of this example: "People might well have no moral qualities at all except the possession of principles and the will (and capacity) to act accordingly."[9] This appears to be a severe indictment for much rule-based ethics.

As we have seen, the sanctions of a rule-based ethics, in its popular religious form, are primarily external: rewards for those who do good and punishment for those who do evil. (Contemporary Christian ethical theory of course avoids this simple barter system of ethics, but one cannot deny that this is at the basis of popular religious belief.) This may lead to a mere moralism rather than a genuine morality based on internal sanctions and the view that virtue is its own reward. Most people would agree that the latter is a more admirable form of ethical motivation, and we have seen that internal sanctions maximize utility. Most traditional religious ethics teaches us the wrong reasons to be moral. We should become moral so as to become a better person and be an example to others, rather than for the purely selfish reasons of avoiding punishment. Moral action should flow naturally from our selves; we should not have to be bribed to be moral. Justice will not be achieved by following rules; it will only be attained, as Plato, Confucius, the Buddha, and Gandhi envisioned, by people with balanced and harmonious souls and the particular just acts that comes from such harmony.

Another concern about duty ethics is the problem of legalism. True morality should be the foundation of law, and the virtues, as prior to law, would then serve as a guide and check to any law. Humans acted courageously, justly, beneficently before they laid down rules regulating human behavior. A rule-based ethics reverses this order. It speaks of law, usually divine law, first, and moral rules that come directly from the mind and mouth of the lawgiver. But true morality must always serve as a check for the possibility of unjust laws. If law and morality are the same, then this crucial idea of morality as the guardian of just law is undermined. For example, most of my students are able to condemn Zeus and other Greek gods as immoral deities because of the basic intuition, central to virtue ethics, that virtue precedes law. The king, earthly or heavenly, is not always right, and we must always guard against the false identity of the legislator and the source of the Good.

For Aristotle the virtues are dispositions that we freely choose to develop, and every day we have to fine tune the moral means that are relative to us and our situations. (It is true that after a short while the virtues become habits *[ethikē]*, but we are still fully responsible for actions that proceed from them.) Rule morality recognizes no middle way and no variation on an absolute right. Virtue ethics always aims at a personal mean that is a creative choice for each individual. Such an approach engages the imagination and personalizes and intensifies moral responsibility. While there can be no process of self-discovery in rule ethics, virtue ethics requires us to confront a growing, dynamic self in ever changing conditions. Here again is the reason for embracing the Buddhist self as opposed to the static self of Hinduism and Stoicism, or any of their philosophical descendants.

Before we move on to Gandhi on virility and virtues, I would like to present one more argument in favor of virtue ethics. Thomas Aquinas is generally considered a solid supporter of natural law theory and the rule ethics that this view implies. Indeed, Aquinas's logical proof for the first law of morality is, even with its problems, a veritable *tour de force*. Defining for the first time the distinction between analytic and synthetic propositions, Aquinas attempts to prove that basic moral propositions are self-evident—namely, they prove themselves. In *Summa Theologica* Aquinas applies the law of contradiction (A always excludes non-A) to metaphysics and concludes that being always excludes nonbeing.[10] Drawing on the neo-Platonic view of evil as nonbeing, the application in axiology gives him the First Law of Practical Reason: one should always pursue good and avoid evil.

The easiest way to explain this argument for students is to have them negate the predicate of the Sixth Commandment and observe the absurdity that results if they make it a rule for their action. Aquinas's argument is brilliant and elegant, but many of our moral intuitions undermine the necessity of this law. Interestingly enough, one does not have to leave the Roman Church to find counter arguments. It is supremely ironic that the Doctrine of Double Effect, profoundly influenced by Thomistic intentionism, sanctioned what Aquinas never would have permitted—namely, to proceed, under certain conditions, with good intentions even though one is aware of evil consequences.[11] In other words, pursuing good does not always exclude evil.

Aquinas undermines any form of moral absolutism by allowing the virtues to complement moral law. Most people do not realize that Aquinas agreed with Aristotle that most of the passions are already directed toward the good; they simply need to be disciplined and finally perfected by grace—an obvious break with Aristotle. Aquinas and the Buddha, however, were more aware of the dangers of disordered desires—lust for Aquinas in particular and craving for views for the Buddha. More significantly, Aquinas acknowledged the role of *prudentia* in what we have called (in chapter 5) concrete appropriation: "[P]ersons are in different conditions with respect to their passions. And, therefore, it is necessary that the rightness of reason in the passions be established with respect to us, who are moved with the passions."[12] Here we can hear the echo of Aristotle's definition of a moral virtue: "Virtue is a state of character concerned with choice, lying in a mean, i.e. the mean relative to us, this being determined by *phronēsis*. ..."[13]

This means that Aquinas's moral laws are only formal truths, abstract ideals whose content can only be supplied by individuals acting out of their own passions and in their own situations. Jean Porter gives Thomistic ethics a contextual pragmatic reading: the virtues will have an open-ended quality that "will give them sufficient flexibility to be applied to persons in different conditions."[14] Thomistic mindfulness, described by Josef Pieper as "the ability of the psyche to listen in silent attention to the language of reality,"[15] is especially important for the affective virtues that are self-referential. Justice, for example, involves not only self-knowledge but knowing the interests of many parties. Fortitude, "holding to one's true good in the face of danger or death," is uniquely self-referential. The foregoing analysis allows a stronger conclusion: the virtues do not merely complement moral rules; rather, they provide otherwise empty rules with particular moral content. In short, they provide personal meaning and empower the proper appropriation of general moral laws.

Virtue and Virility

In the ancient world virtue was thoroughly gendered. There was a strong connection between self-mastery, freedom, and virility. (The Latin *virtus* stems from *vir,* meaning "manhood," so that Roman virtue meant "excellence of manly qualities.") Aristotle's conception of woman as an ill-formed and irrational man was almost universally accepted. Lacking reason, women could not instill reason in those things without it, which of course virtuous men could. (This meant that virtuous men could control their sexual appetites but women could not.) Greco-Roman ethics was, according to Foucault, an "ethics of men made for men, ...a structure of virility that related oneself to oneself."[16]

Foucault also demonstrates that there was a close alliance among sexual, ethical, and social virility. The social hierarchy of virility and mastery produced interesting anomalies, such as the wife of the house being more masculine than the male slaves. Here the virtuous wife has these qualities only because she has imitated male self-mastery. Foucault gives the example of Ischomachus's wife in Zenophon's *Oeconomicus,* who displays "masculine understanding" and is so well trained by her husband that she, like Plutarch's barking dog, need hear his commands only once.[17] *Fourth Maccabees,* a Hellenistic Jewish text, portrays the brave mother of seven boys as more masculine than Antiochus Epiphanes, the tyrant who tortures her sons to death.[18]

In both the Chinese and Indian traditions there is an intimate relationship between virtue and male power, although the *Daodejing* is one text that generally subverts male dominance. In a famous passage Mencius connects the power of *qi* energy with the virtue of courage. The retention and concentration of *qi* is a central focus of the Chinese marital arts and spiritual discipline in general. In Asia there is a near universal dictum that the one who preserves his semen is the one who increases his spiritual power. In some

Asian traditions it is thought that a man loses a little of his soul every time he ejaculates.

Interestingly enough, the only Hindu god who is allowed to be depicted with muscles is the celibate Hanuman, the patron god of wrestlers. Hanuman always preserves his *tejas,* the power of the male gods. (*Vīrya,* linked to the Latin *virtus,* is another Sanskrit word for male power, with its meanings of manliness, heroism, and male seed.) *Tejas* is not only an attribute of the gods and antigods *(asuras),* but it is also found in the Manus, sages, priests, kings, and ordinary men. The priest "takes on a physical form of brilliant energy *(tejas)* and attains the supreme condition..."; the king is "made from particles of these lords and gods, therefore he surpasses all living beings in brilliant energy *(tejas).*"[19] *Tejas* ebbs and flows, as can be seen in the man who breaks a vow of chastity, dissipates his semen, and loses his *tejas* back to the gods.[20] Also significant is the case of the man who loses even more *tejas* by having sex with a menstruating woman, and the priest who loses his vitality by looking at a woman "putting on her eye make-up, rubbing oil on herself, undressed, or giving birth.[21] Even in their misogyny the authors of the *Laws of Manu* give a backhanded compliment to the power of woman.

Initially one's impression of Gandhi is that he conforms to this traditional fusion of virtue and virility. In fact, commentators have said that one of Gandhi's greatest achievements was that he destroyed the Orientialist prejudice that Europe and America were masculine and Asia was feminine—summed up aptly in John Strachey's observations of India and "the extraordinary effeminancy" of the Bengalis in particular.[22] Much of Gandhi's rhetoric has strong martial overtones, such as "nonviolent warfare" waged with the "masculine virtues"; and "nonviolence...does not mean cowardice. It means the spirit of manliness in its perfection."[23]

Gandhi also draws on the Indian ascetic tradition in which the yogi is trained to turn his semen into spiritual power. Saying the Rāmanama also has the power to change semen into the life spirit. Gandhi follows the traditional Hindu belief that the life force is contained within the seminal fluid: "All power comes from the preservation and sublimation of the vitality that is responsible for the creation of life. ... Perfectly controlled thought is itself power of the highest potency and becomes self-acting.... Such power is impossible in one who dissipates his energy in any way whatsoever."[24] As we shall see, Gandhi disagrees with the traditional practice of the yogi's total self-withdrawal from society; indeed, this practice "robbed us of our manliness."[25]

The young Gandhi was very much attracted to British manly virtue and he was initially convinced of the widely held view that meat eating was essential for nourishing a man's vital energies. His experiments with meat eating were a disaster and the recovery of his Hindu heritage (thanks to the theosophists in London) and his dramatic reconversion to vegetarianism were major turning points in his life. As a result, a very different way of relating virtue to gender gradually arose in his thinking. As he reflected back on his childhood, the power of self-suffering, modeled perfectly in his devout mother, moved to the center of his struggle to find an acceptable philosophy of political engagement. Transgressions in Gandhi's home were dealt with by self-punishment, which became the model of Gandhi's insistence on performing others' penance for them.

What the young Gandhi feared most at home was his father's self-suffering, not his punishment, and the mature Gandhi had considerable success in applying this technique against the British. As Susanne and Lloyd Rudolph have shown, Gandhi discovered the connection between self-suffering and courage in his South Africa campaigns. The virtues of patience, self-control, and courage were absolutely essential to defeat the temptation to retaliate and respond with violence. Gandhi concluded that aggressive and retaliatory courage demonstrated a complete lack of self-control; it actually shows impotence rather than manliness. *Satyāgrahis* must purge themselves of ill will and their goal must be to bring out the goodness in their opponents.

Let us now move to the crux of the issues of self-suffering, courage, power, and nonviolence. Gandhi made it clear that each of these virtues were found most often in women. The textual and experiential evidence is quite persuasive: "Has she not great intuition, is she not more self-sacrificing, has she not greater powers of endurance, has she not greater courage?"[26] In 1936 Gandhi declared that *ahiṃsā* is embodied in the woman: she is "weak in striking…strong in suffering."[27] The women around Gandhi were amazed at how comfortable they felt in his presence and how much of a woman he had become to them. ("I hope you have not missed the woman in me," he once said.)[28] His grandniece Manu considered Gandhi to be her new mother and simply could not understand all the controversy surrounding their sleeping with one another. The fact that women felt no unease in Gandhi's presence was a sign of his perfection as a *brahmachāri*. Indeed, he appeared more like a Chinese sage, whose perfected *de* pacified wild animals, than the fierce and intimidating sages *(ṛiṣis)* of ancient India.

Gandhi once said that he wanted to convert the woman's capacity for "self-sacrifice and suffering into *śakti*-power."[29] The Sanskrit *śakti* is the power of the Hindu Goddess and, as opposed to *tejas,* is a necessary attribute that the Goddess shares with everything in the universe. The Hindu Goddess theology essentially breaks the vicious cycle of the Vedic maxim, explained superbly by Brian K. Smith,[30] that one gains power only at another's expense. The Vedic power game, as with most patriarchal concepts of power, is a zero-sum game. Those who control the sacrifice, by hook or by crook control *tejas*. The result is constant battles between gods and antigods, gods and ascetics, priests and kings. Goddess theology is radically different; *śakti* is a power that all beings have by virtue of their very existence. Ontologically speaking, *tejas* is a quality (seen most clearly in its meaning as fire, a primary element of the basic substance *[bhuta]*) while *śakti* is the basic substance, or, more accurately, the basic process because Goddess philosophy is clearly more compatible with process, rather than substance, metaphysics.

The Goddess scriptures were written by men and her sacred sites were controlled by male priests, so it should not be surprising that she does not always speak with a woman's voice. More specific and sexist is the North Indian rule that a husband must pay for fourteen recitations of the *Devī-Māhātmya* in order to control an unruly wife, but he only has to pay for twelve recitations to defeat an enemy.[31] A recitation of same text may also protect a Hindu male's genitals and semen and help him get a good wife. Every year, at the beginning of the warring season, Hindu kings sacrificed thousands of animals to the Goddess so that their battles would go well. Mythologically, this translated into the Goddess, with incredible acts of violence and destruction, winning great victories over the enemies of Dharma. At the 1999 Durga festival in Calcutta, clay and straw statues of brave Indian soldiers were added to the traditional neighborhood altars to demonstrate how the Goddess made Indian victory in the Kargil incident possible.

Significantly, Gandhi embraces Goddess theology in a manner more consistent than these traditional views. The most dramatic demonstration of *śakti* power was Gandhi's pacification of the Pathan warriors, whom Kipling praised as the notable exception to the cowardly effeminancy of the Indian people. "Brave they are as a matter of course," said Gandhi, and "to kill and get killed is an ordinary thing in their eyes, and if they are angry with anyone, they will thrash him and sometimes even kill him."[32] Ironically, the Pathan's disposition to anger and uncontrolled retaliation describes the masculine version of the Goddess's action, while Gandhi's unarmed moral courage in front of them is more consistent with the *śakti* view of shared power. Indeed, Gandhi's Goddess does not decapitate, nor does she impale; rather, she disarms and attempts to reconcile warring peoples. Therefore, when Gandhi states that "all power comes from the preservation and sublimation of the vitality that is responsible for the creation of life"[33] he must be referring to *śakti*, not *tejas*. In the last chapter we will find that the charismatic saint has the power of *de,* the closest Chinese equivalent to *śakti*.

When Gandhi describes himself as "half a woman,"[34] an alternative view of masculine and feminine power suggests itself. The Chinese/Jungian view of complementary *yin (anima)* and *yang (animus)* energies is found in this passage: "A man should remain man and yet should learn to become woman; similarly, a woman should remain woman and yet learn to become man."[35] (This view of coequal powers differs ontologically from the view of *śakti* as primary and *tejas* as derivative.) Actually, this view may have had Christian rather than Asian origins. While a young man in England, Gandhi came into contact with the Esoteric Christian Union, whose interpretation of the image of God meant that the individual "must comprise within himself the qualities—masculine and feminine—of existence and be spiritually both man and woman."[36]

Vows and Virtues

Even though Gandhi does speak of the virtues and even nonviolence as one, my attempt to make him a virtue ethicist is complicated by the fact that he emphasized vows more than virtues. As he once said, "It is my conviction that one cannot build one's character without the help of vows."[37] The fact that a person has to make a vow to discourage certain behavior clearly indicates that this person is not naturally inclined to the virtuous action that counters the vice. Even if this person is successful in the vow, the person may still be virtuous only, as I say, under duress—the pressures of temptation to lapse from the vow. Gandhi believed that the greatest human failing is weakness of the will, and the taking of vows is the best cure for *akrasia*.[38] In Aristotle's terms the person who takes a vow is an *akratēs,* literally one without the will to overcome temptation. The *enkratēs* is one who has sufficient will to resist but has not formed the habit of living naturally in the mean of the virtue in question. Aristotle calls the latter a *sōphrōn,* one who, as Confucius said of himself at the age of seventy, "could give [one's] heart-mind free rein without overstepping the boundaries."[39]

Let us illustrate this distinction with the following story.[40] Jack and Jill work as temporary tellers at a bank. The bank has only one permanent teller position open, and either Jack or Jill will be chosen for the job after a probationary period. As soon as he is on the job, Jack finds that he has strong temptations to embezzle funds from his new employers. He finds these temptations so troubling that he decides to take a solemn vow not to follow through with these intentions. The vow works and Jack makes it through the trial period without succumbing. Meanwhile at the other station, Jill goes through her daily routine not once thinking of stealing funds.

Our story obviously makes Jack the *enkratēs* and Jill the *sōphrōn.* (He would be an *akratēs* without the vow.) First, note how absurd it would be for anyone to suggest that Jill needs to take the vow that Jack has taken. Second, both Jack and Jill are deserving of praise, but we would commend Jill for her virtue, while we can praise Jack only for his willpower to resist temptation. We may believe that Jack's action has moral content, and some may even propose that Jack deserves higher praise. (In fact, Immanuel Kant supports this view because we know for sure that Jack is being honest out of duty and not just mere inclination, while Jill's easy virtue obscures her commitment to duty.) But more dramatic examples of duress virtue—the woman who has strong urges to murder every person that she meets but always restrains herself; or the man who wants to rape every woman he meets but desists—demonstrate that there may be little moral value to Jack's heroic efforts. Third, let us say, just for the sake forcing the argument, that the bank managers somehow learn of Jack's temptations. (He frequently mutters to himself and pounds himself on the forehead like Gandhi used to do.) It is clear that bank managers will obviously not be able to trust Jack and that they will offer the job to Jill without hesitation.

The point of the argument thus far is to suggest that an ethics of virtues and a morality of vows are conceptually divergent and may also assume significantly different views of human nature and the nature of evil. It has been said that Aristotle did not fully appreciate the depth and extent of human evil. While he can envision a person with insufficient will to follow the mean, he cannot conceive of a person who deliberately wills evil and certainly not one who would actually take pleasure in it. It is significant that for Aristotle the only one "with will" (the literal meaning of *enkratēs*) is the person who stays in the mean under duress, not the person with the will to deliberately do evil. Aristotle does admit that persistent misfortunate (Oedipus is a good example) can destroy the conditions for personal happiness. Some Stoics, however, read the external world as one of insurmountable misery and the Christian view of original sin further undermined the optimism and perfectionism of the classical Greeks.

The Stoics' contribution to virtue ethics is considerable, but ironically they were responsible for its eventual demise. As we have seen, the Stoics reaffirmed the concept of virtues as skills and the fact that they are whole the entire time they are expressed. However, their devaluation of the affective dimensions of the human soul led to a position where virtue was an internal process of conformation to cosmic reason and its laws. Like most Hindu thinkers the Stoics rejected the empirical ego in favor of a universal self, one, as Epictetus said, who never sleeps, is never deceived, and always knows the good. The Stoics then set the stage for the full decline of virtue ethics in Christian philosophy. There is no good except obedience to law, whether it be given by reason or God, whether it be by divine command or out of the divine nature. Furthermore, the Stoic view that success is not necessary for virtue leads, ironically, from Augustine to Kant, to the view that the virtues are not necessary for morality at all. Only Thomas Aquinas, under Aristotle's profound influence, resisted this destruction of the classical virtue tradition.

Augustine's emphasis on original sin and the omnipotence of God led him to reject the Greek view that we can develop the virtues on our own power. The dual emphasis on sin and omnipotence also results in a paradoxical position on the resolution of evil. For the Greeks, those who experience great misfortune had no recourse except to endure it, and in *Oedipus at Colonus* the hero, comforted by his equally brave daughters, accepts his fate with grace and equanimity. For the Christian, however, the extent and depth of evil is much greater and punishment for sin is infinite torment or at least alienation from God.

Some are surprised to learn that even Kant believed in radical evil, the original sin against the moral law that produces "infinite guilt." As Kant states, "It would seem to follow, then, that because of this infinite guilt all mankind must look forward to endless punishment and exclusion from the Kingdom of God."[41] On the bright side, the promise of God's grace offers final and complete relief from all misfortune and suffering. For the Greeks, the stakes were lower but complete reconciliation was impossible; for Christians the stakes are much higher, but for the sincere person a ready solution is right at hand. As Christine MacKinnon states, "The problem for the agent who disobeys God is that the stakes are so high: the fate of his soul must be the most important thing the agent is to consider when he contemplates his welfare."[42]

Augustine's position also resulted in a distinctively European focus on the will and its alleged freedom, a view of the will that one does not find in ancient philosophy, either Asian or European.[43] (I qualify this freedom because Augustine's God empowers those who turn away from him just as he empowers those to turn to him in grace.) This focus on the will and sin has subtly transformed our intuitions about the *enkratēs* and the *sōphrōn*. It culminates in Kant's position that the *enkratēs* is the only one that we know is conforming to moral law and the only one whose action has moral worth. The emphasis on sin has led us to suspect people like Jill; indeed, for people who like to speak of such things, it is the Devil who prefers to disguise himself as a person of easy virtue and elegant manners. For Christians committed to original sin, the *sōphrōn* must either be an illusion, or at least secretly bad, at worst Satan in disguise, or at best the incarnation of God himself. In such a view perfection of this sort is not of this world.

Returning now to Gandhi, it appears that the taking of vows is necessarily connected to rule ethics rather than virtue ethics. A vow can be best seen as the self-enforcement of a rule. Gandhi is definitely more like Kant than Aristotle if the Rudolphs are correct in saying that he held that "only self-control in the midst of temptation was worthy."[44] Was Gandhi's view of human nature so negative that he concluded that vows rather than the free development of virtues was the only option for humankind? His neo-Vedāntist view of the self and his negative views of the body and the passions align him very closely with the Stoics. As one of my bright ethics students once said, "Duress virtue is the father of natural virtue," so we might think of Gandhi's vows as instruments to train *satyāgrahis* to develop the virtues necessary for world peace. One could envision, especially within the context of Hindu perfectionism, the Gandhian gradually moving from the *enkratēs* state to that of the *sōphrōn*. Theoretically, however, the neo-Vedāntist position requires that we view the Ātman as already morally perfect, so this would be a recovery rather than a developmental view of the virtues. I personally support the latter and that is why I propose that Gandhi's ethics of nonviolence be reformulated along Pāli Buddhist lines, for most Mahāyāna Buddhist schools have reinstated the higher self of Vedānta.

Gandhi's Vows

Returning to the proposal that Gandhi's vows could turn into virtues that people could enjoy, a critic might raise an obvious objection. Why did the Mahātma himself never make this transition and why did he have to struggle with temptation all his life, even to the point of frequently striking out against himself for his failings? His closest associates uniformly attest to frequent outbursts of anger. Here is one of Manu's observations: "While he was pouring out his soul like this [objecting to good wool used as garlands], he looked the very picture of a volcano in eruption."[45] This is not an image of Aristotle's *sōphrōn*, and George Orwell is obviously mistaken when he notes that Gandhi lost his temper only once.[46] Before 1906, when he took the first the vow of *brahmacharya*, he admitted that he was an *akratēs*, one who not only lacked the will to deny himself the pleasures of sexual intercourse but also one who had insufficient faith in the grace of God.[47] Here is strong evidence that Gandhi cannot join Confucius, the Buddha, or Aristotle in a humanistic developmental virtue ethics. With their emphasis on evil and divine grace, the passages above are strong support for a Christian rule and duty ethics.

Gandhi believes that vows "can be taken only on points of universally recognized principles,"[48] and they are taken with the higher self as witness and the lower self and its desires as the object of control. Typically, Gandhi moves from Vedāntist monism to personal theism with no hesitation. God is the perfect model of inflexible resolve, because, as Gandhi explains, "God is the very image of the vow. God would cease to be God if He swerved from His own laws even by a hair's breadth."[49] Gandhi, according to Suman Khanna, believed a vow to be a "sacred commitment to God" and that "breaking a vow is tantamount to a breach of faith with God on the one hand, and being untruthful to oneself on the other."[50] Taking a vow is a way of grabbing hold of the Good (God) and not letting it go.

The Sanskrit word for "vow" is *vrata* and its earliest use in the *Ṛgveda* is linked to divine will or command.[51] For Khanna a vow is an internal sanction, a "commitment to an injunction voluntarily imposed on oneself."[52] For Gandhi a vow means having "unflinching determination [that] helps us against temptation,"[53] so vow taking for him appears to be a form of duress virtue. It is a way of storming the fortress of virtue and overcoming all odds and succeeding. Presumably it is the only possible way to coerce yourself along the way of moral perfection. *Brahmacharya* does not become the effortless disposition required by the *sōphrōn;* rather, "it is like walking on the sword's edge, and I see every moment the necessity for eternal vigilance."[54] (Here again is the Hindu dramatic vision of extremes rather than calm Buddhist Middle Way.) While in South Africa he convinced himself that he could maintain his vows with "no effort" by simply holding to his diet of fruit and nuts, although he did find that adding milk made the vow difficult again. But the suggestion that humans on their own power can consummate their vows is undermined by the strong assertion that *brahmacharya* is "impossible to attain by mere human effort."[55]

Gandhi's language is ambiguous and not always consistent, so it is always difficult to determine whether this is a Vedāntist-Stoic-Kantian model or a traditional Christian one, in which a transcendent God is directing the moral life. The Christian view is seen in Gandhi's strong hints that divine grace is necessary: "Win divine grace for us in good time, and all artificial tastes will then disappear with the realization of the Highest."[56] The Vedāntist Gandhi would of course follow the Stoics and Kant, with Ātman as the immanent divinity giving itself (that is, gracing itself with) the same cosmic laws that others in tune with their higher selves would. When we read that "the straight way to cultivate *brahamacharya* is the Rāmanama [repeating the name of the god Rāma]", or that the initial vow of 1906 was successful only "with faith in the sustaining power of God,"[57] then the theistic perspective appears to dominate.

Before we analyze Gandhi's principal vows, we should discuss the additional vows that Gandhi added, consistent with his contextual pragmatism, for twentieth-century India. The addition of these vows can be seen as the direct result of Gandhi's experiments with truth: they are, as he says, directly "deducible from Truth."[58] Furthermore, each them stands in considerable conflict with traditional Hindu *dharma*. The phrase "deducible from Truth" implies logical deduction and a necessary relation between premisses and conclusions. We have seen, however, that Gandhi's experiments with truth are thoroughly empirical and, in addition, as "they are enjoined by the present age," it is clear that they are fully contingent. Indeed, if the socioeconomic conditions that caused the need for these additional vows change, then the vows would no longer be necessary. Therefore, we can establish a distinction between basic and necessary vows, such as *brahmacharya,* based as they are on certain facts by human nature that will not change, and contingent vows determined by the conditions of the present age.

First and foremost among the contingent vows is Gandhi's demand that all Indians commit themselves to the elimination of untouchability. Although many contemporary Indians still have great difficulty with this imperative, the central government has implemented, with considerable protest from members of the traditional castes, a quota system for the scheduled castes, more generally known today as the Dalits. The second vow of bread labor also conflicts with traditional *dharma* in that it requires all people regardless of caste/class to involve themselves in the dignity-producing activity of physical labor. Indeed, Gandhi recommends that all Indians commit themselves regularly to the lowest menial labor as a gesture to those who have done these jobs for centuries. (Gandhi himself went one step further and prayed that he be reborn an untouchable.) The third vow of *sarvadharma samabhāva* extends the elimination of caste distinction to the tolerance of all religious faiths. The conceptual similarity is deeper at the practical level: Gandhi proposed that we not merely tolerate other religions but actually attempt to step into their precepts and their forms of life.

The fourth and final vow for the present age is *swadeshi,* which is best translated as "self-realization" and is expressed personally and socially in a life of communal self-sufficiency. In the context of Vedāntist philosophy, self-realization is the discovery of the *ātman* common to all people, so that the traditional concept of autonomy is eliminated in the vow "of selfless service...and the purest *ahiṃsā,* i.e., love."[59] Gandhi appears to equivocate on the contingent nature of *swadeshi* when he states that it "stands for the final emancipation of the soul from her earthly bondage."[60] This not only implies a necessary connection to human nature (thus making it a basic vow), but the Vedāntist overtones make this move highly problematic for the social dimensions of *swadeshi* and the fully embodied self that this vow requires.

These fundamental problems are occasion to reaffirm a basic thesis of this book: a Buddhist relational self is much better suited to *swadeshi* in that it prevents the loss of personal identity that all forms of Vedānta imply (and that Advaita Vedānta asserts) and fully situates the self in the body and society. For example, it is hard to understand how "cultivating self-confidence"[61] has any meaning if the individual self is ultimately unreal. This self-confidence, Gandhi claims, is necessary for courage, a virtue that is intelligible only on the basis of personal integrity and agency. To say that *ātman* is fearless, when this entity has, strictly speaking, no qualities, is to say nothing at all. Furthermore, a Buddhist interpretation would bring Gandhi's ethics back from the extremes that his vows tend to take him to and encourages the contemporary Gandhian to follow the Middle Way.

Returning to the basic vows, *brahmacharya* is the supreme *vrata* that essentially includes all the others. It literally means "dwelling in Truth = God *[brahmā]*" and Gandhi explains that it is "conduct that puts one in touch with God."[62] Generally taken to be a vow of chastity, Gandhi insists that it is much broader than that: "Control over the organ of generation is impossible without proper control over all the senses. They are all interdependent. Mind on the lower plane is included in the senses. Without control over the mind, mere physical control, even if it can be attained for a time, is of little or no use."[63] Control of the mind is obtained by taking the vow and initiating willful power over the senses. The goal of *brahmacharya* is nothing less than complete control of "thought, word, and deed."[64] In his autobiography Gandhi claims that *satyāgraha* would not have been possible without first succeeding in this supreme vow.

As we have seen, Gandhi offers a quite provocative connection between *brahmacharya* and nonviolence when he proposes that "lying naked with a naked member of the opposite sex is the ultimate test for not doing violence to another."[65] The axiom appears to be that if you can overcome the temptations of sex, then you will also overcome the temptation to do violence and to retaliate. An English lady, who initially criticized his sleeping with Manu, praised Gandhi: "Your patience in all my follies and humiliations has been amazing. I see in that patience now one of the purest expressions of nonviolence."[66] *Brahmacharya* is also an expression of great courage, especially with Gandhi and the opposition that he encountered with his sleeping with Manu. When it comes to sexual temptations, the isolated ascetic does not fully trust himself. He is really a coward if he does not put his self-control to the ultimate test.

Interestingly enough, Gandhi adds control of the palate *(asvāda)* to the traditional list of Hindu vows. Its literal meaning is not to eat merely for the taste of food. Gandhi firmly believes that food should sustain the body, not please the palate. It is clear that this amounts to more than Aristotle's mean between gluttony and fasting. It also raises the issue about Gandhi's own fasting and perhaps yet another difference between vows and virtues. Vows, at least in Gandhian practice, tend to the extreme whereas classical virtue theory sought the mean in all actions. Aristotle, Confucius, and the Buddha would all agree that Gandhi's fasts unto death would constitute a vice and not a virtue. (It is significant that Aquinas also argued that fasting was a vice.)[67] One could contend that such fasts do in fact violate *asvāda* insofar as its positive implication is that food is required for human nourishment. Gandhi actually sounds very Aristotelian, even Buddhist, when he proposes that we must always be mindful and adjust our food intake according to our own bodily needs.[68] (In terms of our discussion of experiments with truth, we could say that to eat more than we need is to be untruthful—in the strict factual sense that our bodies do not need the extra calories.) The body must therefore be kept fit for spiritual service. This positive imperative of *asvāda* is therefore at odds with a political fast unto death in which the constant worry of course was Gandhi's health.

With regard to the vows of *asteya* (nonstealing) and nonpossesion *(apārigraha)* Gandhi proposed an experiment that tested the full implications of these vows. (The meaning of truth most appropriate for these two vows is the Greek sense of nonconcealment *[aletheia]*). Gandhi's special way to test his own and any possible thief's commitment to *asteya* was to leave all possessions in the full light of day. In his controversial tests of *brahmacharya* he also insisted on open sleeping arrangements to demonstrate that his bed partners were not his sexual possessions. (This seems to imply that the veiling of women is a major violation of *asteya.*) Not concealing your possessions means that you confuse potential thieves in a way that can best help them overcome their temptations. They would also be morally disarmed by your lack of concern for your possessions and this could very well serve as a way of shaming them into realizing their own extreme possessiveness.

It seems to be a rule that the more people possess the more they are forced to conceal and to secure—sometimes at great cost and inconvenience to themselves. Gandhi believes that to look with envy at the possessions of another is to violate *asetya,* and even the one who fasts sins if he casts a desirous eye at any food.[69] Gandhi makes the vow of nonpossession so comprehensive that he concludes that "everyone of us is consciously or unconsciously more or less guilty of theft."[70] Again his ethics of vows tends to the extreme rather than the mean. Even the most accomplished (that is, spiritual) fasters hallucinate about food, so Gandhi appears to be in strict agreement with the *Yoga-Sūtra,* which requires that one not only control all conscious desires but also unconscious ones as well.

The fifth and final vow is fearlessness *(abhaya)* and the fact that this vow is related to the virtue of courage allows us to make a transition from vows to virtues in the next section. Except for *brahmacharya,* each of the vows is expressed with the Indo-European "a" privative: no stealing, no possession, and no fear. This form of expression intensifies the notion of extremes in Gandhi's ethics of vows. For Aristotle, having no fear could be foolhardy and dangerous and would not always be what right reason *(phronēsis)* requires. Khanna, however, argues that Gandhi believes that the virtue (not vow) of humility is a precondition for all the vows. Proper humility prevents foolhardiness because humble people do not overestimate their "resources of courage."[71]

We shall follow Khanna's constructive proposal in the next section, where Gandhi's virtues will be discussed. Before we do so, there is one issue that requires attention. Gandhi claims that *abhaya* "connotes freedom from all external fear"[72] and the key to this freedom is to distinguish between our true spiritual natures and our bodies. The reader should not be surprised that I encourage contemporary Gandhians to reject this advice and embrace a fully embodied self that an ethics of nonviolence and political engagement requires.

Gandhi's Virtues

The evidence for a Gandhian virtue ethics is considerable. Central passages are the following:

> Education, character and religion should be regarded as convertible terms. There is no true education which does not tend to produce character, and there is no true religion which does not determine character. Education should contemplate the whole life.... I have no faith in the so-called system of education which produces men of learning without the backbone of character.
>
> I have felt during the whole of my public life that what we need, what any nation needs, but we perhaps of all the nations of the world need just now, is nothing else and nothing less than character building.
>
> First of all, we shall have to consider how we can realise the self and how serve our country.... For realising the self, the first essential thing is to cultivate a strong moral sense. Morality means acquisition of virtues such as fearlessness, truth, chastity, etc. Service is automatically rendered to the country in this process of cultivating morality.[73]

Refusing to separate the private from the public, Gandhi insisted that spiritual, moral, and civic virtues are all united.

A Buddhist Gandhi would follow the developmental model of virtue formation found in Aristotle and Confucius. The recovery model—found in Plato, the Stoics, a few neo-Confucians, some Māhāyana schools, and Vedānta—holds that moral education involves coming in touch with a higher self that its already perfect. In terms of a Hindu ethics of nonviolence this would mean that one acts out the Ātman of perfect virtue rather than a self-centered *jīva*. In this model a vow is a lifelong requirement to keep the violent ego in control. Only in the perfected yogi would the vows fall away as unnecessary. Khanna suggests the developmental model for Gandhi when she states that the commitment of a vow "becomes effortless, just as the forming of good habits first needs continual effort of the will but later grows into character, from which good choices issue forth with ease."[74]

If we analyze the list of Gandhi's vows and virtues, we notice at least two interesting points. First, Gandhi considers chastity both a vow and a virtue, and in his detailed comments on *Hind Swaraj* Anthony Parel calls the vow of nonpossession a virtue.[75] If these are virtues in the traditional sense of a disposition that becomes habitual rather than constantly self-imposed, then the developmental thesis is supported. Second, humility is a virtue, not a vow, and Gandhi is very careful to distinguish between the two categories with regard to humility. He maintains that one cannot take a vow to become humble. Humility does not involve a specific decision or course of action. As he states, "Humility...does not lend itself to being deliberately practised."[76] Objections immediately arise. Is not reducing ourselves to zero a specific decision and action? Doesn't Gandhi contradict himself when he states that "true humility means most strenuous and constant endeavor entirely directed towards the service of humanity"?[77] We will return to the virtue of humility at the end of this section.

Gandhi joins the ancient virtue traditions by strongly supporting the unity of the virtues. To interpret this doctrine as the claim that the virtues have no differences whatsoever is of course absurd. For the Greeks the virtues were one in the sense that virtue is knowledge. For Aristotle the moral virtues are the same because they are products of *phronēsis,* and they are different because of the many different spheres of action in which *phronēsis* works. *Phronēsis* operating in the sphere of self-worth becomes pride, just as temperance is the result in the area of controlling the appetites. I propose that Gandhi follows Aristotle by having his experiments with truth unify the virtues. Following Jean Porter's analysis of Aquinas, I also concur with her emphasis on the dialectical relation between *phronēsis* and the virtues: the former not only finds the mean for the latter but the development of the moral virtues aids practical reason in clarifying and fine-tuning the goals of the good life.[78] The moral virtues embody truths just as much as practical reason itself does.

Alan Donagan maintains that unifying the virtues in *phronēsis* produces only a trivial truth: "Certainly Thomas' doctrine of the unity of the virtues follows if every virtue is defined as a disposition that accords with right reason. But why so define them—except to secure the result?"[79] It seems to me, however, that as right reason is always relative to individuals and their circumstances, their moral truths are synthetic rather than analytic. These propositions would obviously have specific empirical content as well as formal truth. This makes "Never eat too much" a synthetic a priori proposition, because the formal truth is necessarily joined with unique and distinctive empirical content in every single eater. If the mean between extremes were arithmetic and the same for all persons, a view that Aristotle explicitly rejects,[80] only then would the results of practical reason be trivially true.

In chapter 5 we have argued that Gandhi's experiments with truth is a contextual and pragmatic search for particular moral truths for particular situations. This means that the traditional truths about *brahmacharya* are reconstructed and then reapplied in a constructive postmodern sense. Writing from the Yeravda prison in 1932, Gandhi states that "truth is the end, love is the means thereto,"[81] and courage is following one's own truth even to the point of ridicule and rejection. The virtues of integrity and sincerity, being true to oneself, are also necessary virtues in the search for truth. This would mean that there is a significant difference between a person who regularly tells the truth and a person who is consistently and predictably truthful. We have already proposed a parallel between the relationship of truth to God in Gandhi to the Confucian idea of heaven's sincerity. The sage or saint are sincere in the same way that heaven is: they are both constant and totally predictable; they are both true to themselves and true to the present age.

It is significant that Gandhi speaks much more of self-control than temperance; in fact, the latter is seldom found in his writings. In talk about the virtues the two are often conflated, when in fact they are distinct in a very important sense. The very construction of the phrase "self-control" implies that one is engaging the will to restrain the appetites. This describes the *enkratēs* rather than *sōphrōn*, who is essentially the embodiment of temperance *(sōphrosynē)*, the one who does not have to exert his will to stay in the mean. Gandhi thought that one of the greatest Indian vices was the lack of self-control. The Rudolphs' diagnosis is as follows: "The severe emphasis on self-restraint [in the Indian tradition], on formality and harmlessness, may well be allied to the omnipresent fear of loss of self-control."[82] This emphasis on self-control rather than temperance indicates an ethics of vows and duties rather than virtues.

Raghavan Iyer offers an alternative framework for the Gandhian virtues in his observation that "Gandhi tended to assimilate all the virtues to that of moral courage."[83] Ronald Terchek has also noted that for Gandhi courage is that which makes love and compassion possible, as these virtues appear impossible for a person filled with fear.[84] Furthermore, one must distinguish between physical bravery, where one defends oneself and others with weapons or fists, and true moral courage, which Gandhi would insist is the will to stand unarmed and unresisting before your enemies. (Even in his time Aristotle had realized that courage was more than just the physical bravery of his Greek forefathers, who "strutted their stuff" with drawn swords.) We have seen that Gandhi was able to convince the physically brave Pathan warriors to change their ways by his moral courage. As he explained, "The possession of arms implies an element of fear...but true nonviolence is an impossibility without the possession of unadulterated fearlessness."[85]

It is important to note that habits of physical courage are not thrown away entirely; rather, they are reshaped such that one is just as firm in non-retaliation as one used to be expert in physical attack and defense. Recall that Confucius warned his disciples that many people could be brave without being *ren**, the obvious implication being that truly courageous people know and trust themselves so well that the force of their virtue (the Chinese *de* expresses this idea perfectly) tends to pacify any dangerous situation. In terms of the aesthetics of virtue and the power of *de,* it is significant that Confucius and his disciples were once able to fend off an attack simply by singing.

Gandhi speaks of active nonviolence as both love and truth, so yet another profitable way to see Gandhian virtues is through the virtue of love. Here is a crucial passage: "In its positive form, *ahiṃsā,* means the largest love, the greatest charity. If I am a follower of *ahiṃsā,* I must love my enemy. I must apply the same rule of the wrong doer who is my enemy or a stranger to me, as I would to my wrong doing father or son. This active *ahiṃsā* necessarily includes truth and fearlessness.[86] Here we see the frequent trinity of truth, courage, and *ahiṃsā* as cardinal Gandhian virtues.

Instructive comparisons suggest themselves from both Confucius and Aquinas. For the former *ren** as filial love is the comprehensive virtue that authenticates all the other virtues. Ideally the *ren** person would not and could not dissemble in any of the virtues; it would be impossible for *ren** persons not to be loyal or courageous or not to be true to themselves. A principal difference between Gandhi and Confucius would be the unconditional love of the stranger, a view that obviously makes him closer to the Buddhist or Christian tradition. For Aquinas *caritas* is the ultimate form of all the virtues, including prudence; it, like *ren**, is the comprehensive virtue in which all the others are perfected. Thomist Josef Pieper distinguishes between "natural" and "Christian" prudence such that the latter is a keener insight into "new and invisible realities."[87] Both Aristotle and Confucius would balk at this supernatural extension of practical reason, but Gandhi would most likely embrace the idea. (Even the Buddha would say that ESP was crucial in proving the truth of "those who know causality know the Dharma.") Gandhi would have been particularly sympathetic to Pieper's view that Christian love may very well lead one to hold "as nought all the things of this world."[88]

Gandhi says that people can cultivate truth and love, but they try to make themselves humble only at the risk of hypocrisy and pride. The reason for this odd stance might be the Vedāntist assumptions implied in this passage: "In one who has *ahiṃsā* in him [humility] becomes part of his very nature."[89] In several passages Gandhi states that the true self is nonviolent, so this means that the true self is also humble. (The concept of the self being nonviolent by nature was already critiqued in chapter 4.) This is not quite correct because true humility "should make its possessor realize that he is nothing."[90] But Ātman is not nothing; it is of course everything. It can only be the *jīva* self that is reduced to nothing. Coherence is finally obtained when Gandhi describes the humble self as analogous to a drop in the ocean as *jīva* is to Ātman/Brahman. On the virtue of humility it is obvious that Gandhi again joins the Christian tradition and rejects Aristotle's view that humility is a vice. For Aristotle "reducing oneself to zero" could never be the correct view of one's self-worth.

Chapter 9

The Virtue of Nonviolence

Ahiṃsā *does not displace the practice of other virtues, but renders their practice imperatively necessary before it can be practised even in its rudiments.*

—M. K. Gandhi

I feel that our progress towards the goal will be in exact proportion to the purity of our means.

—M. K. Gandhi

These things, if undertaken and practiced, lead to welfare and happiness, then you should practice them.

—Gatauma Buddha

[Utilitarianism] is a heartless doctrine and has done harm to humanity. The only real, dignified, human doctrine is the greatest good of all (sarvōdaya), *and this can only be achieved by uttermost self-sacrifice.*

—M. K. Gandhi

Nonviolence is the greatest virtue, cowardice the greatest vice.... Nonviolence always suffers, cowardice would always inflict suffering. Perfect nonviolence is the highest bravery.

—M. K. Gandhi

Here at last is the title chapter of the book and it is here where we will determine what sort of virtue nonviolence is, or whether it is a virtue at all. The first section addresses the issue of virtue theory's relationship to consequentialism and concludes that there is no way to avoid the fact that the virtues have value because of their consequences. We will then focus on the character consequentialism found in Buddhism, Confucianism, and Gandhi's thought. The second section discusses the relationship of ends to means, demonstrating that virtue theory insists that ends are internal to means while they are external in utilitarianism. The third section rejects Graham Hayden's thesis that nonviolence cannot be a virtue, capitalizing on some of his own points in making the argument. The fourth section explicates the distinction between enabling and substantive virtues and considers whether nonviolence is in fact an enabling virtue. The fifth section defends Aristotle's proposition that one must always take joy in the virtues and demonstrates that, as a result, virtue ethics has the most intelligible view of moral freedom. The final section distinguishes among the experiences of joy, happiness *(eudaimonia),* and pleasure, arguing that the first two are qualitatively different from pleasure, and that we should take joy, not pleasure, in the virtues. This means that Gandhi's ethical goal of well-being *(sarvōdaya)* can be interpreted as a form of nonegoistic eudaimonism.

Character Consequentialism

A methodological ideal shared by many virtue theorists is that the virtues should stand alone with intrinsic value independent of consequences and moral rules. For example, Michael Slote commits himself to this goal by saying that virtue ethics must have exclusive areteic grounds.[1] The argument that rules are abstractions from virtues is, I believe, quite persuasive, but the challenge of consequentialism is much stronger. In the burning house example discussed above, we saw that the virtue theorist is not bound to the hedonic calculus. Each person will have a unique mean between foolhardiness and cowardice, so no person would lose courage by not saving the children. Virtue theorists can also answer Peter Singer's most provocative challenge. Tying generous acts to a worldwide maximizing of pleasure leads to unacceptable demands on more fortunate people. It is absurd to say that people who give generously to disaster and famine relief now lose their virtue if they do not conform to Singer's strict requirements. Furthermore, utilitarians could never agree on the specific allocation that we would have to set aside for the poor and bereaved.

To conclude, however, that the virtues have no necessary connection to consequences is to miss the point of the challenge. The examples above pertain only to utilitarianism (consequentialism wedded to ethical hedonism); they do not prove that virtues are in every instance independent of any consequence. An implication of our argument that virtues developed before moral rules is that they were chosen because of their good consequences. As Philip. J. Ivanhoe states, "It seems strongly counter-intuitive to suggest there could be legitimate human goals which *always* or even *usually* led to bad consequences."[2] For example, courage would not have the value that it does if it did not have some significant payoff over the millennia. Furthermore, it is clear that there are many values other than pleasure that conduce to human flourishing, a topic to which we will return in the last section.

Agreeing with his Greek contemporaries, the Buddha established an essential link between goodness and truth on the one hand and evil and untruth on the other.[3] Buddhist mindfulness is primarily conseqentialist and, as we have seen, can be expressed as constant experiments with truth in which one notes very carefully those actions that lead to good consequences. We have already seen the major exemptions for *ahiṃsā,* such as the killing of fish and insects so that the conditions of human well-being can achieved. In a famous passage, the Buddha exhorts his disciples to reject all traditional forms of authority. He tells them that they should not accept any claim merely on the basis of appeal to holy scripture or that it was said by a great yogi; rather he says that if your actions "lead to welfare and happiness, then you should practice them."[4] One of the most striking examples of consequentialism in one school of Mahāyāna Buddhism is the provision that Bodhisattvas may kill persons who will, if not stopped, murder others in the future.[5] At least three good consequences result from such preemptive strikes: Bodhisattvas accrue merit that they then can bequeath to others, many innocent lives will be saved, and the would-be murderers are saved from substantial karmic debt. Because Gandhi insists on a fusion of good means and ends, it is clear that he would not agree with the principle of a violent preemptive strike for good ends.

In the last chapter we mentioned Soka Gakkai's Makiguchi and his value trinity of benefit, goodness, and beauty. Interestingly enough, Gandhi seems to agree with Makiguchi on the value of benefit and utility: "Whatever is useful to starving millions is beautiful in my mind."[6] Although rejecting the philosophy of utilitarianism, Gandhi does acknowledge the ultimate value of the well-being of all people, a value he called *sarvōdaya.* This is not a hedonic calculation but a moral and spiritual assessment based on the needs of all members of society. One might call this a "spiritual consequentialism," and Gandhi's ethical calculus is seen most clearly in his defense of mercy killing: "After calm and clear judgment to kill or cause pain to a living being with a view to its spiritual or physical benefit from a pure, selfless intent may be the purest form of *ahiṃsā.*"[7] The phrasing here is significantly different from either Bentham or even Mill.

One might say that Gandhi's lifetime focus was on purity of character, so Philip J. Ivanhoe's character consequentialism will now be offered as the theoretical home for the virtue of nonviolence.[8] Ivanhoe argues that character consequentialism differs from utilitarianism in several significant ways. As opposed to most hedonic calculations, character consequentialism focuses on the long-term benefits that the virtues bring to individuals and society as a whole. Ivanhoe illustrates this distinction between the short-term utility of quarterly results in American corporations and the lifetime commitment of Japanese companies to their employees. What the Japanese lose in terms of quick and large profits, they gain in the form of corporate, civic, and personal virtues of loyalty, perseverance, and benevolence.

One of the weaknesses of the hedonic calculus is the myriad contingencies and uncertainties that make prediction virtually impossible. In stark contrast, the value of the virtues is well attested and the person of character is eminently predictable and reliable. Complex and variable contexts makes the application of rules difficult, but the virtue theorist, always working from concrete particulars, offers moral agents the freedom to adapt and to improvise. Although critics claim that virtue theory is vulnerable to perfectionism, it appears that both rule ethics and utilitarianism have an even greater liability on this point. Their abstract and universal perspective may deceive them into thinking that there must be a solution to every moral dilemma. The particularism and contextualist perspective of virtue theory should save it from this danger. Furthermore, Ivanhoe adds, "If one does not recognize that some moral problems simply have no satisfactory solution, one runs the risk of cultivating a seriously deformed character."[9]

This conclusion leads Ivanhoe to one of his most powerful insights. He is very concerned that both rule ethics and utilitarianism, primarily because both assume a disembodied moral agent, occasionally require actions that ignore the impact on personal integrity and character. Ivanhoe grants that it is conceivable that a few people in isolated situations may be forced to perform gruesome deeds in order to maximize the social good. But there must be something fundamentally wrong with a theory that uses the language of moral necessity in hypothetical actions such as torturing a child to save the lives of ten adults. There is also something terribly wrong with the Kantian rule that it is always wrong to lie, even when lying might save the life of your best friend. The Kantian allows that it is prudent for you to do so but insists that your action has no moral worth. Kant's reasoning has the absurd result that it moves many of our most trying decisions, ones that have the most moral force and difficulty, out of the realm of morality altogether.

The virtue theorist saves nearly all our intuitions by replying, "Yes, practical reason requires that you lie, but this act does indeed have moral worth, and lying once does not in any way undermine your character." But why is it that our intuitions tell us that it is never acceptable to torture a child to save other lives? Lying once does not undermine character, but torturing a child one time does? Is it because noninjury in the flesh is more culpable than noninjury in speech? This does not seem to work with Ivanhoe's best example. It seems right when he says that experimenters who torture animals to market eye shadow will most likely undermine their character, but the utilitarian position appears to have more support when the animal experiment involves a cure for AIDS. Does overwhelming utility sometimes excuse the possible destruction of the character of AIDS researchers? Virtue theory does not seem to support all of our intuitions on these issues. But perhaps we should remind ourselves that a perfect match with intuitions is a methodological goal of modern ethics that a postmodern virtue ethics should reject. The Buddha would reject this goal as a craving to make an imperfect world different from what it really is.

While not a critique of utilitarianism, Gandhi's rejection of passive nonresistance supports Ivanhoe's points about the degradation of character very well. Village fathers who follow the rule of nonretaliation by letting bandits rob them, rape their wives, and kidnap their children, do not embody *ahiṃsā* at all. As we have seen, true nonviolence works together with other essential virtues such as love, compassion, and, above all, courage. The passive village fathers are not only cowards, but they are also lacking in integrity and self-respect, and their inaction will only encourage future failures of nerve and courage. For this situation Gandhi's contextual pragmatism requires courageous self-defense and most likely some form of violence as part of this defense. Here the value of character and virtue trump the negative consequences of violence.

The assumption of an impersonal, disembodied self also allows rule ethics and utilitarianism to ignore the relationships that define a moral agent's place in a historical, cultural world. It is no accident that the Confucian social self goes hand in hand with a focus on family and societal relations. Ivanhoe connects this insight with the Confucian idea of graded love—namely, that it is only natural that people care more for those closest to them. Michael Scriven's rational agapeism, drawn strictly from the logic of game theory, requires that all people count as equals and that, under certain circumstances, people give their lives in order to save the lives of at least two others.[10] Ivanhoe can be cited as a response to Scriven: "But I am uncommonly concerned about my own concerns, in ways that are not only not immoral but necessarily part of what I regard as a good life. I value, in fact cherish, having people who are not only special but *unique* for me. I don't want to treat my mother and father, my wife and dearest friends as 'just other players' in some ethical game theory. Without these special relationships my life would be greatly diminished."[11] It is precisely the value of these familial relationships and the virtues required to maintain them that defines character consequentialism. The values of the true village father, the loving parents, and the true friend cannot be properly measured in the simple mechanics of the hedonic calculus. People simply cannot be required to count strangers as actual moral equals with those whom they love, nor can they be expected to trade hedons and dolors as if they were neutral moral currency. Orwell puts the point even more succinctly than Ivanhoe: "To an ordinary human being, love means nothing if it does not mean loving some people more than others."[12]

In her work on trust, Annette Baier has come to the same conclusions and has discovered some unlikely European allies for our Asian thinkers. Early in her analysis, Baier points out that the virtue of trustworthiness has come about primarily because we are social and dependent beings. People can never be self-sufficient enough to take care of all the needs of the good life. Baier maintains that modern moral philosophers have neglected the importance of trust for a number of reasons. (When they do speak about it, it is the symmetrical trust of coequals in a social contract or the Kingdom of Ends, not the much more prevalent asymmetrical trust of parent and child, faculty and their administrators, or people and their aging parents.) First, the decline in religious faith removed a major model for trust—namely the unconditional trust in God. (The ultimate asymmetrical power relationship has always been a problem for the egalitarian mind.) Second, most moral philosophers ignored those intimate relationships where trust is most needed and is experienced most often. Baier proposes that it is not a coincidence that the few philosophers who recognized a broader range of trust relations were active family men "who could not ignore the virtues and vices of family relationships, male–female relationships, master–slave, and employer–employee relationships [asymmetrical all] as easily as could Hobbes, Butler, Bentham, or Kant."[13]

Baier draws on the research of Carol Gilligan to observe that since women have had much more experience with asymmetrical trust relations, it should not be surprising to find that Gilligan's female subjects were more likely to value relationality over autonomy, dependence over independence, persuasion over coercion, and nonviolence over rationalized violence. Gilligan also noticed that her subjects did very poorly in terms of Laurence Kohlberg's scale of moral development that placed the moral agent who used abstract rules and principles at the top. The moral lives of women evidently are more concrete, more complex, and much richer—the type of life suitable for the requirements of virtue theory. It is significant to note that the feminist essentialism implied in Gilligan's research is empirically disconfirmed by the fact that sexist men from Confucius to Hume privileged relationality and the emotions, and a sexist Buddha and Gandhi joined an ethics of nonviolence to their relational ontologies.

The Means–Ends Relation

One of the most important aspects of Ivanhoe's character consequentialism has to do with the relationship of means to ends. In utilitarianism means are independent from the ends. (Alternative terminology is "external" or "internal" to ends.) Gandhi phrases the distinction succinctly: "One rupee can purchase for us poison or nectar, but knowledge and devotion cannot buy us either salvation or bondage. These are not media of exchange. They are themselves the things we want."[14] As another example let us say that a person's calendar is finally open for a free weekend. Let us say that the options are two days at the new casino, two days hiking up Idaho's Selway River, or a two-day meditation retreat. Let us also say that the hedonic calculus gives exactly the same balance of hedons over dolors. If the person is a utilitarian, there is obviously no preference and a coin might as well be tossed for deciding the weekend's pleasure. If the person is a character conseqentialist, however, the options are definitely not equal in value. For character development and maintenance, gambling is definitely out and the meditation retreat would probably win over the hike. (The fact that Mill would probably agree with this suggests that his qualitative hedonism could be profitably reinterpreted as a character consequentialism.)[15] The point of this example is that, for character consequentialism, means are not independent of ends; rather, they are internal to them. In fact, the virtues, as means to Aristotle's *eudaimonia,* Gandhi's *sarvōdaya,* and the Buddha's *sukha,* share inherent values with their ends. To phrase the means-ends relation in this way does not allow the virtues to stand alone, as Damien Keown argues;[16] rather, the good life is still a consequence of the virtues and the virtues still have value because of their good consequences.

It is quite possible that some utilitarians might agree that their hedonic calculus determines that the virtues are the best means to the good life, but this still does not result in a necessary relationship of means to ends. It is possible that other means might become available that would have more utility than the virtues. The virtues, as Aristotle reminds us, are difficult, whereas utilitarianism requires the most efficient and painless means to maximize pleasure. A student from my virtue ethics seminar makes the point beautifully: "Whereas the virtue ethicist values the virtues as virtues, the [utilitarian] would just as soon abandon them if they lost their utility in delivering the good life, or if a more efficient and less arduous method of attaining the good life were discovered."[17] Since it is impossible to deny that virtues are connected with consequences, we can still declare their value to be supreme and affirm character consequentialism without any compromise to the superiority of virtue ethics. Regarding the modal argument suggested by my student, it seems clear that the value of the virtues tests true for any number of possible or future worlds. For example, the premise of the movie *ET* was that ET was an individual with an appealing ensemble of virtues that, instructively enough, only the children of the movie recognized.

Recall our discussion of Gandhi's view of means and ends at the end of chapter 1. He rejected the views of his fellow nationalists who separated means from ends: "The means may be likened to a seed, the end to a tree; and there is just the same inviolable connection between the means and ends as there is between seed and tree."[18] Maganbhai P. Desi describes Gandhi's position aptly: "Ends and means must match, that means govern and define ends, therefore only good means can realize good ends."[19] It is supremely significant for the thesis of this book that Desi specifies the following as Gandhian means: virtues of honesty, sincerity, love, charity, integrity, and rectitude. Thinking of means as separate from ends, by contrast, the utilitarian can justify violent means to a peaceful end, for example, the atomic bombing of Japan to end World War II. As Ivanhoe has admitted, it is possible that character consequentialists could make such a dramatic choice, but they are not required to pursue this violent course of action as the utilitarian is. Rather, they are bound first and foremost to the preservation of human character and its constitutive virtue.

Another way to formulate the relationship of means and ends is to say that for Gandhi *ahiṃsā* becomes active and engaged with the substantive virtues of love and truth such that means and ends are ultimately fused. As Gandhi states, "Means and ends are convertible terms in my philosophy of life."[20] In this way one could say that the means constitute the ends. A life of virtue is not the means to the good life; it *is* the good life. As Gandhi said above, "These are not media of exchange. They are themselves the things we want."

The problem with the convertibility of means and ends is that it could be read as either the ends justifying the means or vice versa. The latter could turn out as unwise as the former. To pursue nonviolence regardless of the situation and the ends is something that Gandhi always warned against. This means that truth, in terms of being true to oneself and to the situation, always trumps the application of a rule or virtue, even the virtue of nonviolence. Gandhi admits that there will be times when one must commit violence in order not to be a coward, but these occasions will be few and, if one is a virtue theorist, this option carries no moral necessity. Gandhi's policy was to discipline his *satyāgrahis* to the point where they would have sufficient virtue to opt in most cases for self-suffering and active nonviolence.

This theory of means and ends also solves one of the thorniest problems in the revival of classical virtue theory: the alleged Is–Ought problem. Means–ends relations are natural teleological systems. Means and ends are functional concepts in which means are naturally guided by their ends.

For example, if I want to go to Calcutta, I do not buy a ticket to New Delhi, unless I want to go all the way around the world. Lisa Bellantoni phrases the point well: "Functional concepts allow us to factually evaluate objects as good according to how well such objects work."[21] (The meaning of "work" here should be taken in the pragmatic sense and not any utilitarian sense.) As I have argued in chapter 5, we should read the Buddhist maxim "They who know causality know the Dharma" as "They who know the facts of their own personal histories know what they ought to do." This, I submit, is also the basic principle of Gandhi's experiments with truth and the contextual pragmatism we have discovered in ancient virtue ethics.

Recall that Gandhi discovered that rational calculation and persuasion did not work for him; rather, he and his disciples required a transformation of their character before they could succeed in their goals. Josef Pieper's Thomistic view of proper action is instructively similar: "Since we nowadays think that all a man needs for acquisition of truth is to exert his brain more or less vigorously, and since we consider an ascetic approach to knowledge hardly sensible, we have lost the awareness of the close bond that links the knowing of truth to the condition of purity. ..."[22] Pieper also reminds us that Thomas, like Gandhi, believed that chastity produces "unselfishness, objectivity, and realism." Without preparing ourselves spiritually, our practical reason may give us false conclusions because we are not able to see the world correctly. Finally, Gilbert Meilaender, Pieper's American advocate, supports our interpretation of practical reason as Gandhian experiments with truth: "[M]oral truth...is determined by reality itself in all of its complexity, not produced by our decisions of principle."[23]

Is Nonviolence a Virtue at All?

In his analysis of the concept of nonviolence, Graham Hayden defines violence as a negative character trait, specifically the disposition to do injury on a regular basis.[24] Following Aristotle's time-honored method, if we can identify the vice we should be able to identify the corresponding virtue. Hayden, however, believes that given the indefinite nature of the virtues, a clear formation of the virtue of nonviolence is impossible. Hayden sums up his objections to *ahiṃsā* as a virtue by claiming that (1) it is not a disposition that admits of a mean, and (2) it does not have a sufficiently defined domain. Hayden finally returns to rules for his ethics of nonviolence, because he also finds motivational and normative problems with the virtue approach, issues that we will address here and in the following sections.

It appears that Hayden's second objection is easily met: the domain of *ahiṃsā* can be specified as those acts dealing with causing and receiving injury in thought, word, or deed. With regard to the first objection, the deficiency in this domain is the complete passivity that Gandhi condemned in the men who allowed their village to be ransacked by bandits. This deficiency is allied sometimes with the vice of cowardice, while violent acts may be brave but not truly courageous. (Both Gandhi and the Confucians agree on nonmoral and moral expressions of bravery.) Passive nonresistance also becomes a vice when one allows dangerous animals to threaten human lives or when terminally ill animals or persons are suffering great pain at the cost of their personal dignity. Therefore, the moral content and motivation of the true virtue of nonviolence will be determined by the character consequentialism defended in the first section.

The excess in the domain of *ahiṃsā* would of course be the unnecessary use of force. For example, one can remove an offending insect without killing it, and most people can switch to a vegetarian diet without damaging their health. On our river trips in the Idaho wilderness we have found that we can easily remove rattlesnakes from our camps and, because they are such great swimmers, toss them into the river. The nonwilderness environment of Gandhi's ashrams and any urban setting may call for more violent solutions. This example reiterates the truth that the virtues are distinctively personal means that depend on context—Aristotle's right amount, right means, right goal, right time, right situation, right persons, an soon, with "right" always meaning fitting or appropriate. Kathryn P. George's argument that children and lactating women must be exempted from the claims of moral vegetarianism demonstrates the truth of the contextual pragmatism this book supports.[25] In George's argument and the other arguments we have already made, it is objective conditions (for George it is nutritional requirements) that dominate, not personal whim. The Inuit of the Arctic may be excused from moral vegetarianism for obvious geographic reasons.

One can in many cases specify the proper motivation for the virtue of *ahiṃsā* by inference from what is lacking in passive nonresistance, which does not require any virtue at all except the disposition to nonaction. The passive resistor is motivated primarily by fear, but Gandhi's courageous *satyāgrahis* are motivated by love and compassion for the other. Thich Nhat Hanh believes that we should even think kindly of the pirates who raped Vietnamese girls in the South China Sea. Hanh believes that it is far too easy to side with the girls and justify killing the pirates. Agreeing with the Jain method of *anekāntavāda* and Gandhi's maxim that we should learn tolerance from our enemies, Hanh proposes a different approach. We should try as hard as we can to step into the shoes of the pirate and understand his background and why he might be motivated to commit such heinous crimes.[26] Thinking of the context of motivation supports the virtue perspective as much as rule ethics. In fact, the question that often occurs to us when we hear of such atrocities is, What sort of person would do such a thing? The rule that has been violated is not in dispute; rather, we should want to know as much as we can about the character and background of the perpetrator before we pass final judgment. As Hanh states, "When you understand, you cannot help but love. You cannot get angry."[27]

When Hayden relates anger to nonviolence and determines a mean for anger, it is clear that he is conceding that *ahiṃsā* has a mean as well. As he states, "While it is possible to be too angry, and hence too violent, it is also possible to be too little angry, and hence, in a sense, too peaceable." Significantly, Hayden then refers directly to Gandhi and his condemnation of passive nonresistance. Furthermore, he concedes that the mean for nonviolence will depend on "cultural and even subcultural differences as to where the mean should be."[28] Hayden has not supported the Buddhist call for the stilling of all anger, something that even Gandhi never achieved in practice. A truly Buddhist Gandhi would probably have to agree with Hanh on the complete elimination of anger.

Is Nonviolence an Enabling Virtue?

Virtue theorists have generally distinguished between two types of virtues: enabling virtues and the substantive virtues. The enabling virtues include optimism, rationality, self-control, patience, sympathy, foresight, resoluteness, endurance, fortitude, and industry. The substantive virtues are wisdom, courage, justice, truthfulness, temperance, benevolence, and compassion. The substantive virtues have moral content or substance, that is, the right desire to tell the truth or help the needy, whereas the enabling virtues simply require an effort to resist one temptation or another. The substantive virtues require proper motivation toward the good, while the enabling virtues require sufficient willpower to counter evil. Of the four cardinal virtues, only prudence and justice "do the good," as Josef Pieper says, while courage and temperance "create the basis for this realization of the good."[29]

This distinction appears to test true when we think of a thief who is persistent, resolute, patient, and has fantastic self-control. (Thieves without these virtues are usually the ones who get caught!) The fact that we can think of a loyal and courageous villain has led some to argue that these two virtues really ought to be moved to the enabling category. Another psychological test by which one can distinguish the two is to use Aristotle's requirement that one must take pleasure in the virtues. This criterion must apply only to the substantive virtues, because it seems that one is not required to enjoy a courageous act of persevering torture. As Robert C. Roberts quips, "A person who enjoys enduring dangers is better called daredevilish than brave."[30] On the other hand, it makes no sense that a person must dislike being truthful or compassionate. If this analysis is correct, a person could have all the enabling virtues without having a single substantive virtue.

Let us now itemize the criteria for identifying an enabling virtue: (1) It does not have moral content nor does it appeal to a norm; (2) it is not done for its own sake, but for the sake of a substantive virtue; and (3) one does not take pleasure in it as with the substantive virtues. It appears that *ahiṃsā* is not an enabling virtue because the precept ("Do not injure") always guides its implementation. But one can formulate a norm for several other enabling virtues. For example, the rule for patience would be "Always control your temptation to act hastily"; and the norm for fortitude would be "Never give up on a task worth pursuing." Interestingly, the only way to formulate the implied rule in the enabling virtue of rationality is the tautology "Always be rational." Furthermore, the virtue of courage (and most likely others) does not lend itself to any easy formulation along these lines. True to the concrete particularity of the moral virtues, the description would require endless qualification. Even my specifications of patience and fortitude are rather wordy and open to limiting conditions. Therefore, supplying specific norms to the enabling virtues might be problematic. Indeed, active nonviolence may require a Gandhian to injure a person or an animal for the sake of truth, compassion, and justice.

Let us see what sort of arguments we can give for nonviolence as an enabling virtue. We all need a nonviolent disposition if we are to overcome desires to injure, retaliate, and verbally abuse. We also need good self-control and patience. In fact, Gandhi equates impatience with injury *(hiṃsā)*, provocatively implying that impatience is at the root of all violence.[31] (One could object that much violence in the world is done with deliberate, albeit malicious, patience.) Self-control, patience, and noninjury appear to be connected to the will to resist rather than the will to motivate. (Recall the Rudolphs' definition of Gandhi's nonviolent moral courage as the will not to retaliate in the face of violence.) It is also clear that one does not control oneself for the sake of self-control, nor is one nonviolent simply for the sake of noninjury. Furthermore, resisting the temptation of retaliation while enduring the attacks of an aggressor would obviously not be a pleasant activity. Finally, it appears reasonable to reinterpret Gandhi's basic vows as enabling virtues with *brahmacharya* embracing them all as ultimate self-control.

The thesis that *ahiṃsā* is an enabling virtue may explain why it is not listed among the major Buddhist virtues. *Ahiṃsā,* therefore, joins patience, sympathy, and self-control, three other enabling virtues in Buddhist ethics. The Dalai Lama's analysis of the virtues parallels the current discussion in a way that allows a conceptual transition to the final section of our chapter. When he reaffirms that the cessation of suffering is the ultimate goal of the good life, he is simply giving the negative formulation of the Buddhist eudaimonism defended in chapter 5. When he states that faith and compassion are "virtues by way of their own nature," he is essentially identifying them as substantives virtues. And when he describes mindfulness as a virtue "by way of association," I interpret this to mean that it is an enabling virtue.[32] One is not mindful for the sake of mindfulness but for the sake of love and compassion. Like the Buddhists, Gandhi believed that *ahiṃsā* without compassion is nothing, just as gold is an amorphous material without the goldsmith's artistic shape or the root is nothing without the magnificient tree.[33] The enabling virtues are the roots, but the flowering tree of the substantive virtues is the true goal of the good life.

The main problem with viewing *ahiṃsā* as an enabling virtue is that it essentially ignores the lesson we learned about means and ends earlier. While Gandhi does speak of *ahiṃsā* as a means to higher ends, he also sees the relationship as internal and reciprocal, such as the following: "*Ahiṃsā* is my God and Truth is my God. When I look for *Ahiṃsā*, Truth says, 'Find it through me.' When I look for Truth, *Ahiṃsā* says, 'Find it out through me.' "[34] Even though it may be necessary for us to commit violence in order not to become cowards, this act cannot be motivated by hatred or a desire for revenge. This means that *ahiṃsā* is just as motivational and substantial as love and compassion, because they all must come together in the same act.

If nonviolence satisfies the second criterion, *ahiṃsā* is performed not for its own sake but for the sake of another substantive virtue. Gandhi does not endorse passive resistance or inaction, but an *ahiṃsā* that actively upholds the values of compassion and truth. This implies that nonviolent action is not a mere refraining; thus, *ahiṃsā* is much more than self-control and much more than noninjury. It is true to say, however, that *ahiṃsā* is a means to truth; in fact it is the path to seeking social truth and justice. Perhaps *ahiṃsā* satisfies the second criterion because it is performed for the sake of truth. But according to Gandhi, one may not force or coerce others to recognize the truth (of human equality and unity), so nonviolence is the only way to achieve truth, and truth demands nonviolent engagement with others. (The means and ends must be interchangeable.) One does not impose truth on others, but rather insists on truth, without violence, by compassionate appeal to the other's rationality and conscience.

The third criterion—one does not take pleasure in an enabling virtue as one does with the substantive virtues—is also problematic. Earlier we were too quick to conclude that while we usually take no pleasure in remaining nonviolent in the face of an attack, we always take pleasure in the substantial virtues. But may find being truthful extremely unpleasant—when we bring bad tidings, when we act as witnesses at a trial, or when we give bad grades to students whose hard work has not produced the desired result.

Of course, a clear response is that in such cases, the unpleasantness comes from the situation, not the truth telling itself. But the same holds true for the practitioner of *ahiṃsā*. It is not generally unpleasant to practice the virtue of nonviolence, but it is always painful to endure the attacks of an aggressor, however one responds to the situation. It is simply not the case that one must dislike the practice of nonviolence, and in the situation described it is the context not the practice that is disliked. The *satyāgrahis* on the Salt March were hailed as heroes at every town and village, and their practice of *ahiṃsā* was obviously a pleasant activity until they reached the Arabian Sea. Once there and facing a British force that chose to resist them violently, the affirmation of their truth and their *ahiṃsā* became a very painful activity.

It now seems clear that *ahiṃsā* does not meet the three criteria of an enabling virtue. This, however, does not necessarily mean that it is now a substantive virtue. If virtue ethics requires that ends are internal to means, or if they are, as Gandhi insists, actually fused in action, then the distinction between substantive and enabling virtues becomes problematic and unhelpful. We can assume, for example, that Gandhian courage and *brahmacharya,* fused as they are with *ahiṃsā,* truth, and compassion, will not survive as enabling virtues either. The final conclusion, however, depends on how we see the internality of means and ends.

There are at least two types of internal relations: symmetrical internal relations and asymmetrical relations. If A and B have symmetrical internal relations, then both are mutually dependent on each other. A and B are asymmetrically related if B is dependent on A, but A remains independent of B. The arrow of time is a beautiful example of an asymmetrical internal relation: the future (B) is dependent on the past (A) but the past always remains the same regardless of the future. The clear implication in the distinction between enabling and substantive virtues is that while the latter are internal to the former, the former are external to the latter. Enabling virtues are always means and not ends, they have no moral content, and they do not necessarily fall under a moral norm. If nonviolence, patience, courage, and self-control are external to any moral ends, then many people that we consider bad might well have a full complement of the enabling virtues.

In the crucial passage above, however, Gandhi states that *ahiṃsā* and truth are symmetrically related: means and ends are fused; truth and nonviolence are mutually enabling or mutually substantive. In short, the traditional distinction has now lost its explanatory power. This result is actually a salutary one, because we only reluctantly attribute any virtue to a thief or con man. This conclusion is a particularly happy one in that we would never have to countenance a courageous Nazi or terrorist. Dissolving the distinction between substantive and enabling virtues appears to strengthen the case for virtue theory considerably.

The Virtues, Pleasure, and Moral Freedom

Aristotle claimed that a principal sign of having the virtues is that people take pleasure in them. (At the end of this chapter it may be more proper to say that the virtues bring joy, not pleasure.) In his article "Virtue and Pleasure" Jack Kelly has addressed the problems surrounding this claim and also offers solid support for virtue theory in general. First, Kelly reminds us that Aristotle believes that people can be truly virtuous only if their actions are voluntary and only if their hearts are in them. People obviously cannot enjoy actions that they do not want to perform. Second, Kelly questions whether Kantian theory can make sense of moral freedom: "That which can be constrained or compelled is subject to command and, hence, to rules of conduct."[35] Third, he proves, quite handily I believe, that a virtue such as generosity cannot come under a rule and cannot be commanded. One must first develop the requisite dispositions that order desire in such a way that one wants to be generous. Fourth, the Kantian will is always one constrained by reason and immune from wants and inclinations. Dutiful action is therefore action that does not meet our intuitions about moral freedom and it has no necessary connection to pleasure. Indeed, as we saw with our story of Jack and Jill, the presence of pleasure may completely obscure the person's conformation to duty. Finally, Kelly concludes that moral theorists have always failed "to make generosity and the other humanitarian virtues, such as kindliness and benevolence, purely a matter of duty. ..."[36]

Virtues are instilled not by precept and commandment, but by training and example. Children can be command by their parents not to hit others, but they will not develop the virtue of nonviolence until they have the patience, forbearance, and self-control not to strike out. Kelly maintains that children have to develop "certain attitudes and a certain kind of sensitivity,"[37] which the Buddhist would call the virtue of being mindful. If people are doing what they want when they are virtuous, then they are not following a rule; rather, they are following the higher order desires that have been established in their moral development. Furthermore, to repeat Kelly's point, if they are doing what they want, then they naturally will take pleasure in the virtues.

We are now ready to discuss Kelly's solution to the problem that the exercise of some virtues do not produce pleasure at all. Borrowing Anthony Kenny's distinction between performance and activity, Kelly argues that Aristotle must have meant that pleasure occurs only in the completed performance of the virtue, not during the course of its action. This fits nicely with our previous analysis of the Salt March. *Satyāgrahis* normally take pleasure in developing the virtues of courage, truth, compassion, and nonviolence. The pain suffered through rejection by loyalist Indians or by violent attack is situational only; it is not due to some necessary connection between practicing the virtue and experiencing pain.

As we have already noted, passively nonviolent persons who avoid all conflict and withdraw into themselves (is it too unfair to suggest that Jainism does indeed encourage this?) are simply not practicing *ahiṃsā*. We have also seen that a virtue is never isolated from others—in this case love, courage, and compassion; furthermore, it is, in conjunction with other virtues, a performance with a specific goal (Gandhi would say the general welfare); and finally, there is the proviso that although they must be performed, the virtues do not require success. (This is a grateful nod to the Stoic view of the virtues: a person can have courage and fail in every courageous act.) This analysis begins to fill out the powerful truth of Martin Luther King's famous phrase "Peace is not the absence of violence, but the presence of justice." This motto was inspired by Gandhi's insistence on active engagement and his controversial claim that it was better to cause violence than to be a coward and let injustice continue. As he once said, "I would rather have India resort to arms in order to defend her honour than that she should in a cowardly manner become or remain a helpless witness to her own dishonor."[38]

Happiness, Joy, and Pleasure

We will now conclude this chapter with a discussion of Terrance Irwin's hypothesis that Socrates can be best interpreted as a hedonistic eudaimonist. My critical response to Irwin has been developed as a full-length paper, from which I will now extract just enough to make good on an earlier promise about values other than pleasure that conduce to the good life. While my main task will be a criticism of Irwin, let us nevertheless embrace those of his insights that support the general discussion of virtue in this chapter. First, as support for character consequentialism, Irwin reminds us that, for Socrates, the virtues are not only beautiful and good, they are also beneficial. Second, the thesis that virtue is knowledge finds a distinctively personalist expression in the *Critias*. Irwin expresses Socratic mindfulness thus: "If we have self-knowledge, then we will know what is 'our own,' what we deserve, and what is appropriate for us; in the light of this knowledge we will display the appropriate sort of shame and the appropriate sort of quietness."[39] I submit that this view of practical reason is compatible with our earlier discussions about Aristotelian *phronēsis* and Confucian *yi*, which is a personal appropriation that makes the rules of propriety *(li)* one's own, as in the Latin *proprius*.

Quite apart from the epistemological issues that he raises, Irwin must be wrong when he claims that "if pleasure is [the only] completely self-explanatory and self-justifying end, it follows that happiness and pleasure must be identical."[40] I believe that we can, by means of a fairly straightforward analysis, draw out qualitative distinctions not only between pleasure and happiness but joy as well. I also propose that it is joy, not pleasure, that we experience in practicing the virtues, whereas it is the state of happiness that accompanies our entire life. Aristotle says that we should "find enjoyment or pain in the right things; for this is the correct education"; and, more emphatically, "someone who does not enjoy fine actions is not good."[41] The pursuit of happiness may be at times painful, that is, we are obviously not always maximizing pleasure, but nonetheless we take joy in the moral virtues.

Aristotle would have been pleased that *Webster's Tenth Collegiate Dictionary* actually supports his account of happiness as "well-being and contentment." *Webster's* defines pleasure as a "state of sensual gratification" but also as "a source of joy or delight." Except for Epicurus, who qualified pleasure so much that it becomes *eudaimonia,* the ancient hedonists were correct in limiting pleasure to the fulfillment of physical needs. This means that pleasures of the soul are more properly characterized as joy. For our purposes I shall try to preserve a strict definition of the pleasures as those phenomena that ensue from a direct stimulation of the sense organs and satisfy basic physiological needs.

A problem with this definition is that we never experience raw sensation separate from our perceptions and emotions, even, as some would claim, apart from specific cultural conditioning. For example, most people find the taste of beer unpleasant at first and the Chinese simply cannot understand other people's enjoyment of curdled milk. All this notwithstanding, I agree with John Kekes and Martha Nussbaum that some aspects of human nature are universal and unchanging, primarily because we are members of the same biological species, whose sense organs respond to the world in basically the same ways.[42] In addition to basic sensations, perceptions, and emotions, there are also what Kekes calls "primary virtues," such that virtue ethics is not undermined by cultural relativism. Indeed, as I have argued earlier, under the umbrella of international law and the Universal Declaration of Human Rights, each human society can pursue the primary virtues and its own secondary virtues without making virtue theory incoherent or without conceding the priority of the virtues to moral rules.

In the recent winter Olympics we saw, and we heard the winners themselves say, that they experienced great joy in winning their medals. Note that they did not use the language of pleasure to describe their feelings. In fact, if they had said "This medal gives me great pleasure" instead, we would somehow feel that they were not expressing themselves properly. It is also significant that we usually do not use the word "happy" when we are experiencing any of the specific positive emotions; we use the words for those emotions instead. Furthermore, we most often say that our hearts are filled with joy, indicating of course that the location of this feeling is not in or from any of the sense organs. (People would never say that their hearts are filled with pleasure.) Therefore, *Webster's* is correct in defining joy as "the emotion evoked by well-being, success, or good fortune or by the prospect of possessing what one desires." *Webster's* (7th ed.) is also right in distinguishing joy from both pleasure and delight, because joy "may imply a more deep-rooted rapturous emotion than either."

Let us now look at pleasure, joy, and happiness and test them according to various criteria. With regard to duration it is quite clear that if we take happiness to be Aristotle's *eudaimonia,* then both joy and pleasure are momentary and happiness, except for in cases of great misfortune, lasts for a lifetime. With regard to the related issue of their location, pleasure is situated in the sense organs, while joy and happiness are states of the "heart-mind." I am using the Confucian concept of *xin* here in order not to dichotomize human nature in the way that led to the devaluation of the emotions in the first place. Not only does virtue ethics require a fusion of heart and mind, it also posits a somatic soul in which the heart-mind is coextensive with the body and where the body is constitutive of personal identity.

If we think of the causes of the pleasure, joy, and happiness, we should follow Aristotle in holding that *eudaimonia* is caused by the virtues, moral and intellectual, and sufficient health and external goods to meet life's needs. I have already proposed that the causes of pleasure consist in stimulating the sense organs. While it is true that we take joy in pleasing sounds, beautiful sights (nature and great art), and cute babies, each experience inseparable from sense perception, it is equally true that much avant garde art is not pleasing and some children are not very cute at all. (In fact, newborns are generally quite ugly creatures.) Furthermore, the joy that we take in our loved ones and our own successes is not necessarily preceded by pleasant sensations. We must also recognize that much joy is triggered by memory rather than sensation. Memories of my daughter as a young girl give me incredible bursts of joy, just as memories of times that I might have lost her give me great distress.

Pleasure is distinct from both joy and happiness in several distinct ways. First, people never regret joy or happiness, but they may very well regret the pleasures of overeating, drinking too much, taking drugs, and recreational sex. On the other hand, most people would never regret the times they have fallen in love or the joys that they have experienced with their family and friends and their own personal successes. A friend said that he regretted the joy that he felt when hearing about a friend's successful operation and then learned that the doctor had discovered a terminal cancer. But it seems to me that the joy of the successful operation was certainly not the wrong feeling to have at that moment; nor did the succeeding sorrow in any way cancel the momentary value of that enjoyment. With regard to regretting happiness, it seems utterly absurd for one who, after years of moral development, decides to regret the *eudaimonia* that ensues from such an achievement.

Another way in which pleasure differs from joy and happiness lies in the way in which they are achieved. One can decide to stimulate the sense organs in order to experience pleasure, but one cannot aim at having joy or achieving happiness. For example, one cannot experience joy in sexual activity by simply performing intercourse; indeed, couples may experience joy from intimate embraces without ever coming to orgasm. Additionally, we can also be sated with pleasure, but we can never get enough joy or happiness; or alternatively, we can be so sated with a pleasurable activity (such as sex or eating) that it becomes joyless and meaningless. This observation gives considerable plausibility to the hypothesis that pleasure itself cannot give meaning to life, and if it cannot, then ethical hedonism fails as a moral theory.

Except in the case of the masochist, pleasure usually cannot be experienced simultaneously with pain. (The pain of physical conditioning appears to be a good counterexample.) In an illuminating analysis that is as fresh as yesterday, Aristotle shows how taking pleasure in a flute performance makes it impossible to carry on and gain pleasure from a simultaneous conversation.[43] (Aristotle says that it also explains why one does not mind enjoying nuts during the performance of a bad play!) Very different is *eudaimonia,* which continues unabated as that fortress of well-being and contentment that buttresses us against daily travails and disappointments. Robert Solomon observes that while the emotions of joy and depression exclude one another,[44] we can still experience great joy while feeling severe pain. Though the life of the *brahmacharya* fails to maximize pleasure, Gandhi said that for him "it was a matter of ever-increasing joy." Illustrating the austere virtue aesthetics discussed in chapter 7, he added that "everyday revealed a fresh beauty in it."[45]

With regard to means-ends relations, pleasure is external to its means. As we saw with the example of enjoying a weekend, any number of means could produce the same number of hedons. More precisely and physiologically, it is possible to produce sensations and pleasures by directly stimulating parts of the brain, completely bypassing the sense organs themselves. The means–ends relations with regard to joy and happiness are internal. There are a limited number of experiences that produce joy in us, and, according to Aristotle, only the virtues, assuming that our basic needs are taken care of, can produce happiness. Generally speaking, when the physical stimulus for pleasure stops, the pleasure stops. This is not so with joy or happiness; indeed, while some events or even sensations might trigger great joy, there is no specific stimulus for happiness. One cannot simply turn happiness on and off.

If the foregoing analysis is sound, then Irwin's claim that only pleasure is self-justifying and self-explanatory is not supported. If joy and happiness are qualitatively different even in a few of the ways that we have discovered, then these states of heart-mind cannot be explained in terms of pleasure. This means that eudaimonism, as Aristotle assumed, has its own foundations and that happiness is more than just maximizing pleasure. It also means that we have reinforced our thesis that both the Buddha and Gandhi can be said to support a form of eudaimonism. Gandhi once said that "contentment is the best of riches,"[46] and "contentment" is one of *Webster's* definitions happiness. This is the Buddha's goal as well: "May all beings be happy and secure in themselves, truly happy. All in whom breath of life exists...may all these be in themselves truly happy."[47]

Chapter 10

The Saints of Nonviolence: Buddha, Christ, Gandhi, King

Saints should always be judged guilty until they are proved innocent....

—George Orwell

[I was in] the presence of a moral giant, whose pellucid soul is a clear, still lake, in which one sees Truth clearly mirrored.

—Henry S. L. Polack on Gandhi

It is too early...to clothe me in sainthood. I myself do not feel [to be] a saint in any shape or form.

—M. K. Gandhi

[Martin Luther King] helps us to see that to be a saint is not to be morally perfect, but to be exemplary in love.

—Jean Porter

This final chapter will offer a theory of sainthood that best supports our basic intuitions about the great spiritual leaders of human history. The first section begins with George Orwell's critique of Gandhi as a saint and also finds that the virtue of gentleness is not always present in the lives of some saints. The second section analyzes the saintly ideal from utilitarian, Kantian, and Thomistic perspectives. These three theories are attempts to define what Susan Wolf calls the "moral" saint. Robert Neville's view of the saint falls into this category and, even though we will cast him as charismatic saint, Gandhi appears to fulfill Neville's criteria of saintliness in an eminent way. The third section introduces the concept of the charismatic saint, proposing that what we admire in the saint has more to do with charisma than moral perfection. In short, saints preserve and manifest their *de* or, more biblically, are filled with the Holy Spirit or are exemplars of Christ. The Pentecostals and their predecessors are criticized for too much enthusiasm, but they are closest to Chinese *de* and Ferdinand Galen's view that "virtue is enthusiasm"—namely, virtue is vitality and spirit.[1] As Phyllis McGivney observes, "The saints differ from us in their exuberance, the excess of our human talents. Moderation is not their secret. ..."[2]

The theory of the charismatic saint allows us to canonize both M. K. Gandhi and Martin Luther King even though they both had definite moral weaknesses. The fourth section compares the concepts of *mahātma* and *megalopsychia,* poses the challenge of immoral expressions of *de,* and engages the thorny issue of the flawed saint. Finally, we need to recover the basic humanity of both the Buddha and Christ, who have suffered from the flattery of two millennia of very positive public relations. Their deification and reification has in many cases removed them, unfortunately, from the possibility of any true vitality or life. (Regrettably for the ethics of nonviolence, it is the Jain saints who are the furthest removed from the power of *de.*) However, in the Buddha's temptation and Christ's death we do see an example of what we have called "duress virtue," in which the humanity of both may be affirmed.

Saintly Gentleness and Tough Love

George Orwell's famous essay on Gandhi is not an entirely accurate portrayal of the man, and one can sense the deep bias against Indian spirituality and asceticism that many British have held. (It was, of course, the Scotsman David Hume who simply could not see any value in the monkish virtues.) Orwell continues the myth that all Hindus believe that the "world of solid objects is an illusion to be escaped from," which we have already seen is not only not Gandhi's view but also not shared by many other Indian philosophical schools. Orwell is particularly insensitive in his attribution of motive to the ascetic life: "a desire to escape from the pain of living, and above all from love. ..."[3] Finally, it is definitely unfair to Gandhi to claim that he held that "one must choose between God and Man." This is misleading for at least two reasons: (1) both his neo-Vedāntist philosophy and my Buddhist interpretation of him overcome the divine-human divide, and (2) the fusion of spiritual values and political activism was his greatest achievement.

Orwell, however, has good reason to be suspicious of Gandhi and other saints. Gandhi's belief that there is a necessary connection between truth-telling and *ahiṃsā* appears to have its origins in the *Yoga Sūtra,* where the commentator Vyāsa states, "One must reflect with care before uttering a word, and speak only out of love for others."[4] Madhuri Sondhi brings out the relation to *ahiṃsā:* "[Truthfulness is] meaningfully communicating what we see or hear unless...it is hurtful to another."[5] This raises an interesting issue about Gandhi's tough love with his family and his disciples and the fact that this tactic works on the principle that truth sometimes hurts. (This demonstrates once again Gandhi's principle that truth trumps even a vow not to injure.) For example, Gandhi could have been gentle with his wife Kasturbai and not forced her to clean the latrines at the Ahmedabad ashram. But this was definitely not Gandhi's policy; rather, the duties of a spiritual master require that his disciples not be spared the realities of truth. In 1946 near Noakhali when Manu lost Gandhi's special bar of soap, he made her walk back many miles through a dark and dangerous jungle to retrieve it. Gandhi insisted that she learn a lesson from her carelessness even though it put her at great danger from both wild animals and bandits. Gandhi had insisted on complete truthfulness from Manu and threatened to dismiss her if he saw even an inkling of weakness on her part. It is obvious that Manu and others suffered great intimidation, even terror, in their dealings with their stern "Bapu." As Robert Neville wryly notes, "Living with a saint is more grueling than being one."[6]

We usually think of saints (St. Francis comes to mind) as gentle, meek, and mild. We tend to remember Jesus for his gentleness but sometimes forget the harsh rebukes that he handed out to his disciples, his family, and religious authorities. (He seemed to be consistently gentle only with women not related to him.) Indeed, it is the vices of roughness, harshness, and abruptness that we always contrast with gentleness. A *Frontline* documentary on Mother Theresa revealed her as anything but a meek and gentle soul. Furthermore, if Christopher Hitchen's portrayal of her is even partially correct, then this was a woman of not a few vices.[7]

Jean Porter's analysis of gentleness—of how it so often is only a semblance of virtue—reveals how tough love usually rings more truthfully. Trying to capture the true virtue of gentleness shows how essential context, especially a narrative framework, is for an accurate description of the virtues. Also important is how gentleness operates in the realm of a person's entire ensemble of virtues. Porter explains, "If gentleness is a trait of persons, then we must have a sense of how it is displayed in the patterns of activity that go to make up a human life, and we must also have some sense of the context of circumstances and motives by which we can distinguish true gentleness from its counterparts."[8] Porter then tells the story of Anna and her false gentleness. She is timid in front of her husband and boss because she fears them, and she is soft with her son to the point of spoiling him. Working as a nurse, Anna chooses to hide some facts about a daughter from her dying father.

It is clear that in similar circumstances Gandhi would not have been gentle. He would have found Anna totally lacking in courage and integrity. Holding firm to the truth of what many would consider quack medicine, Gandhi almost lost a son because he refused to follow the doctor's advice. One of Hitchen's strongest criticisms of Mother Teresa is that, even though she had sufficient finances (apparently millions of dollars in Swiss accounts) to equip and staff her clinics, they are austere places of death and, as some former sisters claim, covert baptism. The care the patients receive was gentle, but the unnecessary deprivations were harsh, some would say even criminal.

Consistent gentleness does appear to be found in the life of the Buddha, and if skeptics say that this is because of a sanitized biography, the example of the Dalai Lama could be used instead. (Other Buddhist and Hindu holy persons could also be featured.) I know of no indication that this man, at least in his adult life, has ever wavered in his sincerity, humility, gentleness, or compassion. Indeed, Gandhi and Mother Teresa pale in comparison to this paragon of virtue. We will model the saint on the Chinese concept of *de*, and the Daoist preference for childlike simplicity, innocence, and spontaneity is certainly manifest in the Dalai Lama's life. Orwell may not be correct in claiming that the saint must be lovable (he did not think that Gandhi was), but if lovability is indeed a saintly criterion, then the Dalai Lama certainly fulfills it. In what follows we intend to canonize Gandhi and Martin Luther King despite their moral failings, but we do not want to imply that saints are beyond good and evil as Daoist sages and Nietzschean *Übermenschen* are sometimes portrayed.

Utility, Duty, or Infused Charity?

Let us now look at the concept of sainthood from the perspective of utilitarianism, Kantianism, Thomism, and Robert Neville. Each of these theories (except for perhaps the third) has been used to define what Susan Wolf has called the "moral" saint, one "whose every action is as morally good as possible." I will agree with her basic premise thesis that "moral perfection... does not constitute a model of personal well-being toward which it would be particularly rational or good or desirable for a human being to strive."[9] She finds this a disturbing truth because we have always been told, presumably with good reason, to become the very best persons we can be. While Wolf believes that we must change our moral theories to resolve this basic tension, I propose instead that we should change our idea of what kind of person the saint actually is. But even with regard to moral theory, the idea of the charismatic saint happily joins virtue ethics—the Latin *virtus* and Chinese *de* represent both the power and vitality of our saints and the ordered passions that constitute their virtues. When Wolf finds current moral thinking deficient in "dominant passion" and "concrete and specific" vision,[10] it may well be that human excellence and well-being and the virtues that lead to them may be the answer. (To be fair, Wolf's discussion of Aristotle and Nietzsche as alternatives leads ultimately in this direction.) It may also not be just accidental that a renewed philosophical interests in saints has coincided with the revival of virtue ethics.

One of the most provocative claims in J. S. Mill's *On Utility* is the following: "In the golden rule of Jesus of Nazareth, we read the complete spirit of the ethics of utility. To do as one would be done by, and to love one's neighbor as oneself, constitute the ideal perfection of utilitarian morality."[11] This is not a specific definition of a saint in terms of utility, but it serves as a beginning for our analysis. If utilitarianism is defined as consequentialism wedded to ethical hedonism, then Mill must be wrong to imply that Jesus was a utilitarian. If his only claim is that the ethics of Jesus can be interpreted by means of utility, then the point is arguable. (Indeed, some Christian ethicist have moved to this position very eagerly.) With the exception of Epicurus, none of our spiritual leaders, ancient or modern, were hedonists of any kind. This appears to doom the utilitarian interpretation of sainthood from the very start.

Apart from the empirical problem of absence of hedonistic saints, there are also conceptual problems with utilitarian sainthood. We have already mentioned Michael Scriven's rational agapeism in chapter 9. Although Scriven does not apply his theory to saints, initially it looks as if a saint would be the person who would not have to take Scriven's "pill." Taking a pill to overcome humanity's innate selfishness is merely a symbol for what Scriven believes are necessary steps that any society must take if it wishes to maximize happiness. For Scriven the best society will be the one whose members will always be willing, if the conditions call for it, to sacrifice their lives if at least two other lives will be saved. Scriven argues that even if societies are not subjected to war and natural calamities, the fact that their members have been trained from childhood to be selfless will have a large payoff in terms of total hedons. Scriven claims that game theory dictates that the selfish society, subjected to the same conditions, will not maximize utility.[12]

The ironic conclusion of rational agapeism with regard to saints is that everyone would become one. Since everyone is required to undergo indoctrination in selflessness (Scriven does not flinch at the behavior modification required to accomplish this), there would be no chance to see if any person could become selfless without the "pill." Quite apart from the absurdity of universal sainthood, critics may object strongly to the "good ends justify any means" implied in Scriven's support for moral indoctrination, but, as we have seen, utilitarianism does not require that the means and ends be internally related. Some may respond that I have set up a straw man by choosing such an extreme utilitarian representative, but Peter Singer's views are not substantially different from Scriven's.

Many saints have generally supported an ethics of duty, so perhaps a Kantian approach to saints would be more promising. The first problem involves the supererogatory acts that saints regularly perform. As we saw with our burning-house example, the Kantian is strictly bound to reason such that it is just as irrational to do more than your duty than to do less. (Intriguing and contrasting reductios suggest themselves: with regard to self-sacrificial actions Scriven's utilitarianism requires that we all become saints, while Kant requires that none of us should.) A second problem follows from Kant's moral rationalism: the loving intention of the saint that we admire so much can have no moral relevance. For Kant people who reluctantly give to others without passion are the ones that we know for sure are doing their duty. A smiling and effusive Dalai Lama would be, to say the least, a genuine moral puzzle for Kant. Without the passions, the dutiful saint would be only half-human and certainly not the person that we elevate and admire.

If the Kantian saint is, as Wolf suggests, perfectly obedient to moral laws, then not even the Buddha or Christ are saints in this sense. For many Hindus the Buddha was a fallen yogi whose rejection of ascetic and caste rules made him a veritable antinomian. (One version of Vishnu's incarnations explains his coming as the ninth incarnation as a punishment for human sin and the general decline of *dharma*.) Although Christ is portrayed as perfectly obedient to God's will, first-century religious authorities considered him a dangerous revolutionary and religious fanatic. Furthermore, if Paul is correct that the Law was merely created to manifest human sin, then it is the full freedom of the Gospel and divine grace, rather than obedience to law, that are the essence of the Christian life. We must look to criteria other than moral perfection to discover the reason for the saint's attraction to us.

In his response to Susan Wolf, Robert Adams claims that she has made moral perfection too central to the life of the saint. As he states, "Saintliness is not perfectionism.... There is an unusual moral goodness in the saints, but we shall not grasp it by asking whether any of their actions could have been morally worthier."[13] Adams also criticizes Wolf for viewing the saints apart from their religious lives and the transformative role that God allegedly has had on these exemplary persons. Furthermore, from this theological perspective Wolf's emphasis on moral perfection becomes a form of idolatry. The saints sacrifice everything because they have faith that God will provide not only for them, but also for all those who are the object of their beneficent attention. Gandhi is a good example of one who confesses that he is certainly not morally perfect (recall that he did penance not only for others but for himself as well) and the virtue of humility is one of the trademarks of saintliness.

Interestingly enough, it is difficult for utilitarians or Kantians to privilege humility because the latter must never lose their autonomy and self-worth, while the former would always want to maximize both self-interest and other-interest. This means that utilitarian saints would be those rare persons who could develop their own talents and perform many beneficent acts at the same time. Wolf believes that such persons would be "unattractive" and might have to tone down their own achievements so as not to appear "holier than thou."[14] Even though this would be false humility, it would allow others to enjoy themselves in the saint's presence. Such deception would not be immoral because it would maximize everyone's happiness. (Recall that for the utilitarian, pleasurable consequences, not intentions, are the locus of moral value.) It would, of course, always be better to have more saints than fewer. During the Hindu-Muslim conflicts that led to the disaster of Partition, Lord Mountbatten remarked that it required fifty thousand troops to pacify the Punjab, but it took only one Gandhi to keep the peace in Bengal without using a single weapon. Just think of what Mountbatten could have done with consummate utilitarian efficiency if he had had just a few more Gandhis.

To be fair to Wolf, she does offer a broader vision of the saint by adding "personal bearing, creativity, [and] sense of style" to the strictly moral considerations.[15] (Including these and other qualities in the idea of *de* leads to the charismatic saint of the next section.) Adams himself joins in this expanded notion of the saint by suggesting that, since God is a lover of beauty, great artists (even secular greats such as Van Gough) may be unsung saints. An implication of this theistic view is that since God is reflected in every person in some way, all of us are saints in this sense. Adams thwarts such a move by an intriguing comment that although both Vincent Van Gough and Edvard Munch were equally disturbed personalities, there is too much unhappiness in the latter's work to qualify as saintly.[16]

Another means to a broader perspective on saintliness is to study the long list of Christian saints. Again we do not necessarily find moral perfection either explicitly or implicitly. What we see are various apostles, martyrs, mystics, theologians, monks such as St. Francis, and simple folk who have witnessed the appearance of Mary or other miracles. (The Greek Orthodox calendar celebrates a saint every day of the year.) The only type of person we do not find, except for perhaps the very musical Hildegard of Bingen, are artists, a deficiency that Adams would like to repair. Even without an in-depth study, it is safe to say that the common thread linking all of these people is the special presence of God in their lives. The saint is filled with the Holy Spirit in order to do God's work on earth.

This brings us to the third type of saint, whom we may not want to call "moral" for at least two reasons: (1) moral perfection is not present in many of these people, and (2) if moral perfection is possible, it is the result of divine grace. Wolf calls the utilitarian saint "loving," but I believe that it is a better name for saints who love not because of their own power or initiative; rather, they are able to do so because of the presence of divine love in them. Adams claims that the saint of infused charity is one that is not subject to Wolf's long list of objections (discussed more fully in the next section). Furthermore, one could argue that divine grace appears to be the only reason for the ability of these people, some confessing great weaknesses and sins, to perform the actions for which they have been canonized.

Although courage can be acquired through natural powers, the infused courage of the martyr may appear foolhardy. As Aquinas states, "Courage as a virtue makes the mind competent to endure any dangers. But it has not the resources to make us confident of escaping each and every danger; this is the role of that courage which is the Gift of the Holy Spirit."[17] In a guarded defense of Martin Luther King's sainthood (discussed in the next section), Jean Porter observes that the achievements of both Gandhi and King appear to go far beyond the resources of their respective background and character. Like the prophets of old they were, as young men, very unlikely and somewhat reluctant political and spiritual leaders.

Although Robert Neville's concept of saintliness is principally linked with the ideal of moral perfection, there are other features of his view that deserve special attention with regard to Gandhi's sainthood. Neville's discussion of the saint is informed and strengthened by first delineating the requirements for the good soldier and sage. He summarizes his analysis by proposing that while the soldier must have a resolute will and the sage a profound understanding, the saint requires a pure heart. He also acknowledges essential common ground among the three and concludes that "for all their perfected impulses, saints without toughness and thorough understanding are saps."[18] Gandhi was incredibly intense (perhaps too much so) in his self-purification and his will was as resolute as any soldier's, but his understanding was not necessary profound. (Gandhi would have been the first to admit this.) Gandhi's lifelong social and political engagement did not allow "the considerable discipline of intellect" that Neville's sage requires. Finally, Neville speaks of the aesthetic quality of the saint's life and character in ways consonant with our earlier discussions in chapters 6 and 7. He states, "The art of living is a manner of existing so as to gather into one's life the greatest richness of experience possible... and the exercise of creative powers to their utmost."[19]

Neville's saint is also someone with "heroic accomplishments," and Gandhi certainly fulfills this criterion even considering the horrible disaster of Partition. Heroic deeds are often associated with great failures that make even the saint fall into despair, and Neville is keenly aware of how important this emotion is for the saint. Despair might ruin an ordinary person's life, but it sometimes serves as a moral catalyst in the life of the saint. Hindu-Muslim violence in 1946–48 forced Gandhi to focus even more on "absolute values," the ultimate goods of Neville's saint who is pure of heart and free of any individual interests. Making good use of Plato, Neville describes the saint as the world's greatest lover, one who is in love with nothing less than the highest good. The intense focus of the saint's moral vision requires that he or she reconsider the meaning of the perfection of desires. Neville is particularly insightful on this point: "The paradox in the perfection of desires is that such perfection entails the abandonment of the search for perfection in any egoist sense. Saints give up on perfecting many of their desires long before secular egoists realize that their striving to become super people are vain. The perfection of desires begins with abandoning the special interest of having perfect desires. The saints' motive is not self-improvement but service to the desirability of the enhancement of things absolutely."[20] This shift in the meaning of perfection not only changes the focus of moral perfection but it may also explain why the saint's courage may appear foolhardy. It may even explain the saint's eccentricities and failure to conform to social norms.

The Charismatic Saint

As we have already seen, the Greek *aretē* and the Latin *virtus* have their equivalent in the Chinese *de,* which can be translated as "virtue," "power," or "charisma." The original meaning of the Latin *sanctus* was the holy power that the Christian martyrs possessed, a power that continued to reside, according to popular religious imagination, in their bones, body parts, and relics. In Vedic religion we find that Indra's thunderbolt was made of a sage's bones. We will now cultivate the rich comparative soil that this mixture produces.

Etymologically, *de* means to "to get" or "to have," so *de* is that which everything has for its proper functioning. All of the ancients saw this general concept of virtue in nonhuman things as well as human. For the human realm, Ames and Rosemont define *de* as "excelling in becoming one's own person."[21] Ontologically, the many *de* are the individual instantiations of the *dao* itself. (The Chinese, except under the influence of some Buddhist schools, never thought of things as illusory or lacking reality in any sense.) *De* is also intimately related to *qi,* the cosmic energy out of which everything arises and from which all things get their vitality. Ames and Rosemont also draw a comparative link to the Indian *dharma*, so *de,* especially in the Confucian tradition, has a normative dimension that we shall discuss shortly.

In ancient China there arose two schools with regard to the care of one's *qi.*[22] The first school of "closed orifices" assumed that each of us was born with a certain amount of this energy that we must preserve as best we can.

Those who lead disordered lives and dissipate their *qi* out their bodily orifices will distort the *Dao* and die young. The second school of "open orifices" believes that we can replenish our energy by keeping the body open to the constant influx of *qi.* The virtuous person concentrates this energy in the heart-mind *(xin),* where it retains its fine spiritual texture. Disorder in this school comes about when the heart-mind loses its focus and *qi* reverts to its gross physical states. In Chinese medicine illness arises out of the blockage of *qi* in the acupuncture meridians.

The *Daodejing* distinguishes between people who have "lived life...lavishly," thereby dissipating their *de,* and those who have preserved their *de*—the abundant *de* of the child—and will not die prematurely. Therefore, if people will "stop the apertures, close the doors,"[23] then they can save their life *(shen)* even in the face of dangerous animals and humans. With "accumulated *de*" people can, just like Nietzsche's *Übermenschen,* become "all overcoming" and "have long life and enduring vision."[24] The Chinese *shen* can have this meaning of psychophysical self, but it can also refer to gods, spirits, and sometimes sages. In other work I have argued that this does not mean that sages are deified; rather, it means that sages, just as the Christian saints, are "spirit-filled."[25]

There is a passage from *The Mencius* that sums up much of what has been presented in this study thus far. In response to the question of why Yue Zeng is "good and true," Mencius said, "The desirable is called 'good.' To have it in oneself is called 'true.' To possess it fully in oneself is called 'beautiful,' but to shine forth with this possession is called 'great.' To be great and be transformed by this greatness is called 'sage'; to be sage and to transcend the understanding is called *shen.*"[26] Mencius's definition of the good is thoroughly Aristotelian. Gandhi would agree with the Confucians that good people are true to themselves, and he would also embrace Mencius's aesthetics of virtue. The spirit-filled sage is also a courageous person, one who cultivates a floodlike *qi* and who can, figuratively of course, "fill the space between Heaven and Earth." The concept of *de* is now carried within both *qi* and *yi,* which were discussed in chapter 5: "It is *qi* that unites rightness *(yi)* and the *dao.* ... It is born of accumulated rightness. ...[27]

In the first major study of comparative virtue ethics, Lee Yearly lays out points of similarity and contrast between Mencius and Aquinas on courage.[28] They both believe that a fully mature practical reason —Yearly sees this function in *zhi* rather than *yi*—is essential for true courage. They both agree with Aristotle that military courage is at worst a semblance of virtue and at best only an imperfect form. A supremely significant point for the ethics of nonviolence is Yearly's observation that mature courage is perfected by replacing attacking and retaliating with the virtues of endurance and forbearance, which is precisely what Gandhi did in his encounter with the

British and the Pathan warriors. Unlike Aristotle, both Mencius and Aquinas believe that the perfection of virtue requires a transcendent power, although for Mencius the focus is more on the heavenly endowment of virtue "sprouts" than any direct bestowal of divine grace. ("Heaven has given life to and nourished *de* in me...," as Confucius said.)[29] For Mencius the virtues are infused at birth whereas for Aquinas they are bestowed as the spiritual life matures. Finally, both affirm the unity of virtues in such a way that it is difficult to make intelligible the reality of the flawed saint, which is discussed in the next section.

We are now ready to respond more fully to Wolf's critique of the saintly ideal. Adams has already answered the charge that the saint is bland and lifeless, but the concept of the charismatic saint exemplifies the opposite qualities of vitality, passion, and floodlike energy and courage. As we have seen in chapter 6, the Confucians, contrary to the received view of them, were great dancers and singers and the sage would have been most elegant and vital among them. There is, of course, sobriety in the life of the saint, but there are also moments of great joy. Wolf must have forgotten about the "belly" Buddha and the giggling Dalai Lama when she bemoaned the fact that the saint could not enjoy a good laugh.

If Wolf were correct that the saint is perfectly obedient to moral laws, then her claim "there seems to be a limit to how much morality we can stand"[30] would cut to the quick. If she had spent more time around Buddhist monks she might have asked, "When are these people going to get serious?" in response to Zen monks, or in response to the Tantric, "When is this guy going to start behaving himself?" It may be true that some of our saints are not very well rounded (their focus is usually too singular and intense) and some can even be called fanatics, but very few of them fit Wolf's description of "moral fanatic." Finally, her deflation of the saint to the level of aesthetic, sexual, or sports fanatic is a cheap shot and a low blow.

As we have seen, Wolf adds the *de*-like qualities of "personal bearing, creativity, [and] sense of style" and moves us in the direction of the charismatic saint. But she is not happy with this gesture to virtue ethics because she contends that we could never spell out any definite ensemble of virtues that could be labeled, with any certainly, saintly. We have already seen, however, that it is precisely this openness and flexibility that gives virtue theory its advantages. If Wolf and others are right that human life must be ruled by abstract rules and impersonal considerations in order to be reckoned as moral, then perhaps we should then simply declare, "If this is the moral life, then so much the worse for it!" If *de* is "excelling at becoming one's own person," then judging that excellence cannot come under any abstract rule; rather, the judgment is going to be partially aesthetic, partially vitalistic, partially consequentialist, and partially personal.

Although I have emphasized the aesthetic dimension and would insist that the making of a saint/sage is best seen as a creative art form, the virtue theorist should never lay down necessary and sufficient conditions and especially not speak any language of moral necessity. Looking at the huge number of Christian saints, the amazing thing is the great variety of achievements these people encompass. The particular virtues and their arrangement are many times unexpected and sometimes shocking, as our short summary of the Daoist immortals and Buddhist *siddhas* in the next section will reveal. The voluntary and indeterminate nature of the virtues, especially those having family resemblances to the saintly or sagely, fit our intuitions almost perfectly. We are filled with great admiration, sometimes awe, by saints and sages, but we realize that we not only cannot be like them but that *we do not have to become like them*. All of us to some extent are filled with the power of *de* or the Holy Spirit, but some of us simply do not have this miraculous power in sufficient quantity or quality to do what we expect saints to do.

How many of us have felt guilty because we have not become a saint? I suspect that there are very few people who feel this way. (In fact, the person who aspires to sainthood and obviously does not have the *de* to do it is usually considered at best foolish and at worst pathological.) Our intuitions appear to be different about how we generally feel about not conforming to moral rules. Here many of us unfortunately do feel unnecessary guilt, a guilt that could be mitigated by less emphasis on moral rules and more training in the virtues. Kantian and utilitarians can only condemn most of us as failed saints, but virtue theorists would praise us for our ordinary virtues and our wisdom for not attempting acts that are inappropriate for us (*phronēsis* or *yi* working here) or too difficult for us to achieve.

While the Kantian unreasonably demands moral perfection, the utilitarian would insist that the saint produce consistent and maximal results. But the principle that success is not necessary for the practice of the virtues applies to the saint/sage as well as to the ordinary person. One could argue that the disaster of Partition dramatically upset the hedonic balance sheet of Gandhi's achievements. (He at least thought this was a catastrophic failure for which he took responsibility.) Perhaps Gandhi was terribly unrealistic and hopelessly naive to think that he could get radical Muslim separatists like Jinnah to agree to a united Indian subcontinent. The facts could certainly support the conclusion that if Gandhi had let the Muslim extremists go their own way earlier and if Nehru had allowed Muslim Kashmir to join Pakistan, there would be have been far less violence then as well as since the bloody days of 1947–48. (The hedonic calculation for Gandhi's long-term success as a prophet of active nonviolence is obviously much more positive.) Less controversially, I am confident that the sober utilitarian could not very easily get a balance of hedons over dolors from the work of Mother Teresa. Many souls have been comforted (but perhaps deceptively baptized), but very few lives have been saved or even serious attempts have been made to do so. Therefore, when Adams declares that "goodness was present in [Gandhi] in exceptional power,"[31] this is not the goodness of moral perfection or the greatest happiness for the greatest number; rather, it is the goodness of *de* or *śakti,* the Sanskrit equivalent that is appropriate for Gandhi.

Mahātma, *Megalopsychia,* and the Flawed Saint

One of the most imposing challenges for virtue ethics is the question of the relativity of the virtues. Which virtues shall we choose? The heroic warrior virtues of Homer and Nietzsche, the virtues of the Athenian gentleman, the weak virtues of Jesus, the Buddha, and the Daoist, the utilitarian virtues of Ben Franklin, or the strong entrepreneurial virtues of modern capitalism? The conflict most mentioned is the alleged irreconcilability between Greek pride *(megalopsychia)* and Christian humility. Aristotle defined pride as knowing one's own self-worth, which constitutes a mean between undervaluing oneself and overrating one's achievements. Commentators have also assumed that in this schema humility will always come out as a vice. Our task is not to solve this dilemma, but to see what we can learn about the saint from the issues involved.

One way of making the unity of the virtues intelligible is to say that they are unified in the activity of practical reason. Following Martha Nussbaum's analysis in her "Non-Relative Virtue," one can say that the virtues actually differ only in terms of their sphere of action. *Phronēsis* operating in the sphere of acting in the face of danger or challenge becomes courage, while its function with regard to controlling the senses would produce the virtue of temperance. Furthermore, Nussbaum argues that the fact that Aristotle had no name for some of the virtues/vices and that he recognized differences in conceptions of courage demonstrate that he saw the virtues as general types with many possible culturally specific tokens. It seems, however, that with regard to expressing one's own self-worth, pride and humility may be competing types and not tokens of one general virtue. Therefore, while we may agree with Nussbaum that each of the virtues exemplifies the same areas of heart-mind and human action, this still does not solve the question of which virtues to favor or how to judge deficiencies or excesses properly.

As we start the analysis, let us first consider these facts: (1) Although he replaced pride with humility, Aquinas preserved the idea of the great person in the virtues of magnanimity and magnificence, which he thought were parts of courage; (2) Gandhi was called the Mahātma—great soul—the exact linguistic equivalent of *megalopsychia;* (3) the Buddha was called *mahāpuruṣa,* another Sanskrit word for "great soul"; and (4) the Chinese sages were so expansive in their virtue that they were said to take up, figuratively of course, the space between heaven and earth.

Let us look at each of the concepts of great soul in turn. For the Vedāntist the Mahātma would be the person who most truly reveals Ātman, the essence of the Godhead (Brahman) that is in us. This interpretation, however, does not really explain why such a title should be appropriate for someone such as Gandhi or any other person who performs great deeds for humankind. Ātman is an eternal, unchanging spiritual substance; it is not an individual agent (it does not act at all) and does not have any qualities. The Vedic meaning of *ātman* is "individuated life force" and it is essentially indistinguishable from the *jīva* self. The etymological roots of *ātman* are the same as the Greek *psychē* and the Hebrew *nephesh,* which is the "breath of life." (*Ruah,* the word for "divine spirit" in Hebrew, gives a more theistic view of human vitality.) On this view one could say that the great soul is the one who embodies and expresses this life force (Chinese *qi* or Sanskrit *śakti*) in an especially eminent way. The Chinese sages are admired for the same reason: they have preserved and channeled their *de* in such a way that it affects everyone around them. Therefore, as *ātman* has no agency or vitality, I propose that Hindus return to either Vedic views or the Buddhist *jīva* to explain the charisma of their saints.

In other work I have argued that the Buddha was a *mahāpuruṣa,* not because he was divine or even because he was morally perfect, but only in the sense that he had overcome all craving and found the mean in all actions and thoughts.[32] This means that his *jīva* (the Buddha never rejected this idea, just the *ātman*) was a harmonic attunement of the five *skandhas*. In the Pāli scriptures the most the Buddha had achieved was an Aristotelian *sōphrōn* or a sage of perfected *de* and *ren**. The *sōphrōn* is also the *eudaimon,* literally, the one with the good soul.

Gandhi at least affirmed his potential to become a Mahātma: "It is my full conviction that if only I had lived a life of unbroken *brahmacharya* all through, my energy and enthusiasm would have been a thousand fold greater...."[33] (Note how Gandhi confirms the concept of the charismatic saint, explaining it in the vitalistic terms of *śakti.*) Specific evidence indicates that he reached this state of perfection more often and more consistently than he would have ever admitted, although he once said that he was a better *bhramachāri* than any of his associates.[34] One of the assumptions for his sexual experiments with Manu was that it would take a perfect yogi to have the composure that he presumably maintained during all the nights he spent with her. (His goal was not only to reach perfection himself, but also to make Manu an ideal *brahmachāri* as well.)[35] The fact that many women at various points in time attested to his nonthreatening womanliness or sexlessness also demonstrates that he had reached the perfection of *de* that would, as both the *Yoga-Sūtra* and the *Daodejing* claim, pacify not only humans but even wild animals.

We have seen that Ames and Rosemont imply that *de* has normative content (as the "right" act as opposed to another) by comparing it to *dharma*. The Greek *aretē* and the Latin *virtus* are also value laden because of Aristotle's cosmic teleology. Aquinas explains his favorite philosopher: "A virtue implies the perfection of a power...Now, it is necessary that the end of which any power is capable is good, because every evil implies a certain defect. ... Hence, human virtue, which is an operative habit, is a good habit, and is productive of the good."[36] Aquinas's argumentation is usually impeccable, but this looks like a piece of circular reasoning if one does not grant the truth of Aristotle's teleology. The functional argument formulated in chapter 9 appears to be the best answer to the charge of circularity and the best argument for teleology and virtue ethics in general.

There also remains the empirical challenge of virtuoso performers on stage and off, who have not embodied or pursued anything we could call good. Using the Daoist immortals as the most dramatic examples of the power of *de,* Lu Dongbin, although virtuous in nearly all other respects, seduced the maiden He Xiengu (White Peony) and Cao Guojin was a drunken geomancer. Some of the Buddhist Siddhas appear even more sinful. In a fit of anger Kāṇḥapa killed a young girl with his yogic powers. He of course performed penance for this heinous deed and has nonetheless continued to hold his place among the eighty-four Buddhist saints of this type.[37]

We have now reached the conundrum, some say outright paradox, of the flawed saint. Jean Porter raises this issue within the Thomistic framework and struggles sympathetically with the case of Martin Luther King. Porter believes that there is a theoretical opening for understanding the sinful saint in Aquinas's distinction between acquired versus infused virtues. The latter are not carefully developed habits as the former are, so this means that it is entirely possible for a person in a state of infused charity to commit a vice. As Porter states, "[B]ad habits may continue and break through the infusion of grace from time to time."[38] (Luther's fully dialectical *simul iustus et peccator* is more radical, but they are both in the same place conceptually and theologically.) This concession also implies that Aquinas's commitment to the unity of the virtues is not as strong as we would think. Indeed, this unity appears to hold only for the cardinal virtues, and even more variable is his view that some virtues are not appropriate in certain circumstances or certain life stages.

King's sexual sins were very specific and limited, but habitual and regular. (For academics the examples of plagiarism might be taken as worse.)

Porter is right about the near perfection of his other virtues. His commitment to nonviolence was just as consistent as Gandhi's and his sense of justice and courage were equal to any other saint that we know. King and Gandhi were also convinced that a divine power had made these achievements possible. Interestingly enough, King's self-control was firm when it came to not seeking prestige and wealth, but it failed regularly with regard to sexual temptation. Ultimately, as Porter sadly concedes (hers is a very passionate and sympathetic analysis), King cannot be a Thomistic saint because of the doctrine that grace is removed by the mortal sin of sexual promiscuity. Porter refuses to give up on King's sainthood, but she cannot resolve the paradox short of rejecting a major church doctrine. There is another paradox, however, that Porter does not acknowledge: God's grace continues to be present to perfect King's virtues of compassion, justice, and courage, but the same grace cannot be present because of his sins. At one point Porter seems willing to reject church doctrine altogether because of her strong belief in King's saintliness.

Returning to Gandhi's experiments in *brahmacharya* and the use of young women as subjects, let us take a less charitable approach. Even though Manu was nineteen years old, she was described as a very immature and innocent girl. In most legal jurisdictions, King's extramarital affairs were not crimes and were done with consenting partners. Gandhi's experiences with Manu and other young women, however, could be called a form of child abuse. (Abduhl Ghaffar Khan defended Gandhi by describing Manu as innocent as a "six months' babe,"[39] but many today may not take that in the way Khan intended it.) One then could conclude that Gandhi's sexual sins were greater than King's. Manu never complained and presumably has not yet regretted these intimate acts of nonsexual intercourse. Nor has it come to anyone's attention, as far as I know, that she has suffered any psychological problems because of these activities. These facts mitigate the damaging implications of this less favorable interpretation, but they do not eliminate the worry altogether.

Particularly significant and problematic is that King admitted that what he had done was a great sin, while Gandhi insisted that he was performing a sacrifice *(yajña)* for his own and Manu's spiritual purification and for the "full practice of truth." In fact, in response to one critic, he said that "it is not an experiment but an integral part of my *yajña*. One may forgo an experiment, but one cannot forgo one's duty."[40] When he boasted to Thakkar Bapu in February of 1947 that he would sleep with thousands of women if duty required it, Gandhi defended himself a little too enthusiastically. Interestingly enough, at this point Manu offered to stop the practice and Gandhi agreed but only in light of her "inexperience" not, presumably, because of any failing on his part.

The sexual license that men of power have allowed themselves over the centuries has just as much to do with a deep need for control as it does with any sexual urge. This need to control and to dominate seemed to be much stronger in Gandhi than in King. Anecdotal evidence indicates that it is sometimes the impotent man who dominates and abuses both the men and women who are drawn to pornography and prostitution. (Here misogyny may also play a pervasive and devastating role.) Even stronger evidence appears in the power that eunuchs have wielded over the centuries as those essential middle managers of the royal inner quarters. Significantly enough, during the debate about Manu, Gandhi refers to himself, borrowing a New Testament idea, as a eunuch for the Kingdom of Heaven.

Dante's intuitions about the gradations of sin appear to be confirmed in humanity as a whole. The sexual sinners are at the higher levels of hell, while those who dominate and control are at the deepest levels. The prideful Satan, as one who would always rule and never serve, was encased in ice at the center of hell. Such relative judgments about sin appear to be the reason why Americans still condemn Richard Nixon more harshly than Bill Clinton. (Porter's insight that we would never think of having a King holiday if he had performed regular acts of cruelty further confirms our basic intuitions.) The foregoing observations do not in any way imply that Gandhi was corrupt, but abuses of power need not be venal or vicious to be culpable.

Aquinas's doctrine of mortal sin reflects a defective view of power as a zero-sum game. The issue of power is radically skewed if one being, namely God, has all of it and we have none of it. (The delegation of divine power, as far as I can ascertain, has never been given an intelligible explanation.[41]) It also creates incredible problems with regard to evil. If God is the only originative power in the cosmos, then all acts, good or evil, must stem from God. Second Isaiah and Luther were willing to embrace this conclusion outright: "I form light and I create darkness. I produce well-being and I create evil. I Yahweh do all these things."[42] Augustine does a brilliant job of developing the view that evil is privation but he dooms the free-will defense for the moral evil of Adam and Eve when he indirectly concedes that the first parents had deficient wills because they were made by God ex nihilo.[43] Even though one might argue that Adam and Eve were authors of their own acts (divine omnicausality makes this claim problematic), they obviously were not responsible for their defective wills.

We have seen that *śakti* power is not a zero-sum game and that all things share in it by virtue of their existence. (In contrast, if the Hindu gods have all the masculine *tejas,* the demons are then impotent.) The power of the *dao* can be seen in a very similar way. Indeed, one could say that the *dao* is nothing but all *de*-containing beings in the interdependent web of existence. A very different view of evil comes from such a cosmology. Evil is not privation, as the neo-Platonist saw it, nor is it a dark separate power opposed to good as Mani believed; rather, evil is imbalance and discord. *Yin* and *yang* are never evil in themselves or by nature; evil is the result of their disharmony. The soul of the sage, then, is much like the Platonic soul with its constituent parts in perfect harmony.

Even here, however, we still have the charge that the habitual womanizer or even a onetime murderer must have a seriously disordered soul, and therefore could not be counted among the saints or sages. The Chinese view at least does give us more perspective on the balance of good and evil in people's lives. Specifically, it would never embrace a view that a few evil acts completely undermine a person's moral value. The Buddhist analogy of a spoon of salt in a glass (an evil act in a sinful person) versus the ocean (same act in a saint), while problematic in its possible rationalization of great evils, nonetheless demonstrates the contextual pragmatism of Buddhist ethics.[44]

Gandhi's manipulation of those closest to him and his anger were his only major weaknesses, and King's sins were limited to extramarital sex and plagiarism. The balance of good in both lives was exceedingly great, just as it was in the stories of the Daoist immortals and the Buddhist Siddhas. Like King and Gandhi, they are also honored for their lifelong commitment to the poor and the oppressed. No person should be called out after only one strike or even three. Perhaps consequentialism wins in the end: we naturally weigh the good and the bad and, for the most part—confirming character consequentialism—we count the virtues far more than simple pleasures or even much pain. Gandhi was convinced that he would weather the Manu crisis with his reputation intact, and it looks as if he was correct in that assessment. Except for some conservative critics, King's reputation has held up equally well.

Charles Taylor's concept of the "strong evaluator" helps us refine the idea of the charismatic saint in at least one important way. The strong evaluator has a broad vision of cultural, political, moral, and spiritual possibilities. Taylor explains that this vision is "unavailable to one whose sympathies and horizons are so narrow that he can conceive of only one way of life."[45] Adding an insight from virtue theory, one could also say that strong evaluators also possess a very strong sense of self, which is embodied in virtues such as integrity and constancy that come from a unified narrative idea of their lives. (The personal histories of Gandhi and King will help to explain both their weaknesses and their strengths.) Gandhi's commitment to recognizing the good in every religion and every person, along with his strong empathy even for his enemies, make him a superb candidate for Taylor's ideal. (I also suggest that a contemporary appropriation of the Confucian *junzi* would also track well with the strong evaluator.) I contend that there is much conceptual overlap between the saint/sage and the strong evaluator that bears further reflection and analysis, but let us suffice with one specific judgment. It seems clear, even without Hitchen's critical work in the picture, that Mother Teresa, with her narrow and rigid view of the world, was not a strong evaluator. Finally, it is equally clear that the Buddha and Christ were both saints and strong evaluators according to Taylor's criteria.

Buddha, Christ, and Duress Virtue

It is truly ironic that the most famous gods who have lived on earth—Gautama, Kṛṣṇa, and Jesus—began their religious careers as human beings. In his sermons Gautama Buddha made it clear that he had come only to teach the Dharma and that his disciples were not to worship him as god or savior. Although a few commentators choose to read divine attributes into the earliest reference, the *Chāndogya Upaniṣad* describes Kṛṣṇa as a man, the son of Vasudeva and Devakī.[46] The Jesus of the Synoptic Gospels speaks of himself as a good Jew would, making a clear distinction between himself and God. Once he rebuked those who called him "good," for "no one is good but God alone."[47] An early and widespread Christology was "adoptionism," the view that Jesus was just a human being, approved and adopted by God at his baptism. It is doubly ironic that Kṛṣṇa and Gautama actually became higher than the Vedic gods: the Buddha is called "God beyond the gods" *(devatīdeva)* and Kṛṣṇa becomes the highest expression of divinity, surpassing even Brahman itself.

When the Pāli texts call the Buddha "great person" *(mahāpurisa)*, the authors mean at the very most that he was a perfect human only. In a detailed study of the *mahāpurisa*, Bellanwila Wimalaratana concludes that early Buddhists did not follow the prototype of the Vedic *puruṣa*, one from which a cosmic yogi and divine Kṛṣṇa emerges; rather, they followed another early tradition that used the perfect marks *(lakṣaṇa)* of the *mahāpurisa* for moral diagnostics only.[48] Beginning with the Sanskrit *Mahāvastu*, the Buddha attributes the term *mahāpuruṣa* to himself and elevates himself far above earlier views. In later Mahāyāna schools the Buddha is fully deified and in China the cosmic meaning of *mahāpuruṣa* is fully entrenched. The consequences for the humanity of the Buddha are catastrophic. For Asaṅga and Vasubandhu, for example, the true Buddha-mind has none of the qualities that we do: no desires, no intentions, no dreams, no anticipation, no memory. For them the Buddha only appeared to inhabit a body, take nourishment from food, get tired, and sleep.

The Jain saints, as well as the yogis of Sāṃkhya-Yoga, were equally separate from the world and alienated from their humanity. The liberated ones reside at the top of the universe independent from any body and cut off from all other saints. (These two major pluralistic schools are far different from Vedāntist monism.) While in the world, they only appeared to be like ordinary humans. This meant that the Jain savior Mahāvīra possessed "such a body and such an organ of speech that he will be able to impart the knowledge of truth without engaging in a volitional act."[49] According to some accounts, Mahāvīra did not preach with ordinary words, but simply emitted mysterious sounds, which were intelligible only to his closest disciples. Mahāvīra's omniscience consisted in simultaneous knowledge of all six substances in all of their modes and in all three aspects of time. Equally troublesome is the impassibility of the Indian saints and Christ. Drawing on a Greek attribute for divine perfection, the doctrine of divine immutability made the Passion of Christ and its redemptive powers unintelligible. When the early Church condemned the patripassians (literally "father suffering") as heretics and limited the suffering of Christ to his human nature, the logic of Christian redemption was shattered. The sacrifice of God the father is now an illusion and a sham.

These models of sainthood are surely not suitable for a Gandhian theory of nonviolent, political activism. They give us an *ahiṃsā* that is perfect, but it requires no effort, has no content, and does not bring any love or justice to the world. It is far preferable to have a flawed human saint/sage than an inaccessible spiritual Titan. Most of us appear willing to jettison moral perfection and the unity of the virtues for saints of flesh, blood, and even moral flaws. We prefer that our saints have vitality *(de)*, even though this life force is sometimes channeled in the wrong direction. Wolf phrases it nicely: "A person may be perfectly wonderful [filled with *de*] without being perfectly moral."[50]

As we close the chapter and the book, we shall choose two events from the lives of Christ and Buddha—their temptations and their deaths—and determine the role of duress virtue in these incidents. ("Duress" virtue is an alternative way of describing the *enkratēs,* the one who is tempted but has sufficient will to resist evil.) The stories of their respective temptations are overlaid with legend. In his excellent biography of the Buddha, one that emphasizes his humanity, Daisaku Ikeda is most likely correct that the account of the temptation is an allegory about the Buddha's own inner turmoil.[51] (One could of course read the Temptation of Christ in the same way.) Against Mara and his demonic forces the Buddha waged a great struggle, which required considerable aid from the earth goddess and the serpent gods. (The serpents actually aided him while the earth goddess may have just stood as a witness to his right to claim to be the Buddha.) In stark contrast Christ remained unflappable throughout Satan's wagers in the desert. (His humanity is apparent only in the fact that he became hungry.) Satan appeared easily defeated by rebuke rather than spiritual or physical force. In their temptations Christ had natural virtue while the Buddha may be said to have possessed duress virtue. In Aristotle's terms Christ was a *sōphrōn* and the Buddha was an *enkratēs*.

In facing death, however, the experiences are reversed: the Buddha as a *sōphrōn* was calm, trying his best to comfort his emotional disciples, but Jesus cried out in despair that God had forsaken him. (To explain the difference, one might say that Jesus suffered a far more gruesome death than the Buddha did.) Jesus also appeared weak in the Garden of Gethsemane, where one might conclude that God's will took over Jesus' will so that the redemption of Christ could be fulfilled. (Was Jesus even at a lower level, an *akratēs* having no will to proceed?) Therefore, we have found natural virtue in the Buddha's death but duress virtue in Jesus' end. The fact that we have found weaknesses in stories that have strong mythological content is telling and significant. Even with the strongest attempts to deify and reify these savior figures, their basic humanity shines through. If they were true deities, they would have never faltered, and our exercise has simply proved that virtues are for humans, not for gods.

Let us now refer to both the literary and scholarly imagination to test our intuitions concerning alternative lives of Christ. One of the most famous versions is Kazantzakis's *Last Temptation of Christ,* which presents us with a Jesus who had sexual desire for Mary Magdalene. Morton Smith's hypothesis about Jesus initiating the naked young man in Mark 14 has been hotly disputed, but at least Smith offered a scholarly argument from manuscript evidence.[52] If either or both of these events were true, the Church would certainly suffer a credibility crisis. My sense, however, is that, based on the consensus that sexual infractions are lesser sins, the confirmation of Hugh Schonfield's "passover plot" or a similar view based on the Shroud of Turin that question the basis for the Resurrection[53] would shake Christian foundations much more seriously.

The Buddha and Christ are clearly our foremost ancient practitioners of nonviolence. Christ's message that we are to love even those who hate us is essentially the message of the Buddha. Both knew very well that hate figuratively burns a hole in the heart. Equally remarkable, particularly because we know their personal histories and weaknesses so well, are the lives of Gandhi and King. Taking the ancient saints of nonviolence or the more human twentieth-century sages of *ahiṃsā* as our models, let us all try to develop the virtue of nonviolence until it becomes as natural as taking a breath.

Notes

Introduction

1. Gandhi, *Non-Violence in Peace and War,* vol. 1 (Ahmedabad: Navajivan, 1942), p. 48; originally in *Young India* 7 (October 8, 1925): 346.

2. Mark Juergensmeyer, "Shoring Up the Saint: Some Suggestions for Improving Satyāgarha," in *Gandhi's Significance For Today,* ed. John Hick and L. C. Hempel (New York: St. Martin's Press, 1989), p. 45.

3. Ibid., p. 46.

4. Jay L. Garfield, *Empty Words: Buddhist Philosophy and Cross-Cultural Interpretation* (New York: Oxford University Press, 2002), p. 220.

5. Ibid.

6. Raghavan Iyer, "Civilization and Religion," in *Gandhi's Significance for Today,* p. 132.

7. Luis O. Gomez, "Nonviolence and the Self in Early Buddhism," in *Inner Peace, World Peace,* ed. Kenneth Kraft (Albany, N.Y.: State University of New York Press, 1992), p. 46. In contrast to Gomez I will give a more robust view of the Buddhist self as a real, albeit changing, moral agent in the world.

8. Excerpted in *The Words of Wisdom of Mahatma Gandhi,* ed. Shall Sinha (Edmonton, Alberta: SKS Publishers, 2002), p. 283.

9. N. F. Gier, *Spiritual Titanism: Indian, Chinese, and Western Perspectives* (Albany, N.Y.: State University of New York Press, 2000), chapters 2, 9–11.

10. Michael Slote, *From Morality to Virtue* (New York: Oxford University Press, 1992), p. 10.

11. Wendy Doniger O'Flaherty, *Asceticism and Eroticism in the Mythology of Śiva* (Oxford: Oxford University Press, 1973), p. 82.

12. See Nair Pyarelal, *Mahatma Gandhi: The Last Phase,* vol. 1 (Ahmedabad: Navajivan, 1958), p. 579; 2nd ed. (1966) vol. 1, bk. 2, p. 219.

13. Shree Chand Rampuria, *The Cult of Ahiṃsā: A Jain View-Point* (Calcutta: Sri Jain Setamber Terapanthi Mahasabha, 1947); Atulya Ghosh, *Ahimsa and Gandhi* (Calcutta: Congress Bhawan, 1954); George Kotturan, *Ahiṃsā: Gautama to Gandhi* (New Delhi: Sterling Publishers, 1973); Koshelya Walli, *The Conception of Ahiṃsā in Indian Thought According to the Sanskrit Sources* (Varanasi: Bharata Manisha, 1974); Unto Tähtinen, *Ahiṃsā: Non-Violence in Indian Tradition* (London: Rider and Company, 1976); Indu Mala Ghosh, *Ahiṃsā: Buddhist and Gandhian* (Delhi: Indian Bibliographies Bureau, 1988). There is also a special issue of *Journal of Dharma* 16, no. 3 (July–September, 1991) devoted to *ahiṃsā* and ecology. Nathaniel Altman's *Ahimsa: Dynamic Compassion* (Wheaton: Theosophical Publishing House, 1980) is just an anthology of materials relating to nonviolence.

14. Tähtinen, *Ahiṃsā: Non-Violence in Indian Tradition,* p. 44. He argues that the inconsistencies among the three views can be overcome by moving from ontology to axiology, where Vedāntist totality is seen as "an ideal to be observed in action, not as a fact of reality" (p. 44) Tähtinen himself realizes that this is not the view of Vedānta, at least in its nondualist versions.

15. Gandhi, *Young India* 12 (February 13, 1930): 56; *Young India* 8 (July 8, 1926): 244.

16. Raghavan Iyer, *The Moral and Political Thought of Mahatma Gandhi* (New York: Oxford University Press, 1973), pp. 131–32. There is no equivalent to Socratic *daimon* in Buddhism either, at least in the Pāli scriptures. See I. B. Horner, *The Early Buddhist Theory of Man Perfected: A Study of the Arahant* (London: Williams & Norgate, 1936), p. 146.

17. Gandhi, *Young India* 12 (February 13, 1930): 56. "My claim to hear the Voice of God is no new claim. Unfortunately, there is no way that I know of proving the claim except through results" (*Harijan* 1 [May 6, 1933]: 4).

18. Gandhi, *Harijan* 1 (July 8, 1933): 4. "Before one is able to listen to that Voice, one has to go through a long and fairly severe course of training, and when it is the Inner Voice that speaks, it is unmistakable" (*Harijan* 1 [March 18, 1933]: 8). When Gandhi describes the Voice as coming upon him and causing "a terrific struggle" in him, this is more in line with a new view of Socrates' *daimon* as the voice of God. This interpretation challenges the view that Socrates saw his inner voice as the dictates of autonomous moral reason. (See Giovanni Reale, *A History of Ancient Philosophy: From the Origins to Socrates,* ed. and trans. John R. Catan, vol. 1 [Albany, N.Y.: State University of New York Press, 1987], pp. 232–35.) Gandhi's theism is especially strong in one article in which he says that although some may call conscience the "dictates of reason," it is really God's direct command (*Bombay Chronicle,* November 18, 1933, reprinted in *Truth is God,* p. 29).

19. Iyer, "Civilization and Religion," p. 123.

20. Pyarelal, *The Last Phase,* vol. 1, p. 581; 2nd ed., vol. 1, bk. 2, p. 221. Kripalani's repetition of the Kantian principle that one should never use a person as means to an end reveals a deep discomfort about Gandhi's actions. Therefore, his assertion "you have never exploited her" simply does not ring true.

21. Gandhi, *Harijan* 6 (January 28, 1939): 445.

Chapter 1. Gandhi as a Postmodern Thinker

1. Sarvepalli Gopal, *Radhakrishnan: A Biography* (Delhi: Oxford University Press, 1989), pp. 27–28. George Orwell concurs: "[H]is medievalist program was obviously not viable in a backward, starving, overpopulated country" (*Shooting an Elephant and Other Essays* [1949], excerpted as "Reflections on Gandhi" in *Vice and Virtue in Everyday Life,* ed. Christina Sommers and Fred Sommers (San Diego: Harcourt Brace Jovanovich, 1989), p. 477.

2. Drawing on process and pragmatic traditions, David L. Hall and Roger T. Ames give Confucius a constructive postmodern interpretation in their *Thinking Through Confucius* (Albany, N.Y.: State University of New York Press, 1987), pp. 1–25. For a constructive postmodern Buddha see David J. Kalupahana, *A History of Buddhist*

Philosophy (Honolulu: University of Hawaii Press, 1992). For Zhuangzi's postmodernism and more on the Buddha see my *Spiritual Titanism*, chapter 11 and pp. 54–57. This chapter is adapted from the first section of the second chapter of *Spiritual Titanism*.

3. For example, Som Raj Gupta proposes that "when, following Śaṅkara, a student analyzes the Upaniṣadic statements about reality he finds that they cancel each other, that whatever they proclaim about reality they subsequently disclaim, that Upaniṣadic statements too are, in the final analysis, false fabrications..." (*The Word Speaks to Faustian Man* [New Delhi: Motilal Banarsidass, 1991], pp. x–xi). Gupta seems to be suggesting that Śaṅkara holds something like the Buddhist dialectical identification of Saṃsara and Nirvāṇa, a doctrine that Nāgārjuna formulates in terms that do anticipate postmodern thought. Because Buddhism is more clearly antisubstance and antiessentialist, a postmodern interpretation of Buddhism has a much better chance of succeeding. See David J. Kalupahana, *Nāgārjuna: Philosophy of the Middle Way* (Albany, N.Y.: State University of New York Press, 1986); and Ian W. Mabbett, "Nāgārjuna and Deconstruction," *Philosophy East & West* 45, no. 2 (April, 1995): 203–226. Kalupahana's interpretation is constructive postmodernism while Mabbett's reading is à la Derrida.

4. Gandhi, *Hind Swaraj and Other Writings*, ed. Anthony J. Parel (New Delhi: Foundation Books, 1997), chap. 13, p. 71.

5. Gandhi, *The Collected Works of Mahātma Gandhi* (New Delhi: Government of India Publications, 1959), vol. 13, p. 524; vol. 14, p. 513. Of the untouchables Gandhi said, "They are more cultured than we, their lives are more righteous than ours" (*Young India* 3 [May 4, 1921]: 143).

6. Gandhi, *Harijan* 5 (March 6, 1937): 27.

7. Gandhi, *Collected Works*, vol. 12, p. 375.

8. Ibid., vol. 12, p. 165. "We are born in sin, and we are enslaved in the body, because of our sinful deeds" (*Collected Works*, vol. 12, p. 375; a letter of March 7, 1914).

9. Gandhi, *Young India* 8 (January 21, 1926): 121.

10. "The enemy is first of all oneself..." (*Selections from Gandhi*, p. 159); *Young India* 3 (November 17, 1921): 367.

11. See Gandhi, *Harijan* 5 (May 8, 1937): 104.

12. Pyarelal, *The Last Phase*, vol. 1, p. 593; 2nd ed., vol. 1, bk. 2, pp. 231–32.

13. Bhikhu Parekh, *Gandhi's Political Philosophy* (London: Macmillan, 1989), p. 52.

14. Quoted in Jayantanuja Bandyopadhyaya, *Social and Political Thought of Mahātma Gandhi* (Bombay: Allied Publishers, 1969), p. 72.

15. Gandhi, *Harijan* 9 (February 1, 1942): 27, excerpted in *Democracy: Real and Deceptive* (Ahmedabad: Navajivan, 1961), p. 31.

16. N. K. Bose, "Interview with Gandhi," cited in Joan V. Bondurant, *The Conquest of Violence* (Princeton: Princeton University Press, 1988), p. 175.

17. Recently A. L. Herman has made such an attempt in his "Karma, Saviors, and Communities," a paper presented at the Eight International Vedānta Congress, Miami University, October, 1996.

18. Gandhi, *Harijan* 10 (Feburary 10, 1946), cited in Madhuri S. Sondhi, *Modernity, Morality, and the Mahātma* (New Delhi: Haranand Publications, 1997), p. 104.

19. I am indebted to Avidam Chakravarty of the philosophy department at the University of New Delhi for this insight.

20. Gandhi, *Indian Opinion* (August 16, 1913); *Collected Works,* vol. 11, p. 166.

21. Gandhi, *Harijan* 7 (August 19, 1939): 237, excerpted in *Truth is God,* p. 43. See also *Harijan* 12 (February 15, 1948): 34.

22. Gandhi, *Harijan* 11 (March 16, 1947): 63; see also *Hind Swaraj,* ed. Parel, chap. 10, p. 52.

23. Ronald J. Terchek, "Gandhi and Moral Autonomy," *Gandhi Marg* 13, no. 4 (Jan.–Mar., 1992): 45.

24. See Terchek, *Gandhi: Struggling for Autonomy* (Totowa, N.J.: Rowman & Littlefield, 1998), p. 14. It is clear from Tercheck's remarks that he, like so many other thinkers, can conceive of only one type of postmodernism, namely, French deconstruction.

25. Gandhi, *Collected Works*, vol. 68, p. 265.

26. Huiyyun Wang, "Gandhi's Contesting Discourse," *Gandhi Marg* 17, no. 3 (October–December, 1995), p. 262. I am indebted to Wang for the initial inspiration to think about Gandhian postmodernism, but Gandhi's constructive postmodernism is much more sophisticated than the New Age movement that Wang compares him to.

27. Anthony J. Parel, "Gandhi's Idea of Nation in *Hind Swaraj,*" *Gandhi Marg* 13, no. 3 (Oct.–Dec., 1991): 261–281. Parel observes that the Hindi translation of *Hind Swaraj* renders *praja* as *rashtra* and therefore obscures an important difference that Gandhi wished to maintain.

28. Gandhi, *Collected Works,* vol. 16, p. 187. "We were one nation before they [the British] came to India" (*Hind Swaraj*, ed. Parel, chap. 9, p. 48). Here Gandhi goes on to explain national unity in terms of shared sacred places.

29. Parel, "Gandhi's Idea of Nation," p. 287.

30. Parekh, *Gandhi's Political Philosophy,* pp. 115–16.

31. Eleanor MacDonald, "Derrida and the Politics of Interpretation," in *The Socialist Register 1990: The Retreat of the Intellectuals,* ed. R. Miliband and L. Panitch (London: Merlin Press, 1990), p. 230. MacDonald surmises that Derrida would hold that "individuals are unable to represent their own interests, even to themselves" (p. 230).

32. Bondurant, *The Conquest of Violence*, pp. 177–78.

33. Gandhi, *Collected Works*, vol. 58, p. 219.

34. Gandhi, *Hindu Dharma* (New Delhi: Vision Books, 1987), p. 8. Gandhi was very impressed with Tolstoy's dictum that one must "obey reason in the pursuit of the good" (Bondurant, *The Conquest of Violence,* p. 179); see her earlier discussion of reason in Gandhi.

35. Gandhi, *An Autobiography,* introduction.

36. Richard B. Gregg, "Gandhi as a Social Scientist" in *M. Gandhi,* ed. S. Radha Krishnan (London, 1939), p. 80. Gandhi thanked the American people for giving him such a great teacher in Henry David Thoreau, "who furnished me, through his essay *On the Duty of Civil Disobedience* scientific confirmation of what I was doing in South Africa" (D. G. Tendulkar, *The Life of Mahatma Gandhi* [Delhi: Government Publications Office, 1960], vol. 6, p. 177).

37. See David Ray Griffin, ed., *The Reenchantment of Science: Postmodern Proposals* (Albany, N.Y.: State University of New York Press, 1988).

38. Ramashray Roy, "The Modern Predicament and Gandhi," in *Contemporary Crisis and Gandhi,* ed. R. Roy (Delhi: Discovery Publishing House, 1986), p. 57.

39. Ibid.

40. Parekh, *Gandhi's Political Philosophy,* p. 26.

41. Vivek Pinto, *Gandhi's Vision and Values* (New Delhi: Sage Publications, 1998), p. 20; Sondhi, *Modernity, Morality, and the Mahātma*, p. 74

42. Thomas Pantham, "Gandhi, Nehru, and Modernity," in *Crisis and Change in Contemporary India,* ed. U. Baxi and B. Parekh (New Delhi: Sage Publications, 1995), p. 109.

43. Maduri Wadhwa, *Gandhi Between Tradition and Modernity* (New Delhi: Deep & Deep, 1991), pp. 2, 12fn; Sanford Krolick and Betty Cannon, eds. *Gandhi in the "Postmodern" Age: Issues in War and Peace* (Golden, Col. Colorado School of Mines Press, 1984). The authors of the latter volume are even more misinformed about the meaning of "postmodern."

44. Heinrich Zimmer, *Philosophies of India,* ed. Joseph Campbell (Cleveland, Ohio: World Publishing Co., 1956), p. 400fn.

45. Karl H. Potter, *Presuppositions of India's Philosophies* (Westport, Conn.: Greenwood Press, 1963), p. 3.

46. Ibid., p. 95. This means that, contrary to Parekh's thesis that anthropocentrism characterizes only Euro-American thought, this central problem is present in Indian philosophy as well.

47. Gandhi, *Young India* 2 (December 5, 1920); *Selections from Gandhi,* p. 159.

48. Susanne H. Rudolph and Lloyd I. Rudolph, *Gandhi: The Traditional Roots of Charisma* (Hyderabad: Orient Longman, 1987), p. viii. See also Lloyd L. Rudolph, "Contesting Civilizations," *Gandhi Marg* 13, no. 4 (January–March, 1992): 419–431.

49. Douglas Allen, "Gandhi's Philosophy: The Struggle over Many Contradictory Philosophies," *Social Theory and Practice* 19, no. 3 (fall, 1993), pp. 306, 307.

50. Richard G. Fox, *Gandhian Utopia: Experiments with Culture* (Boston: Beacon Press, 1989), p. 73.

51. Ibid., pp. 13, 15.

52. Gandhi, *Harijan* 9 (June 7, 1942), p. 177. Gandhi appears to be speaking metaphysically here, that is, about the human nature of the British. The context is whether or not the British "can ever do justice voluntarily." Of course there are other passages where Gandhi speaks of both God and the self as having immutable natures, so there is no way I can make a case for a consistent idea of a Buddhist "no-self." Incidentally, Gandhi seems to have changed his mind about a mutable British nature. Nearly forty years earlier he said that "when the tiger changes his nature, the Englishmen will change theirs" (*Hind Swaraj*, ed. Parel, p. 27).

53. Gandhi, *Selected Works,* vol. 4, p. 247.

54. See chapter 2 of *Spiritual Titanism.*

55. See K. R. Rao, *Gandhi and Pragmatism* (Calcutta: Oxford and IBH Publishing Co., 1968).

56. Immanuel Kant, *Fundamental Principles of the Metaphysics of Morals,* trans. T. K. Abbott (London: Longmans, Green, 1898) p. 25.

57. See my "*Ahiṃsā,* the Self, and Postmodernism," *International Philosophical Quarterly* 35, no. 1 (March 1995): 72–75; "On the Deification of Confucius," *Asian Philosophy* 1, no. 3 (1993): 51–52; and with Johnson Petta, "Hebrew and Buddhist

Skandhas," presented at the Pacific Northwest Division of the American Academy of Religion, May 2002.

58. Quoted in Bondurant, *The Conquest of Violence*, p. 175.

59. A. T. Nuyen has joined other scholars in rejecting the charge that French post-struturalism implies complete relativism and skepticism. Therefore, he contends that David Griffin is wrong to distinguish between constructive or revisionary postmodernism, on the one hand, and deconstructive or eliminative postmodernism on the other. Specifically, he claims that Mark C. Taylor, an American theologian and disciple of Derrida, is not an eliminative postmodernist, because for him meaning is still found in a "productive and primordial causality" ("Postmodern Theology and Postmodern Philosophy," *International Journal for the Philosophy of Religion* 30, no. 1 [January, 1991]: 70). Much more needs to be said in response to Nuyen's significant article, but it appears that he has eliminated the difference between Griffin and Taylor by making Taylor into a constructive postmodernist. In my mind this is not possible.

60. Suzi Gablick, "The Reenchantment of Art: Reflections on the Two Postmodernisms," in *Sacred Interconnections: Postmodern Spirituality, Political Economy, and Art*, ed. David R. Griffin (Albany, N.Y.: State University of New York Press, 1990), pp. 179–80.

61. Wang, "Gandhi's Contesting Discourse," p. 271.

62. Gandhi, *Harijan* 10 (July 28, 1946): 236.

63. As paraphrased by Maganbhai P. Desai, "Ends and Means in Politics," in *Facets of Mahātma Gandhi: Ethics, Religion, and Culture*, eds. S. Mukherjee and S. Ramaswamy (New Delhi: Deep & Deep, 1996), vol. 4, p. 27; originally appeared in *Gandhi Marg* 1, no. 2 (April, 1957): 153–57.

64. See David Ray Griffin's series introduction in any of the State University of New York Press titles in the Series in Constructive Postmodern Thought.

65. Gandhi, *The Hindu* (September 12, 1927), in *Collected Works*, vol. 34, p. 505. The preceding sentence, "there is no distinction whatever between individual growth and corporate growth," might imply absolute monism, but the context makes it clear what Gandhi's meaning is. The emphasis is clearly on the individual when he repeats the old adage that no chain is stronger than any one of its links.

66. Gandhi, *Hind Swaraj*, ed. Parel, chap. 13, p. 67.

67. Ibid., p. 67, note 124.

68. Gandhi, *Collected Works*, vol.10, p. 70.

69. Philippa Foot, *The Virtues and the Vices and Other Essays in Moral Philosophy* (Berkeley: University of California Press, 1987), pp. 5–7.

70. William Galston, *Liberal Purposes: Goods, Virtues, and Diversity in the Liberal State* (Cambridge: Cambridge University Press, 1991), *passim*, p. 230 for a revised view of the self; Galston, "Liberal Virtues and the Formation of Civic Character," in *The Seedbeds of Virtue: Sources of Competence, Character, and Citizenship in American Society*, eds. M. A. Glendon and D. Blankenhorn (Lanham, Md.: Madison Books, 1995), pp. 35–60. See also David L. Norton, *Democracy and Moral Development: A Politics of Virtue* (Berkeley: University of California Press, 1991); and Stephen Macedo, *Liberal Virtues* (Oxford: Oxford University Press, 1990), *passim*, pp. 220–221 for "situated autonomy."

Chapter 2. Nonviolence in Jainism and Hinduism

1. Prem Suman Jain, "The Ethics of Jainism," in *World Religions and Global Ethics*, ed. S. Cromwell Crawford (New York: Paragon House, 1989), p. 55.

2. Quoted in Kotturan, *Ahiṃsā: Gautama to Gandhi*, p. 13. "No matter whether he is Śvetambara, or Digambara, a Buddhist or follower of any other creed, one who looks on all creatures as his own self, attains salvation" (quoted in ibid., p. 12).

3. Bhargava, "Some Chief Characteristics of the Jain Concept of Nonviolence," p. 124.

4. Ibid., p. 122. Jyoti Prasad Jain takes a more Buddhist approach when he states that "piety is rooted in active compassion" (*The Essence of Jainism* [Varanasi: Shuchita Publications, n. d.], p. 16).

5. Gandhi, *Navajivan* (March 31, 1929), trans. in *Collected Works*, vol. 40, pp. 191–92.

6. See Stephen N. Hay, "Jain Influences on Gandhi's Early Thought," in *Gandhi, India, and the World*, ed. S. Ray (Bombay: Nachiketa Publishers, 1970), pp. 14–23; and "Jain Goals and Disciplines in Gandhi's Pursuit of Swaraj," in *Rule, Protest, and Identity*, ed. Peter Robb and David Taylor (London: Curzon Press, 1978), pp. 120–132.

7. Gandhi, *Young India* 10 (October 25, 1928): 356.

8. George Kotturan, *Ahiṃsā: Gautama to Gandhi*, p. 54.

9. Gandhi, *Young India* 7 (October 8, 1925): 345.

10. See Tähtinen, *Ahiṃsā: Non-Violoence in Indian Tradition*, p. 24.

11. Gandhi, *Young India* 8 (January 21, 1926): 30.

12. The Dalai Lama, *The Dalai Lama at Harvard: Lectures on the Buddhist Path to Peace* (Ithaca, N.Y.: Snow Lion Publications, 1988), p. 185.

13. Nathmal Tatia's commentary on the *Tattvārtha Sūtra*, p. 281. Tatia acknowledges that the saint's omniscience is a major exception to *anekāntavāda* (p. xvii).

14. See P. S. Jaini, *The Jaina Path of Purification*, p. 142.

15. Ibid., p. 96.

16. Christopher Key Chapple, *Nonviolence to Animals, Earth, and Self in Asian Traditions* (Albany, N.Y.: State University of New York Press, 1993), chap. 5.

17. D. K. Bedekar, *Towards Understanding Gandhi*, ed. R. Gawande (Bombay: Popular Prakashan, 1975), p. 80. In a very insightful analysis, Bedekar suggests that Gandhi discovered that the "spell" of Vedānta had compromised his commitment to individual agency and engagement (p. 115). According to Stephen Hay, Raichand uses the term *ātman* only to start a dialogue with the Hindu Gandhi, not to adopt it as his own ("Jain Influences on Gandhi's Early Thought," p. 19). In terms of Hay's thesis of Jain influence it is significant that Gandhi did not adopt Jain terminology.

18. Gandhi, letter to Bhai Prithvi Singh, October 2, 1941, in *The Moral and Political Writings of Mahatma Gandhi*, ed. Raghavan Iyer, vol. 2, (Oxford University Press, 1986), p. 251. Elsewhere he states that "*ahiṃsā* is the attribute of the soul" (*Harijan* 8 [March 2, 1940]: 19).

19. "Nevertheless, *ahiṃsā* is the means, Truth is the end" (*From Yeravda Mandir*, trans. V. G. Desai [Ahmedabad: Navajivan, 1945], p. 8). In his autobiography, Gandhi says that the "only means for the realization of Truth is *ahiṃsā*...." (*An Autobiography*, p. 419; cf. p. 230).

20. Gandhi, *Harijan* 8 (September 1, 1940): 266. He also says that *anasakti* "transcends *ahiṃsā*." Elsewhere he states, "We find that the fulfilment of *ahiṃsā* is impossible without utter selflessness. *Ahiṃsā* means Universal Love" (*From Yeravda Mandir*, p. 10).

21. Gandhi, *From Yeravda Mandir,* p. 8.

22. Tähtinen, "Values, Non-Violence and Ecology: Two Approaches," *Journal of Dharma* 16, no. 3 (July–September, 1991): 216.

23. Smith, "Eaters, Food, and Hierarchy," *Journal of the American Academy of Religion* 48, no. 2 (summer 1990): 196fn.

24. Klaus K. Klostermaier, "Bhakti, *Ahiṃsā*, and Ecology," *Journal of Dharma* 16, no. 3 (July–September 1991): 249.

25. *The Laws of Manu*, trans. Wendy Doniger O'Flaherty (New Delhi: Penguin Books, 1991), 5.44, 45, 51.

26. *Chāndogya Upaniṣad,* trans. R. C. Zaehner, in *Hindu Scriptures* (London: Dent & Sons, 1966), 3.17.4; 8.15.1. According to Uno Tähtinen the earliest Hindu reference to *ahiṃsā* is the pre-Upaniṣadic *Kapisthalla-Katha-Samhita* (*Ahiṃsā in Indian Tradition,* p. 2).

27. See Tähtinen, *Ahiṃsā: Non-Violence in Indian Tradition*, p. 77.

28. See *Mahābhārata, Ādi Parva* 11.12.12 and *Anuśasāna Parva* 115.25; *Kūrma-Purāṇa* 2.29.31; and *Vārāha-Purāṇa* 117.38.

29. *Katha Upaniṣad* 2.20–23 and *Mundaka Upaniṣad* 3.2.3.

30. *Śvetāśvatāra Upaniṣad* 3.8, 9.

31. *Bhagavad-gītā* 15.15, 18 (Zaehner trans.).

32. Ibid., 11.13; 10.2; 11.52.

33. Ibid., 14.3, 27.

34. *The Bhagavad-gītā,* commentary and trans. R. C. Zaehner (New York: Oxford University Press, 1973), p. 368.

35. See Robert S. Minor, *An Exegetical Commentary of the "Bhagavad-gītā"* (New Delhi: Heritage Publishers, 1982), p. 429.

36. Gandhi, *The Bhagavad-gītā* (New Delhi: Orient Paperbacks, 1980), p. 13; Gandhi, *Gītā the Mother*, pp. 172, 155, 160.

37. Ibid., pp. 12–13.

38. Ibid., p. 14.

39. Gandhi, *Hindu Dharma* (Ahmedabad: Navajivan, 1960), p. 162.

40. *The Bhagavad-gītā* 3.25 (Zaehner trans.).

Chapter 3. Vedānta, *Ātman,* and Gandhi

1. "God, ourselves and all objects in the universe are in essence one reality. Even God vanishes and we have only *neti, neti*" (*Collected Works,* vol. 32, p. 218). By also affirming *dvaita* (that is dualism), Gandhi is being more than equivocal. See his speech at Tanjore on September 16, 1927, in *Collected Works,* vol. 35, p. 1. Also feeling "one with God" is "the principle of *advaita*" is not its technical meaning in Śaṅkara. See speech on March 9, 1929, in *Young India* 11 (April 4, 1929), excerpted in Iyer, *The Moral and Political Writings*, vol. 1, p. 59). Gandhi's statement that "the sum total of this life is God" (*Harijan* 12 [February 15, 1948]: 33) is definitely not the Advaitin position.

2. Gandhi, Speech at Tanjore on September 16, 1927, in *Collected Works*, vol. 35, p. 1.

3. Gandhi, *Young India* 6 (September 25, 1924), p. 313; cf. his comments on the unity of life in *Young India* 4 (February 16, 1922): 104. S. K. Saxena's insightful discussion of Gandhi's self-suffering also assumes the Advaitin position (*Ever Unto God: Essays on Gandhi and Religion* [New Delhi: Indian Council of Philosophical Research, 1988], chap. 5).

4. Gandhi, *Harijan* 12 (February 15, 1948): 33.

5. Gandhi, letter to Jamnalal Bajaj, March 16, 1922 in Iyer, *Moral and Political Writings*, vol. 2, p. 194.

6. Verma, *The Metaphysical Foundations of Gandhi's Thought*, p. 80.

7. Parekh, *Gandhi's Political Philosophy*, p. 94.

8. Ramashray Roy, *Self and Society: A Study in Gandhian Thought* (New Delhi: Sage Publications, 1985), p. 95.

9. Ibid., p. 108.

10. Roy, *Gandhi: Soundings in Political Philosophy* (Delhi: Chanakya Publications, 1984), p. 14.

11. Gandhi, *The Hindu* (September 12, 1927), in *Collected Works*, vol. 34, p. 505. The preceding sentence "there is no distinction whatever between individual growth and corporate growth" might imply absolute monism, but the sentence cited makes it clear what Gandhi's meaning is.

12. Roy, *Gandhi: Soundings in Political Philosophy*, p. 14.

13. John D. White, "God and the World from the Viewpoint of Advaita Vedānta: A Critical Assessment," *International Philosophical Quarterly* 30, no. 2 (June 1981): 185–193.

14. See Rex Ambler, "Gandhi's Concept of Truth," in *Gandhi's Significance for Today*, p. 93.

15. Lance E. Nelson, "Reverence for Nature or the Irrelevance of Nature? Advaita Vedānta and Ecological Concern," *Journal of Dharma* 16, no. 3 (July–Sept. 1991): 299.

16. Glyn Richard, "Gandhi's Concept of Truth and the *Advaita* Tradition," *Religious Studies* 22, no. 1 (March 1986): 1–14.

17. Chatterjee, *Gandhi's Religious Thought*, pp. 134, 104. There are of course passages that do imply the *māyā* doctrine, where, for example, he agrees with the statement "Brahma alone is real; all else is nonexistent" (*Collected Works*, vol. 14, p. 97; from a letter dated November 22, 1917).

18. *Discourses on the Gītā*, trans. V. G. Desai (Ahmedabad: Navajivan, 1960), pp. 22, 34. See A. L. Herman, *Introduction to Indian Thought* (Englewood Cliffs, N.J.: Prentice-Hall, 1976), pp. 63, 107, 108–109, 137, 138, 145, 164, 191–192, 207–209, 220, 256, 278.

19. See Lance E. Nelson, "Living Liberation in Shankara and Advaita Vedānta," in *Living Liberation in Hindu Thought*, ed. Andrew O. Fort and Patricia Y. Mumme (Albany, N.Y.: State University of New York Press, 1996), pp. 17–62.

20. Bedekar, *Towards Understanding Gandhi*, p. 115.

21. Ibid., p. 117; Gandhi, *An Autobiography, introduction*. p. xi.

22. Roy, *Self and Society*, p. 74.

23. Gandhi, *Collected Works*, vol. 12, p. 396; from a letter dated March 22, 1914. "The only condition of a successful use of this force is a recognition of the

existence of the soul as apart from the body and its permanent nature" (*Selections from Gandhi,* pp. 30–31).

24. Roy, *Self and Society,* p. 66.

25. Lovers of the orangutan will not appreciate Gandhi's reference to this peaceful creature as an example of what will happen to us if we do not practice *ahiṃsā.* See *Harijan* (October 8, 1938): 282.

26. Gandhi, *Young India* 8 (July 8, 1926): 244.

27. Roy, *Understanding Gandhi,* p. 106, note 67.

28. Gandhi, *Harijan* 12 (February 15, 1948): 33.

29. Gandhi, letter to Bhai Prithvi Singh (October 2, 1941) in Iyer, *Moral and Political Writings,* vol. 2, p. 250.

30. Bedekar, *Towards Understanding Gandhi,* p. 81.

31. Gandhi, *The Hindu* (September 12, 1927) in *Collected Works,* vol. 34, p. 505.

32. Gandhi, *Harijan* 2 (September 28, 1934): 258.

33. Gandhi, *The Collected Works,* vol. 19, p. 175.

34. Gandhi, *Young India* 8 (January 21, 1926): 30. The long passage here is filled with unfortunate implications of differences "inherent in human nature" and the "law of heredity." These comments mitigate the effect of his otherwise laudable comments about a brahmin doing a śudra's work.

35. Gandhi, *Harijan* 5 (March 6, 1937): 27. In the same source a questioner counters that, according to this logic, Abraham Lincoln should not have aspired to become president of the United States. Gandhi only deflects the question by answering, unsatisfactorily, that the scavenger, as long as he keeps his profession, can otherwise be anything that he wants to be. Gandhi does allow one exception to the Law of Varna: we must follow the professions of our fathers "in so far as that traditional calling is not inconsistent with fundamental ethics" (*Young India* 9 [October 20, 1927]: 355).

36. Rem B. Edwards, *Reason and Religion* (New York: Harcourt, Brace, Jovanovich, 1972), p. 211.

37. Roy, *Self and Society,* p. 92.

38. Ibid., p. 93.

39. Ibid., p. 100.

Chapter 4. The Buddha and Pragmatic Nonviolence

1. Gandhi, *Collected Works,* vol. 40, p. 160; speech at a Buddha Jayanti meeting in Bombay on May 18, 1924, in *The Collected Works,* vol. 24, p. 86.

2. Albert Schweitzer, *Indian Thought and Its Development,* trans. Mrs. Charles E. B. Russell (Bombay: Wilco Publishing House, 1960), p. 231.

3. Iyer, *The Moral and Political Thought,* p. 49.

4. Chatterjee, *Gandhi's Religious Thought,* pp. 43, 105, 27.

5. Paul Williams, *Mahayana Buddhism: Doctrinal Foundations* (London: Routledge, 1989), p. 145. Robert Thurman reminds us that "even if he has to take life in order to save life, he does not do so aggressively. He acts with regret and love toward the person he must kill." Thurman, however, stretches the point too far when he rationalizes this violence, much like the Hindus justified animal sacrifice: "If we defined violence as force used in connection with hatred, anger, or aggression, then

the taking of life by the Bodhisattva is not violence" ("Tibet and the Monastic Army of Peace," in *Inner Peace, World Peace,* p. 78).

6. S. Tachibana, *The Ethics of Buddhism* (London: Cruzon Press, 1926), p. 184.

7. N. H. Samtani, "Non-Violence vis-à-vis *Maitri*: Buddhist and Jain Approaches," in *The Contributions of Jainism to Indian Culture,* p. 135.

8. *Arthavinishcaya-sūtra,* quoted in ibid., p. 139.

9. Luis O. Gomez reminds us that this might very well be an instance of ritualistic nonviolence rather than a command not to kill snakes. Gomez finds many examples of vows of nonviolence among other promises made on particular holy days, including not wearing garlands, playing musical instruments, and watching theater. In the case of the snakes it is most likely a ritualistic charm for protection rather than a universal ethics of nonviolence. Even so, Gomez admits that the monk is still required to form a nonviolent intention towards the snakes in order for the charm to work. See Gomez, "Nonviolence and the Self in Early Buddhism," in *Inner Peace, World Peace,* pp. 36–37.

10. Gandhi, *Collected Works,* vol. 13, p. 232.

11. Gandhi, *Collected Works,* vol. 28, p. 3.

12. Gandhi, *Young India* 8 (November 18, 1926): 395.

13. Gandhi, *Young India* 8 (November 4, 1926): 385.

14. Gandhi, *Harijan* 4 (March 28, 1936): 49.

15. Gandhi, *An Autobiography,* chap. 20.

16. Quoted in Iyer, *The Moral the Political Thought,* p. 226. In 1929 Gandhi told an audience in Mandalay that it should use Buddhism to "explore the limitless possibilities of nonviolence" (*The Collected Works,* vol. 40, p. 159).

17. Gandhi, Speech at a Public Meeting in Rangoon (March 8, 1929), in *Collected Works,* vol. 40, p. 104. The comment about his son is in a speech that he gave in Sri Lanka. See *Young India* 9 (November 24, 1927): 392.

18. Gandhi, Speech at a Public Meeting in Toungo (Sri Lanka), in *Collected Works,* vol. 40, p. 161.

19. Gandhi, *Young India* 9 (November 24, 1927); 392.

20. Gandhi, *Hindu Dharma,* p. 34.

21. Gandhi, *Selected Works,* vol. 4, p. 247.

22. Gandhi, *Young India* 9 (November 24, 1927): 392.

23. Surendra Verma, *The Metaphysical Foundations of Gandhi's Thought* (New Delhi: Orient Longmans, 1970), p. 107.

24. Gandhi, *Young India* 9 (November 24, 1927): 393.

25. Gandhi, *Harijan* 7 (August 19, 1939): 237. I have supplied a capital *S* on each of the original "selves." Raghavan Iyer describes Gandhian prayer quite accurately: "The noblest and purest petition is that one should become outwardly what one is inwardly—that one's thoughts, words and deeds should ever more fully express the soul's core of Truth and nonviolence.... Prayer is truly an intense supplication towards one's inmost ineffable nature, the source of one's being and strength, the touchstone of one's active life" ("Civilization and Religion," p. 132). Many people would call this meditation rather than prayer.

26. Gandhi, *The Essence of Hinduism* (Ahmedabad: Navajivan, 1987), p. 176.

27. Gandhi, *Harijan* 7 (August 19, 1939): 237; *Harijan* 12 (February 15, 1948): 34.

28. Gandhi, *Harijan* 11 (August 17, 1947): 281.

29. Madadev Desai, "At Sevagram," in *Gandhiji: His Life and Work,* ed. D. G. Tendulkar et al. (Bombay: Karnatak, 1944), pp. 204–5. Contemporary followers of Nichiren use the mantra *Nam myoho renge kyo* instead of what stands in this text.

30. See *Harijan* 8 (September 8, 1940): 277, where there is a long discussion of *tapasyā.*

31. See Chatterjee, *Gandhi's Religious Thought,* p. 83.

32. Gandhi, *Young India* 13 (October 29, 1931): 325. Iyer describes this position quite aptly: "Gandhi believed that if one man gains spiritually, the whole world gains with him and if one man falls, the whole world falls to that extent" ("Civilization and Religion," p. 133).

33. Gandhi, *The Bombay Chronicle* (April 8, 1929); quoted in Manmohan Choudhuri, *Exploring Gandhi* (New Delhi: Gandhi Peace Foundation, 1989), p. 23.

34. Chatterjee, *Gandhi's Religious Thought,* p. 25.

35. Gandhi, *Young India* 4 (February 16, 1922): 103. Also see S. K. Saxena, "The Fabric of Self-Suffering: A Study in Gandhi," in *Suffering: Indian Perspectives,* ed. Kapil N. Tiwari (Delhi: Motilal Banarsidass, 1986), p. 232.

36. Quoted in K. P. Karunakaran, *Gandhi Interpretations* (New Delhi: Gitanjali Publishing House, 1985), p. 17.

37. Gandhi, *Young India* 2 (December 5, 1920); *Selections from Gandhi,* p. 159.

38. Gandhi, *Collected Works,* vol. 14, p. 475.

39. Marie B. Bayles, "The Buddha and the Mahatma," *Gandhi Marg* 6, no. 2 (April, 1962): 126.

40. The leading scholars here are David J. Kalupahana (*Buddhist Philosophy: A Historical Analysis* [Honolulu: University of Hawaii Press, 1976]; and *A History of Buddhist Philosophy: Continuities and Discontinuities* [Honolulu: University of Hawaii Press, 1992]); Peter Harvey ("The Mind-Body Relationship in Pali Buddhism: A Philosophical Investigation," *Asian Philosophy* 3, no. 1 [1993]); and Daisaku Ikeda (*Unlocking the Mysteries of Birth and Death: Buddhism in the Contemporary World* [London: MacDonald, 1988], pp. 141–42). A contemporary follower of Nichiren Daishonin, Ikeda has one of the most positive views of the body in Mahāyāna Buddhism.

41. *Majjhima-nikāya* II, 6; *The Middle Length Sayings,* trans. I. B. Horner (London: Luzac & Co., 1970), vol. 2, p. 207.

42. Gandhi, *Amrita Bazar Patrika,* June 30, 1944.

43. Quoted in Pyarelal, *The Last Phase,* vol. 2, p. 143. See also Gandhi, *Young India* 9 (November 24, 1927): 90, 93; and *Harijan* 4 (August 29, 1936): 226.

44. Ramjee Singh, "Gandhi and the Bodhisattva Ideal," in *New Dimensions and Perspectives in Gandhism,* vol. 4, p. 186.

45. Śāntideva, *Śikṣā Samuccaya,* trans. Cecil Bendall and W. H. D. Rouse (Delhi: Motilal Banarsidass, 1971), pp. 256–257.

46. Gandhi, *Young India* 3 (May 4, 1921), p. 144.

47. Śāntideva, *Bodhicaryāvatāra,* excerpted in *The Teachings of the Compassionate Buddha,* ed. E. A. Burtt (New York: Mentor Books, 1966), p. 140.

48. Gandhi, *Young India* 9 (March 24, 1927): 93.

49. See Gandhi, *Harijan* 8 (October 13, 1940): 322.

50. Ibid.; *Harijan* 8 (September 8, 1940): 277.

51. Madan Gandhi, "Metaphysical Basis of Gandhism," p. 211.

52. Joan Bondurant, *The Conquest of Violence,* p. 114.

53. Gandhi, *Young India* 4 (February 16, 1922): 103.

54. See E. Stanley Jones, *Mahatma Gandhi: An Interpretation* (London: Hodder & Stoughton, 1948), p. 143.

55. For the best comparative studies of the Buddha and Hume, see L. Stafford Betty, "The Buddhist-Humean Parallels: Postmortem," *Philosophy East and West* 21, no. 3 (July 1971): 237–254; and James Giles, "The No-Self Theory: Hume, Buddhism, and Personal Identity," *Philosophy East and West* 43, no. 2 (April, 1993): 175–200.

56. See Gier and Petta, "Hebrew and Buddhist Skandhas." I follow Ames' and Hall's convention of distinguishing between the virtue *ren** and homophonic *ren*.

57. Kalupahana, *The Principles of Buddhist Psychology*, pp. 20–21. Kalupahana's Pāli has been changed to Sanskrit.

58. Harvey, "The Mind-Body Relationship in Pāli Buddhism," p. 31

59. Verma, *The Metaphysical Foundations of Gandhi's Thought*, p. 7.

60. Gandhi, *Harijan* 9 (June 7, 1942): 177. Gandhi is not consistent on this idea of a mutable self, as he refers to an immutable self and an immutable God several times (*Harijan* 7 [August 19, 1939]: 237; excerpted in *Truth is God*, p. 43). Gandhi's continual references to becoming as well as being show a basic process orientation in his thought.

61. Gandhi, letter to Purushottam Gandhi, May 12, 1932, in Iyer, *Moral and Political Writings*, vol. 2, p. 235.

62. See Daisaku Ikeda, *Buddhism: The First Millennium* (Tokyo: Kodansha International, 1978), p. 140.

63. Thich Nhat Hanh, *Being Peace* (Berkeley, Calif.: Parallax Press, 1987), p. 39.

64. For more on Buddhism and humanism see Gier, *Spiritual Titanism*, pp. 158–161; and Gier, "The Virtues of Asian Humanism," *Journal of Oriental Studies* 12 (October, 2002): 14–28.

65. Kalupahana, "Buddhism and Chinese Humanism," p. 11.

66. Ibid., p. 12.

67. See *Free Inquiry* 3, no. 4 (fall 1983): 7. A list of the members of the Humanist Pantheon and the Academy of Humanism appears on the back cover of every recent issue.

68. Kalupahana, "Buddhism and Chinese Humanism," p. 1.

69. Daisaku Ikeda, *The Living Buddha: An Interpretative Biography*, trans. Burton Watson (New York: Weatherhill, 1976).

70. Nichiren Daishonin, "The True Aspect of All Phenomena," in *The Writings of Nichiren Daishonin* (Tokyo: Soka Gakkei, 1999), p. 384.

Chapter 5. Experiments with Truth

1. Nolan Pliny Jacobson, *Buddhism and the Contemporary World: Change and Self-Correction* (Carbondale and Edwardsville: Southern Illinois University Press, 1983), p. 148.

2. See Raimond Gaita, "Virtues, Human Good, and the Unity of Life," *Inquiry* 26 (1983): 424, n. 18. "An ethics centered on the notion of flourishing *[eudaimonia]* can have little to say on those in severe and ineradicable affliction" (ibid.).

3. Aristotle, *Nicomachean Ethics*, 1178a8.

4. Ibid., 1169a3.
5. Ibid., 1143b13; 1144a30.
6. Ibid., 1141a20–1.
7. Ibid., 1141b8–9.
8. Ibid., 1143b19.
9. Ibid., 1144a3.
10. John Kekes, *Moral Wisdom and Good Lives* (Ithaca, N.Y.: Cornell University Press, 1995), p. 17.
11. Aristotle, *Nicomachean Ethics,* 1140b6–7.
12. Ibid., 1122a25–6.
13. Ibid., 1142a10ff.
14. Ibid., 1142a23–5.
15. Ibid., 1143b13.
16. Nancy Sherman, *The Fabric of Character: Aristotle's Theory of Virtue* (Oxford: Oxford University Press, 1989), pp. 13–22. Alasdair MacIntyre claims that for one to apply the law one requires the virtue of justice—"to give each person what each deserves"—which is known only through *phronēsis* (*After Virtue* [Notre Dame, Ind.: Notre Dame University Press, 1984], p. 152). I am indebted to Jiyuan Yu, "Virtue: Confucius and Aristotle," *Philosophy East and West* 48, no. 2 (April 1998): 329–30, for the ideas for this summary.
17. Confucius, *Analects* 4.10. Ames and Rosemont, *The Analects of Confucius: A Philosophical Translation* (New York: Ballantine Books, 1998); D. C. Lau, *Confucius: The Analects* (Harmondsworth: Penguin Books, 1979). Henceforth the Roger Ames and Henry Rosemont translation will be cited in the text unless the D. C. Lau translation is indicated. I follow David Hall's and Ames's convention of distinguishing homophones by using an asterisk as in *ren* as a human person and *ren** as the virtue; and *yi** as "meaning deriving" and *yi* as "meaning bestowing." See Hall and Ames, *Thinking Through Confucius* (Albany, N.Y.: State University of New York Press, 1987).
18. Confucius, *The Analects,* 16.11.
19. Ibid., 17.23.
20. Ibid., 15.18.
21. Ames and Rosemont, *The Analects,* p. 51. The reference to the Latin *proprius* is theirs.
22. Yu, "Virtue: Confucius and Aristotle," p. 331.
23. Ibid., note 22.
24. Confucius, *The Analects,* 12.5.
25. Ibid., 4.10; 19.11.
26. Ibid., 2.4.
27. Ibid., 17.23; 14.4.
28. Tu Weiming, *Centrality and Commonality* (Albany, N.Y.: State University of New York Press, 1989), p. 52. Benjamin Schwartz agrees that *yi* is "situation-oriented" and that "it is the capacity to act correctly in all the complex circumstances of...human life" (*The World of Thought in Ancient China* [Cambridge, Mass.: Harvard University Press, 1985], pp. 266, 264). D. C. Lau agrees with Hall and Ames in the bilateral application of *yi:* "[W]hether an act is *yi* does not depend only on the motive, but also on whether it is fitting in the situation" (*Mencius,* p. 253).
29. Michel Foucault, *The Use of Pleasure,* vol. 2 of *The History of Sexuality,* trans. Robert Hurley (New York: Pantheon Books, 1985), p. 29.

30. Foucault, "The Ethic of Care for the Self as a Practice of Freedom," *Philosophy and Social Criticism* (summer 1987): 117.

31. Sherman, *The Fabric of Character,* p. 36.

32. Hall and Ames, *Thinking Through Confucius,* p. 96. In their only reference to Aristotle Hall and Ames state that "*yi* is 'divided' into itself and *yi** in much the same fashion as Aristotle divides *praxis* and *technē*" (p. 348). In a personal communication, John Makeham of the University of Adelaide contends that Hall and Ames have failed to prove this distinction between *yi* and *yi**.

33. Confucius, *The Analects,* 4.3 (Lau trans.).

34. Ibid., 15.27.

35. Ibid., 13.24; cf. 17.24.

36. Wing-tsit Chan, *Source Book in Chinese Philosophy,* p. 25n53. We should also note that Ames and Rosemont go beyond premoral liking and disliking in their translation of 4.3: "The *ren** person alone has the wherewithal to properly discriminate the good person from the bad."

37. H. V. Guethner, *Philosophy and Psychology in the Abhidharma* (Berkeley, Calif.: Shambala, 1976), p. 37.

38. Robert C. Roberts, "Will Power and the Virtues," *Philosophical Review* (April 1984): 227–247. Excerpted and extensively revised in *Vice and Virtue in Everyday Life,* ed. Christina Sommers and Fred Sommers (San Diego: Harcourt Brace Jovanovich, 1989), p. 240.

39. *The Mencius* 2a6 (van Norden trans.).

40. *The Analects* 17.26.

41. Given the fact that *yi* sometimes indicates a premoral comprehension of likes and dislikes, Lee Yearly's proposal that *zhi* is more comparable to *phronēsis* deserves serious consideration. See Yearly's *Mencius and Aquinas: Theories of Virtue and Conceptions of Courage* (Albany, N.Y.: State University of New York Press, 1990), pp. 40–41. In Mencian terms *yi* as a premoral disposition to like or dislike that matures as *zhi,* the realization of right from wrong.

42. *The Analects* 6.22.

43. Ibid., 15.32 (Lau trans.).

44. Ibid., 8.9.

45. *The Mencius* 5a1; 2a6.

46. *The Analects* 2.24.

47. *The Mencius* 4a27.

48. See David J. Kalupahana, *A History of Buddhist Philosophy,* chapter 10; *Ethics in Early Buddhism* (Honolulu: University of Hawaii Press, 1995).

49. See Damien Keown, "Karma, Character, and Consequentialism," *Journal of Religious Ethics* 24, no. 2 [fall 1996]: 348); *The Nature of Buddhist Ethics* (New York: St. Martin's Press, 1992), p.112; see also pp. 38–43, passim.

50. Keown cites the Croom Robertson passage from Mrs. Rhys Davids, *The Birth of Indian Psychology and its Development in Buddhism* (London: Luzac, 1936), p. 268.

51. Keown observes that *kusala* can also mean technical excellence as in a good carpenter (*The Nature of Buddhist Ethics,* p. 118). The good life is something that is crafted, something that takes a certain skill to achieve.

52. *Majjhima-nikāya* I.190–1, quoted in Kalupahana, *Buddhist Philosophy,* p. 64.

53. Kalupahana, *Buddhist Philosophy,* p. 63; *Ethics in Early Buddhism,* p. 44.

54. Meilaender, *The Theory and Practice of Virtue* (Notre Dame, Ind.: Notre Dame University, 1984), p. 8.

55. Ibid., pp. 34, 29, 22. Meilaender is paraphrasing the work of Josef Pieper, a German Roman Catholic philosopher.

56. *Mulamadyamakakarika,* translated by Nancy McCagney in *Nagarjuna and the Philosophy of Openness* (Totowa, NJ.: Rowman & Littlefield, 1997).

57. Ames and Rosemont, *The Analects,* p. 57.

58. See the *Śalistramba Sūtra,* trans. N. Ross Reat (Delhi: Motilal Banarsidass, 1993), §3, p. 28.

59. Keown, *The Nature of Buddhist Ethics,* p. 226.

60. *Mahāvedallasutta,* I.293.

61. Kalupahana, *Ethics in Early Buddhism,* p. 45.

62. *Mahāvedallasutta,* I.15.

63. A. J. Bahm, *The Philosophy of the Buddha* (New York: Capricorn Books, 1958), p. 82.

64. Ibid., p. 83.

65. Keown, *The Nature of Buddhist Ethics,* p. 220.

66. Aristotle, *Nicomachean Ethics* 1122a25–6.

67. Bahm, *The Philosophy of the Buddha,* p. 86.

68. Ames and Rosemont, *The Analects,* p. 5.

69. *The Analects* 11.22.

70. Bedekar, *Towards Understanding Gandhi,* pp. 117, 119.

Chapter 6. The Aesthetics of Virtue

1. Peter Brown, "Saint as Exemplar in Late Antiquity," in *Saints and Virtues,* pp. 3–14.

2. Michel Foucault, "On the Genealogy of Ethics," interview in *The Foucault Reader,* ed. Paul Rabinow (New York: Pantheon Books, 1984), p. 351.

3. Foucault, "The Concern for Truth," in *Michel Foucault: Politics, Philosophy and Culture,* ed. L. Kritzman (London: Routledge, 1988), p. 262n32; and "The Return to Morality" in *Michel Foucault: Politics, Philosophy and Culture,* ed. Kritzman, p. 50n2. For clarity in the last citation I have changed the order of the phrase "with a disciplinary structure."

4. Foucault, "The Ethic of Care for the Self as a Practice of Freedom," p. 117.

5. Foucault, *The Use of Pleasure,* pp. 250–51.

6. Tu Weiming, *Confucian Thought: Selfhood as Creative Self-Transformation* (Albany, N.Y.: State University of New York Press, 1985), chap. 5.

7. Yu, "Virtue: Aristotle and Confucius," p. 335.

8. D. C. Lau, *The Mencius* (Harmondsworth: Penguin Books, 1970), 7a21. The Lau translation will be cited in the text unless otherwise indicated.

9. Wing-tsit Chan, *Source Book in Chinese Philosophy* (Princeton, N.J.: Princeton University Press, 1963), pp. 89–90.

10. See Tu Weiming, *Confucian Thought,* pp. 97, 98.

11. Foucault, "On the Genealogy of Ethics," p. 348.

12. Foucault, *The Care of the Self,* vol. 3 of *The History of Sexuality,* trans. Robert Hurley (New York: Pantheon Books, 1986), pp. 51, 53.

13. I am indebted to Chan (*Source Book in Chinese Philosophy,* p. 27) for his reference to Liu Baonan's linkage between *Analects* 4.15 and 6.28.

14. Tu Weiming, *Centrality and Commonality* (Albany, N.Y.: State University of New York Press, 1989), p. 27.

15. Foucault, "The Ethic of Care for the Self as a Practice of Freedom," p. 118.

16. John B. Cobb, *The Structure of Christian Existence* (Philadelphia: Westminster Press, 1967), p. 133.

17. Flint Shier, "Hume and the Aesthetics of Agency," *Proceedings of the Aristotelian Society* 87 (1986–87): 121.

18. For more on synthetic reason see my *Wittgenstein and Phenomenology* (Albany, N.Y.: State University of New York Press, 1981), chapter 8; and the updated discussion in my "Synthetic Reason, Aesthetic Order, and the Grammar of Virtue," *Journal of Indian Council of Philosophical Research* 18, no. 4 (2001): 13–28. The principal inspiration for this idea came from Merleau-Ponty's "Hegel's Existentialism" in *Sense and Non-Sense,* trans. H. L. and P. A. Dreyfus (Evanston, Ill.: Northwestern University Press, 1964), p. 63.

19. I have used the principle of subisitutability from Hall and Ames but the examples and formulations are my own (Hall and Ames, *Thinking Through Confucius,* pp. 131–137). Hall has informed me that my use of aesthetic order is more rational than his because I believe that aesthetic order has structure, a view that I will continue to defend.

20. Confucius, *The Analects* 13.23.

21. Hall & Ames, *Thinking Through Confucius,* pp. 165–66.

22. Aristotle, *Politics* 1287a28–32; *Nicomachean Ethics* 1137b26–7.

23. This means that Henry Rosemont may be incorrect when he states that *yi* "denotes rational order" ("Confucian and Feminist Perspectives of the Self," in *Culture and Self,* ed. Douglas Allen [Boulder, Colo.: Westview Press, 1997], p. 66).

24. Robert Eno, *The Confucian Creation of Heaven* (Albany, N.Y.: State University of New York Press, 1990), pp. 192–93.

25. Ibid., pp. 22, 53.

26. Cited in ibid., p. 59.

27. Robert C. Neville, *The Tao and the Daimon* (Albany, N.Y.: State University of New York Press, 1982), p. 151.

28. Confucius, *The Analects,* 3.23.

29. Ibid., 7.14.

30. Ibid., 9.15.

31. There is, however, one indication that Confucius believes that beauty does not necessarily imply goodness. He once declared that *The Succession,* a piece of Shun dance music, was both "perfectly beautiful and perfectly good," whereas *Military Exploits,* dance music from King Wu, was "perfectly beautiful but not perfectly good" (3.25, Lau). As a Zhou ruler there is no question that Wu was a man of virtue, but the fact that he assumed his position through military force made his actions less than perfectly good. This example, therefore, does not undermine the general unity of the good and the beautiful.

32. *Analects* 1.12 (following Lau, Huang, Leys, and Waley with "beauty" rather than Chan's "excellence"); 4.1 (following P. J. Ivanhoe's private translation); 3.3; 13.3; 8.8.

33. *The Mencius,* 6a8; 7b25.

34. Ibid., 7b33.

35. Marcia Eaton comments on the intimate connection between aesthetic and ethical delight. The former results from perception and reflection of intrinsic features of objects and events, while for the latter it is action of ourselves and others that gives delight. See Eaton's *Aesthetics and the Good Life* (Cranbury, N.J.: Farleigh Dickinson University Press, 1989), p. 153.

36. *The Mencius,* 4a27.

37. Watson, *The Complete Works of Chuang Tzu,* p. 140.

38. See *Xunzi* 21.22.

39. *Xunzi,* 20; *Hsün Tzu: Basic Writings,* trans. Burton Watson (New York: Columbia University Press, 1963), p. 117.

40. *Xunzi* 8.86–87, Eno's translation and insertion.

41. *Xunzi* 20; Watson, p. 118.

42. Edward Machle, *Nature and Heaven in the "Xunzi"* (Albany, N.Y.: State University of New York Press, 1993), p. 181.

43. James F. Cahill, "Confucian Elements in the Theory of Painting," in *Confucianism and Chinese Civilization,* ed. Arthur F. Wright (Stanford, Calif.: Stanford University Press, 1959), pp. 84ff.

44. Zhou Dunyi, *Penetrating the Book of Changes,* chap. 17.1; trans. Chan, *Source Book in Chinese Philosophy,* pp. 472–3.

45. Ibid., chap. 28, p. 476.

46. Ibid.

47. *The Mencius* 5a1.

48. Aristotle, *Nicomachean Ethics* 1140a20–21. Yu sees a link between *hexis* with the literal meaning of "having" and *de,* which means "to get." Both are essential for the cultivation—that is, the "getting" and "having" of virtue ("Virtue: Aristotle and Confucius," p. 337).

49. Confucius, *The Analects* 8.9.

50. Aristotle, *Nicomachean Ethics* 1140b5–7.

51. Julia Annas, *The Morality of Happiness* (New York: Oxford University Press, 1993), p. 70.

52. Anthony Kenny, *Action, Emotion, and Will* (London: Routledge & Kegan Paul, 1963), pp. 172–178.

53. R. G. Collingwood, *The Principles of Art* (Oxford: Clarendon Press, 1938), pp. 15–16, 20.

54. Roberts, "Will Power and the Virtues," p. 240.

55. *Doctrine of the Mean,* chap. 13; Chan, *Source Book in Chinese Philosophy,* pp. 100–01.

56. Confucius, *The Analects,* 16.11.

57. A. C. Graham, *Chuang-Tzu: The Inner Chapters* (London: Unwin Paperbacks, 1986), p. 98.

58. Eno, *The Confucian Creation of Heaven,* p. 143.

59. Watson, *The Complete Works of Chuang Tzu,* p. 97.

60. Scott Cook demonstrates the close connection between a Confucian and Daoist virtue aesthetics in "Zhuang Zi and Carving the Confucian Ox," *Philosophy East & West* 47, no. 3 (October 1997): 521–553.

61. Annas, *The Morality of Happiness,* p. 72.

62. Josef Pieper, *The Four Cardinal Virtues* (Notre Dame, Ind.: Notre Dame University Press, 1966), p. 30; cited in Meilaender, *The Theory and Practice of Virtue,* p. 37.

63. James D. Wallace, "Ethics and the Craft Analogy," in *Midwest Studies in Philosophy* (Notre Dame, Ind.: Notre Dame University Press, 1988), vol. 13, pp. 223–232.

64. John Fowles, *The French Lieutenant's Woman* (New York: New American Library, 1969). "The novelist is still god, since he creates.... What has changed is that we are no longer the gods of the Victorian image, omniscient and decreeing; but in the new theological image, with freedom our first principle, not authority" (p. 82).

65. Flint Schier, "Hume and the Aesthetics of Agency," p. 122.

66. Using the term "epistemic multiplism" and using the example of reading a musical score, Michael Krausz brilliantly defends this position. See Krausz, *Rightness and Reasons: Interpretation in Cultural Practices* (Ithaca, N.Y.: Cornell University Press, 1993), chapter 1.

67. Confucius, *The Analects,* 3.23.

Chapter 7. Gandhi, Confucius, and Virtue Aesthetics

1. Cited in Fung Yulan, *A History of Chinese Philosophy,* vol. 2 (Princeton, N.J.: Princeton University Press, 1973), pp. 610–11.

2. Confucius, *The Analects,* 12.11.

3. Ibid., 12.5.

4. See Ames and Rosemont, *The Analects,* p. 250, note 192.

5. Confucius, *The Analects,* 3.17.

6. Ibid., 14.34.

7. See Gandhi, *Young India* 9 (October 20, 1927): 355.

8. Confucius, *The Analects* 11.9.

9. Ibid., 6.28.

10. Ibid., 2.3.

11. Gandhi, *Collected Works,* vol. 13, p. 295.

12. Quoted in Philip. J. Ivanhoe, *Confucian Moral Self Cultivation* (Indianapolis, Ind.: Hackett Publishing Co., 2000), p. xiii.

13. *Mencius* 7b31 (van Norden trans.)

14. Ivanhoe, *Confucian Moral Self Cultivation,* p. xiii.

15. "Because of [the king's] willingness to put himself in danger on behalf of another, his *de* is magnified" (quoted in Ivanhoe, *Confucian Moral Self Cultivation,* p. xv).

16. Confucius, *The Analects* 20.1.

17. Ibid., 9.13.

18. Graham Parkes, "The Wandering Dance: Chuang Tzu and Zarathustra," *Philosophy East and West* 33, no. 3 (July, 1983), p. 245.

19. See Gier, *Spiritual Titanism*, end of introduction and *passim*.

20. Parkes, "The Wandering Dance," p. 246.

21. Gandhi, *Harijan* 5 (June 16, 1937): 192.

22. Confucius, *The Analects* 2.4.

23. Gandhi, *Young India* 12 (September 11, 1930): 1.

24. John S. Hawley, "Introduction: Saints and Virtues," in Hawley, ed. *Saints and Virtues* (Berkeley, Calif.: University of California Press, 1987), p. xvi.

25. Geoffrey Ashe, *Gandhi: A Study in Revolution* (New Delhi: Asia Publishing House, 1968), p. 370.

26. See Pyarelal, *The Last Phase,* vol. 1, p. 589. In his defense Gandhi also mentioned the Gopis stripped naked, standing unembarrassed in front of their Lord Krishna (ibid., vol. 1, p. 585).

27. Confucius, *The Analects* 6.28.

28. Ibid., 17.23.

29. Ibid., 5.7.

30. Gandhi, *Young India* 12 (September 11, 1930): 1.

31. Dayle M. Bethel, ed., *Education for Creative Living: Ideas and Proposals of Tsunesaburo Makiguchi,* trans. Alfred Birnbaum (Ames: Iowa State University Press, 1989), pp. 75, 82.

32. Gandhi, *Young India* 6 (November 20, 1924): 386.

33. Gandhi, *Harijan* 6 (February 19, 1938): 10.

34. Gandhi, *Young India* 6 (November 13, 1924): 377.

35. Gandhi, *Young India* 6 (November 20, 1924): 386.

36. Cited in Madan Gandhi, *A Gandhian Aesthetics* (Chandigarh: Vikas Bharati, 1969), p. 69.

37. Gandhi, *Young India* 6 (November 13, 1924): 377.

38. Ibid.

39. M. Kirti Singh, *Philosophical Import of Gandhism* (New Delhi: South Asian Publishers, 1994), p. 136, note 3.

40. Cited in ibid., p. 135.

41. *The Complete Works of Chuang Tzu,* trans. Burton Watson, p. 72.

42. Cited in Albert O'Hara, *The Position of Women in Ancient China* (Washington, D. C.: The Catholic University of America, 1945), p. 76.

43. Gandhi, *Young India* 6 (November 13, 1924): 377.

44. Ibid.

45. *The Mencius* 4b25.

46. Jawaharlal Nehru, *Mahatma Gandhi* (Calcutta: Signet Press, 1949), p. 159.

47. Robert Payne, *The Life and Death of Mahatma Gandhi* (New York: Dutton, 1969), p. 14.

48. Confucius, *The Analects* 2.1.

Chapter 8. Rules, Vows, and Virtues

1. See Ian Tattersall, *The Last Neanderthal* (Boulder, Colo.: Westview Press, 1999), p. 169–70.

2. Michael L. Spangle and Kent E. Menzel, "Symbol, Metaphor, and Myth: the Origin and Impact of Spoken Language," Seventh Annual Meeting of the Language

Origins in DeKalb, Illinois, 1991; http://baserv.uci.kun.nl/~los/Meetings/Dekalb/Articles/24-MENZEL.htm. Studies have shown that deaf people do not score very well in some areas of abstract reasoning (see Helmer R. Mykelbust, *The Psychology of Deafness* [New York: Northwestern University Press, 1966], pp. 85–89). I am indebted to Shane Sheffner, student in my seminar on virtue ethics, for these references.

3. This argument for the priority of the divine virtues works only within the framework of classical theology, because God without the world is not possible in process theology. Whitehead believes that physical laws are simply the habits of the universe, so it would follow that moral laws are derived from the habitual behaviors—the vices and the virtues of humankind. Moral laws would not exist in God either because the Whiteheadian God—committed to the aesthetic values of harmony and intensity—could not be a moral legislator or judge. If we make God a personal society of occasions, which is Hartshorne's position, we can then speak more confidently of a full complement of divine virtues, although the traditional view of divine justice is not supported. God is not the same as a terrestrial or even extraterrestrial person—for example, the cosmos is God's body only by analogy—so God would embody and act on the virtues in a uniquely divine way. However, God's conscious inclusion of all experience in the consequent nature is the epitome of compassion and unconditional love. As opposed to the classical doctrine of divine impassivity, God can truly empathize with the suffering of the cosmos in the same way that we are aware of the pain in our bodies. Theological ethics should consider thinking of God's virtues as a model for human action rather than God the judge, rewarding and punishing according to a set of divine rules.

4. Leslie Stephen, *The Science of Ethics,* quoted in Louis P. Pojman, *Ethics: Discovering Right and Wrong* (Belmont, Calif.: Wadsworth Publishing Co., 1990), p. 114. The following four-part critique of rule and duty ethics is derived from Pojman's chapter.

5. Nussbaum, "Non-Relative Virtues," p. 44.

6. Annette Baier, "Trust and Anti-Trust," *Ethics* 96 (January, 1986): 231–260.

7. Gandhi, *Young India* 10 (September 13, 1928): 308.

8. Nussbaum, "Non-Relative Virtues," p. 44.

9. Bernard Mayo, *Ethics and the Moral Life,* excerpted in Christina and Fred Sommers, eds, *Vice and Virtue in Everyday Life* (San Diego: Harcourt Brace Jovanovich, 1989), p. 199.

10. Thomas Aquinas, *Summa Theologica* I–II. 94.2.

11. Ibid., 20.5.

12. Ibid., 64.2.

13. Aristotle, *Nicomachean Ethics* 1106b36 (Ross trans.).

14. Jean Porter, *The Recovery of Virtue: The Relevance of Aquinas for Christian Ethics* (Louisville, Ky.: Westminster/John Knox Press, 1990), p. 116. Porter does not actually embrace the view, held by D. M. Nelson, that Aquinas joins Aristotle in championing the priority of virtue. See Nelson's *The Priority of Prudence* (University Park, Penn.: Penn State University Press, 1992).

15. Josef Pieper, *The Silence of Saint Thomas* (New York: Pantheon Books, 1957), p. 20; cited in Meilaender, *The Theory and Practice of Virtue,* p. 23.

16. Foucault, *The Use of Pleasure,* p. 83.

17. Ibid., p. 84.

18. See Stephen D. Moore and Janice Capel Anderson, "Taking it Like a Man: Masculinity in 4 Maccabees," *Journal of Biblical Literature* 117, no. 2 (1998): 249–273.

19. *The Laws of Manu*, 3.93; 7.5. Most of this paragraph is taken from my *Spiritual Titanism*, p. 122.

20. Ibid., 11.122.

21. Ibid., 4:41, 44.

22. John Strachey, *India: Its Adminstration and Progress* (London: Macmillan, 1888), p. 412; cited in Susanne H. and Lloyd I. Rudolph, *The Modernity of Tradition: Political Development in India* (Chicago: University of Chicago Press, 1967), p. 165.

23. Gandhi, *Collected Works*, vol. 19, p. 12.

24. Gandhi, *Harijan* 6 (July 23, 1938): 192.

25. Gandhi, *Collected Works*, vol. 14, p. 504.

26. Gandhi, *Women's Role in Society*, p. 8.

27. Gandhi, *Harijan* 4 (November 14, 1936): 316. "Woman is the incarnation of *ahiṃsā*. *Ahiṃsā* means infinite love, which again means infinite capacity for suffering" (*Harijan* 8 [February 24, 1940]: 13). "If only the women of the world would come together they could display such heroic nonviolence as to kick away the atom bomb like a mere ball.... If the women of Asia wake up, they will dazzle the world. My experiment in nonviolence would be instantly successful if I could secure women's help" ("Message to Chinese Women, New Delhi, July 18, 1947, excerpted in Iyer, *Moral and Political Writings*, vol. 3, p. 409).

28. Pyarelal, *The Last Phase*, vol. 1, p. 595; 2nd ed., vol. 1, bk. 2, p. 234. A Mrs. Polak noted a "trait of sexlessness" even in his South Africa day (*Gandiji as We Know Him*, p. 47). C. Shukla said that "there are some things relating to our lives that we women can speak of...with no man....But while speaking to Gandhiji we somehow forgot the fact that he was a man" (C. Shukla, *Gandhiji's View of Life* [Bombay, 1951], p. 199).

29. Pyarelal, *The Last Phase*, vol. 1, p. 574; 2nd ed., vol. 1, bk. 2, p. 214.

30. Brian K. Smith, "Eaters, Food, and Social Hierarchy in Ancient India," *Journal of the American Academy of Religion* 58, no. 2 (summer 1990), pp. 177, 178.

31. Thomas B. Coburn, *Encountering the Goddess* (Albany, N.Y.: State University of New York Press, 1991), p. 222fn.

32. Gandhi, *Selected Works*, vol. 3, p. 223.

33. Gandhi, *Harijan* 6 (July 23, 1938): 192.

34. Quoted in Pyarelal, *The Last Phase*, vol. 1, p. 577; 2nd ed., vol. 1, bk. 2, p. 217.

35. *Gandhi's Letters to Ashram Sisters*, ed. K. Kalelkar and trans. A. L. Mazmudar 2nd ed. rev. (Ahmedabad: Navajivan, 1960), p. 94.

36. Pyrarelal, vol. 1, p. 581; 2nd ed., vol. 1, bk. 2, p. 223.

37. Gandhi, *Collected Works*, vol. 14, p. 97; from a letter dated November 22, 1917.

38. See Iyer, *The Moral and Political Thought*, p. 69.

39. Confucius, *The Analects* 2.4.

40. I have elaborated greatly on Louis Pojman's example in *Ethics: Discovering Right and Wrong*, p. 114–15.

41. Kant, *Religion within the Limits of Religion Alone,* trans. Theodore M. Greene and Hoyt H. Hudson (New York: Harper & Row, 1960), p. 66.

42. Christine McKinnon, *Character, Virtue Theories, and the Vices* (Peterborough, Ontario: Broadview Press, 1999), p. 105.

43. See N. F. Gier and Paul K. Kjellberg, "Buddhism and the Freedom of the Will" in *Freedom and Determinism: Topics in Contemporary Philosophy,* ed. J. K. Campbell, D. Shier, M. O'Rourke (New York: MIT Press, 2004).

44. The Rudolphs, *The Modernity of Tradition,* p. 212.

45. Pyarelal, *The Last Phase,* vol. 1, p. 552; 2nd ed, vol. 1, bk. 2, p. 192.

46. George Orwell, "Reflections on Gandhi," p. 479.

47. Gandhi, *An Autobiography,* III.7.

48. *Selected Works*, vol. 4, p. 248.

49. Ibid., p. 250.

50. Suman Khanna, *Gandhi and the Good Life* (Delhi: B. R. Publishing Corporation, 2nd ed., 1996), p. 60. I am indebted to Khanna for both insights and references.

51. See V. M. Bedekar, "The *Vrata* in Ancient Indian Culture and Gandhi" in *Quest for Gandhi,* ed. G. Ramachandran and T. K. Mahadevan (New Delhi: Gandhi Peace Foundation, 1970), p. 15.

52. Khanna, *Gandhi and the Good Life,* p. 59.

53. Gandhi, *Selected Works,* vol. 4, p. 248.

54. Gandhi, *An Autobiography,* III.8.

55. Ibid.

56. Gandhi, *Selected Works*, p. 226.

57. Gandhi, *Harijan* 11 (June 22 & 29, 1947): 200, 212; *An Autobiography,* III.7.

58. Quoted without reference in Khanna, p. 75, but vows as "derived from Truth" is found in *Harijan* 11 (June 8, 1947): 180.

59. Gandhi, *Selected Works,* vol. 4, p. 256.

60. Ibid.

61. Ibid., p. 233.

62. Gandhi, *Harijan* 4 (June 13, 1936): 137.

63. Ibid.

64. Gandhi, *An Autobiography,* III.8.

65. Pyarelal, *The Last Phase,* vol. 1, p. 591; 2nd ed., vol. 1, bk. 2, p. 230.

66. Ibid., p. 592/231.

67. Aquinas, *Summa Theologia* II–II.147.1ad2.

68. Gandhi, *Selected Works,* vol. 4, p. 226.

69. "One who takes no food, physically speaking, is generally said to be fasting, but he is guilty of theft as well as a breach of his fast, if he gives himself up to a mental contemplation of pleasure, when he sees others taking their meals" (ibid., p. 228). It is a widely known fact that even the spiritual masters have vivid hallucinations about devouring great amounts of food, a reaction that appears to be completely involuntary.

70. Gandhi, *Selected Works,* p. 227.

71. Khanna, *Gandhi and the Good Life,* p. 71.

72. Gandhi, *Selected Works,* vol. 4, p. 232.

73. Gandhi, *Collected Works,* vol. 37, p. 362; vol. 13, p. 225.; vol.10, p. 70; see also vol. 10, pp. 206–08.

74. Khanna, *Gandhi and the Good Life,* pp. 59–60.
75. Gandhi, *Hind Swaraj,* ed. Anthony J. Parel, note 193.
76. *Selected Works,* vol. 4, p.245.
77. Ibid., p. 247.
78. Porter, *The Recovery of Virtue,* chapter 4.
79. Cited in Jean Porter, "Virtue and Sin: The Connection of the Virtues and the Case of the Flawed Saint," *Journal of Religion* 75, no. 4 (October 1995): 522.
80. Aristotle, *Nicomachean Ethics* 1106a35.
81. *Selected Works,* vol. 4, p. 226.
82. The Rudolphs, *The Modernity of Tradition,* p. 190.
83. Iyer, *The Moral and Political Thought,* p. 69.
84. Terchek, *Gandhi: Struggling for Autonomy,* p. 193.
85. Gandhi, *Harijan* 7 (July 15, 1939), p. 201.
86. Gandhi, *Collected Works,* vol. 13, p. 295.
87. Josef Pieper, "On the Christian Idea of Man," cited in Meilaender, *The Theory and Practice of Virtue,* p. 29.
88. Ibid.
89. *Selected Works,* vol. 4, p. 245.
90. Ibid., p. 246.

Chapter 9. The Virtue of Nonviolence

1. Michael Slote, *From Morality to Virtue* (New York: Oxford University Press, 1992).
2. Philip. J. Ivanhoe, "Character Consequentialism: An Early Confucian Contribution to Contemporary Ethical Theory," *Journal of Religious Ethics* 19, no. 1 (spring 1991): 56.
3. See Kalupahana, *Buddhist Philosophy,* p. 63.
4. *Aṅguttara-nikāya* 3.65.
5. See Paul Williams, *Mahayana Buddhism,* p. 145.
6. Gandhi, *Young India* 6 (November 20, 1924): 386.
7. Gandhi, *Collected Works,* vol. 37, p. 313.
8. P. J. Ivanhoe, "Character Consequentialism," pp. 55–70.
9. Ibid., p. 62.
10. Michael Scriven, *Primary Philosophy* (New York: McGraw-Hill, 1966), pp. 238–258.
11. Ivanhoe, "Character Consequentialism," p. 63–64.
12. Orwell, "Reflections on Gandhi, " p. 480.
13. Baier, "Trust and Anti-Trust," p. 48.
14. Gandhi, *Hindu Dharma,* p. 161.
15. John Stuart Mill, *Utilitarianism* (London: Longmans, Green, 1897), chap. 2, p. 12.
16. Damien Keown, "Karma, Character, and Consequentialism," pp. 329–350.
17. Jonathan MacIntosh, "Confucianism, Consequentialism, and Modal Thinking," from Virtue Talk (March 1, 2001), a threaded discussion for Philosophy 490 still available at www.class.uidaho.edu/ngier/490/490.htm.

18. *Selections from Gandhi,* p. 36.

19. Desai, "Ends and Means in Politics," p. 27.

20. Gandhi, *Young India* 6 (December 12, 1924): 424.

21. Lisa Bellantoni, *Moral Progress: A Process Critique of MacIntyre* (Albany, N.Y.: State University of New York Press, 2000), p. 11.

22. Josef Pieper, *The Silence of Saint Thomas,* pp. 19ff.

23. Meilaender, *The Theory and Practice of Virtue,* p. 26. 34. Roberts, "Will Power and the Virtues," p. 236.

24. Graham Haydon, *Values, Virtues, and Violence: Education and the Public Understanding of Morality* (Oxford: Blackwell, 1999), p. 55.

25. See Kathyrn Paxton George, *Animal, Vegetable, or Woman* (Albany, N.Y.: State University of New York Press, 2000).

26. Thich Nhat Hanh, *Being Peace,* pp. 62ff.

27. Ibid., p. 14.

28. Haydon, *Values, Virtues, and Violence,* p. 70.

29. Josef Pieper, *The Four Cardinal Virtues,* p. 147; cited in Meilaender, *The Theory and Practice of Virtues,* p. 39.

30. Roberts, "Will Power and the Virtues," p. 236.

31. See Khanna, *Gandhi and the Good Life,* p. 62n15.

32. Dalai Lama, *The Dalai Lama at Harvard,* p. 61.

33. Gandhi, *Navajivan* (March 31, 1929), trans. in *The Collected Works of Mahatma Gandhi,* vol. 40, pp. 191–92.

34. Gandhi, *Truth is God,* ed. R. K. Prabhu (Ahmedabad: Navajivan, 1955), p. 4.

35. Jack Kelly, "Virtue and Pleasure," *Mind* 82 (1973): 403.

36. Ibid.

37. Ibid.

38. *Selections from Gandhi,* p. 162. "I do believe that, when there is only a choice between cowardice and violence, I would advise violence. Thus when my eldest son asked me what he should have done, had he been present when I was almost fatally assaulted in 1908, whether he should have run away and seen me killed or whether he should have used his physical force, which he could and wanted to use, and defend me. I told him that it was his duty to defend me even by using violence" (*Young India* 2 [August 11, 1920]: 3). Gandhi gave other examples: If one man with a sword fights a bunch of bandits he is "fighting nonviolently." Also a woman's "primary duty is self protection. She is at liberty to employ every method or means that come to her mind in order to defend her honour. God has given her nails and teeth. She must use them with all her strength and, if need be, die in the effort" (*Harijan* 9 [March 1, 1942]: 60).

39. Terrance Irwin, *Plato's Ethics* (New York: Oxford University Press, 1995), p. 39.

40. Ibid., p. 88.

41. Aristotle, *Nicomachean Ethics* 1104b12–13; 1099a18.19 (Irwin's trans.).

42. Kekes, *Moral Wisdom and Good Lives*; Nussbaum, "Non-Relative Virtue."

43. Aristotle, *Nicomachean Ethics* 1175b5–7.

44. Robert C. Solomon, *The Passions* (Garden City, N.Y.: Doubleday Anchor, 1977), pp. 335–337.

45. Gandhi, *An Autobiography,* III.8; see also Pyarelal, *The Last Phase,* vol. 1, p. 604; 2nd ed., vol. 1, bk.2, p. 242.

46. Gandhi, *Selected Works*, vol. 5, p. 486.

47. *Mettā Sutta* in *Suttanipāta*, cited in Gomez, "Violence and the Self in Early Buddhism," p. 40. Gomez's comments on this passage are instructive: "This passage is more subtle than it may seem. It offers no motivation for compassion beyond compassion itself, nor any goal besides the happiness of living beings."

Chapter 10. The Saints of Nonviolence: Buddha, Christ, Gandhi, King

1. Quoted in Lester H. Hunt, "Generosity and the Diversity of the Virtues," in *The Virtues: Contemporary Essays on Moral Character*, ed. R. B. Kruschwitz and Robert C. Roberts (Belmont, Calif.: Wadsworth, 1987), p. 225.

2. Phyllis McGinley, *Saint Watching* (New York: Viking Press, 1969), p. 19.

3. Orwell, "Reflections on Gandhi," pp. 479, 481.

4. Jean Varenne, *Yoga and the Hindu Tradition* (Delhi, 1989), p. 10; cited in Sondhi, *Modernity, Morality, and Tradition*, p. 77.

5. Sondhi, *Modernity, Morality, and Tradition*, p. 77.

6. Robert Neville, *Solider, Sage, Saint* (New York: Fordham University Press, 1987), p. 89.

7. Christopher Hitchens, *The Missionary Position: Mother Theresa in Theory and Practice* (New York: Verso, 1995).

8. Porter, *The Recovery of Virtue*, p. 108.

9. Susan Wolf, "Moral Saints," *Journal of Philosophy* 79, no. 8 (August 1982): 419–439; excerpted in Sommers and Sommers, p. 445.

10. Ibid., p. 449.

11. John Stuart Mill, *Utilitarianism*, chap. 3, p. 41.

12. Scriven, *Primary Philosophy*, pp. 238–258.

13. Robert M. Adams, "Saints," *Journal of Philosophy* (July 1984): 392–401; excerpted in Sommers and Sommers, p. 469.

14. Wolf, "Moral Saints," p. 453.

15. Ibid., p. 459.

16. Adams, "Saints," p. 472.

17. Aquinas, *Summa Theologica* II–II. 139.1.1.

18. Robert Neville, *Solider, Sage, Saint*, p. 71.

19. Ibid., p. 117.

20. Ibid., p. 83.

21. Ames and Rosemont, *The Analects*, p. 57.

22. This paragraph is a summary of D. C. Lau's account in *Mencius* (Harmondsworth: Penguin Books, 1970), pp. 24–25.

23. *Daodejing*, chap. 50 (LaFargue trans.).

24. *Daodejing*, chap. 59 (Ellen Chen trans.).

25. *Spiritual Titanism*, chap. 9; for the principal Mencius passage, see pp. 184–89.

26. *Mencius* 7b25 (Lau trans.).

27. *Mencius* 2a2 (Lau trans.).

28. Lee Yearly, *Mencius and Aquinas*, chap. 4.

29. Confucius, *The Analects* 7.23.
30. Wolf, "Moral Saints," p. 449.
31. Adams, "Saints," p. 469.
32. See Gier, *Spiritual Titanism*, pp. 161–164.
33. Gandhi, *Self-Restraint vs. Self-Indulgence* (Ahmedabad, 1958), p. 56. In this passage he grants this potential to every person: "I believe it to be possible for every human being to attain that blessed and indescribable sinless state in which he feels within himself the presence of God to the exclusion of everything else" (*Young India* 3 [November 17, 1921]: 367).
34. Pyarelal, *The Last Phase*, vol. 1, p. 588; 2nd edition, vol. 1, bk. 2, p. 228.
35. "If out of by becoming an ideal mother to you, I shall thereby have rendered a unique service to womankind. Only by becoming a perfect Brahmachari can one truly serve the woman" (quoted in Pyarelal, 2nd ed., vol. 1, bk. 2, p. 217).
36. Aquinas, *Summa Theologica* I–II. 55.3.
37. James B. Robinson, ed. and trans., *The Buddha's Lions: The Lives of the Eighty-Four Siddhas* (Berkeley, Calif.: Dharma Publishing, 1979), p. 84.
38. Porter, "Virtue and Sin," p. 530.
39. Pyarelal, *The Last Phase*, vol. 1, p. 591; 2nd ed., vol. 1, bk. 2, p. 230.
40. Pyarelal, *The Last Phase*, vol. 1, pp. 582, 583; 2nd ed., vol. 1, bk. 2, pp. 224–225.
41. See Gier, "Three Types of Divine Power," *Process Studies* 20, no. 4 (winter 1991): 221–232.
42. Isaiah 45.7 in the Anchor Bible translation. Since "God is excluded from no place," Luther concludes that "then he is in the devil, too...Yes, and essentially" (*Luther's Works*, eds. Pelikan and Lehman, vol. 54 [St. Louis: Concordia, 1955–67], p. 32). In his *Lecture on Romans* Luther states that "it is true that God wills evil and sin" (ed. W. Pauk [Philadelphia: Westminster, 1961], p. 29).
43. Augustine, *The City of God*, xiv, 13.
44. "A certain person has not properly cultivated his body, behavior, thought, and intelligence; [he] is inferior and insignificant and his life is short and miserable; of such a person...even a trifling evil deed done leads him to hell. In the case of a person who has proper culture of the body, behavior, thought, and intelligence, who is superior and not insignificant, and who is endowed with long life, the consequences of a similar evil deed are to be experienced in this very life, and sometimes may not appear at all" (quoted in Kalupahana, *Buddhist Philosophy*, p. 48).
45. Charles Taylor, "What's Wrong with Negative Liberty?" in *Philosophy and the Human Sciences: Philosophical Papers*, vol. 2 (Cambridge: Cambridge University Press, 1985), p. 20. Mark Juergensmeyer defines the saint as a strong evaluator in the following statements: "For what makes a saint a saint is not just the honorable virtues he or she exhibits but the vision of a remarkably different way to live that the saint projects. The images of saintly figures are appealing precisely because they are not lists of moral rules or techniques for action; they are portrayals of persons" ("Shoring up the Saint," p. 48). The saint as embodying a distinctive "style of living" fits perfectly with the personal and narrative aspects of virtue theory, especially as it has been reenvisioned by MacIntyre.
46. *Chāndogya Upaniṣad* 3.17.6.
47. *Mark* 10.18.

48. Bellanwila Wimalaratana, "A Study of the Concept of the *Mahāpurisa* in Buddhist Literature and Iconography," University of Lancaster dissertation, 1980, p. 267.

49. Cited in P. S. Jaini, "On the *Sarvajñatva* of Mahāvīra and the Buddha," in *Buddhist Studies in Honour of I. B. Horner* (Dortrecht: Reidel, 1974), p. 79.

50. Wolf, "Moral Saints," p. 461. Wolf's italics have been deleted.

51. Daisaku Ikeda, *The Living Buddha,* p. 59.

52. Morton Smith, *The Secret Gospel* (New York: Harper & Row, 1973). For a good summary of the reception of this book, see Shawn Eyer, "The Strange Case of the Secret Gospel according to Mark," at www.globaltown.com/shawn/pubs/secmark.html.

53. Hugh J. Schonfield, *The Passover Plot* (London: Hutchison, 1965); Hoger Kersten and Elmar R. Gruber, *The Jesus Conspiracy: The Turin Shroud and the Truth about the Resurrection* (Shaftesbury, Dorset: Element Books, 1992).

Glossary of Foreign Terms

Note: For transliterating Chinese terms the Pin Yin system is used.

Advaita Vedānta. A school of Vedāntist philosophy founded by Śaṅkara, an eighth-century philosopher who believed that Brahman and Ātman were completely identical and constituted the only true reality. In this book this position is also called "absolute monism" or "nondualism" (the literal meaning of *advaita*).

Aretē. Greek for "virtue" in the broad sense of a thing's potential to function properly. Comparable to the Chinese *de.*

Ahiṃsā. Sanskrit for "noninjury," usually implying noninjury in thought, speech, and action.

Akratēs. Greek for "no will," identifying the person who does not have sufficient will power to overcome temptation.

Anatman. Sanskrit for "no self." For Pali Buddhists this meant a rejection of any soul substance *(ātman)* but not the self *(jīva)* that comes about because of the functions of the five *skandhas* (see below).

Anekāntavāda. Sanskrit for "way of many sides." This is the Jain theory that knowledge is always relative to the individual knower and it therefore can never be absolute.

Ātman. Sanskrit for the eternal, unchanging soul substance that for most Vedāntist philosophers is identical with Brahman, the very substance (or Godhead) of the universe itself.

Avidyā. Sanskrit for "ignorance," which for all Indian religions is the basic reason why most beings remain trapped in the cycles of death and rebirth.

Brahmacharya. Sanskrit for the basic vow of chastity taken by Indian ascetics, who then become *brahmacharis.* Gandhi broadens this vow to encompass self-restraint in all areas of human activity.

Brahman. Sanskrit for the fundamental substance of the universe, which, according to the Upaniṣads, is found in the *ātman* of all things.

Cetanā. Nearest Sanskrit equivalent to the English "will," but it is not separate from either the mind or the emotions.

Dāna. Sanskrit for the moral virtue of benevolence, sometimes more specific as the giving of alms.

Dao. Chinese for the moral way in Confucianism but nature's way in Daoism.

De. Chinese for a thing's special function or power. Morally it means "virtue" or "charisma."

Dharma. Sanskrit for "moral law," but its metaphysical meaning is "true reality." Gandhi's translators usually translate *dharma* in his texts as "religion."

Enkratēs. Greek for "having the will" to overcome temptation.

Ethos. Greek for general customs that through the context-specific use of *phronēsis* constitute the particular character *(ēthos)* of any person. The Chinese equivalent is *li.*

Eudaimonia. Greek for "having a good spirit." Usually translated as "happiness," but more accurately it is "personal well-being" or "contentment."

Hundun. Chinese for the amorphous being that some Daoists believe represents the epitome of *wu wei* (see below).

Jīva. Sanskrit for "empirical self" as opposed to the Vedāntist view that *ātman* is the real self. Pali Buddhists accept *jīva* as the only self. Jains use *jīva* as an equivalent for *ātman,* but it is an individual substantial self that is not part of a greater cosmic self such as Brahman.

Junzi. Chinese for the perfected person, viewed as even more excellent than the person of *ren** (see below).

Li. Chinese for "social customs" or the "proper acts," hence "propriety" as the best English translation.

Logos. Greek for "cosmic order" or more specifically as the logic of both things and thought. Equivalent to Chinese *dao* and Sanskrit dharma.

Māyā. Sanskrit for Brahman's uncanny power. Means "illusion" only for followers of Advaita Vedānta (see above).

Nous. Greek for "reason," from which both practical *(phronēsis)* and theoretical *(sophia)* reason originates.

Qi. Chinese for the basic energy of the universe.

Phronēsis. Greek for Aristotle's concept of practical reason.

Poēsis. Greek for Aristotle's concept of productive knowledge.

Polis. Greek for the "city-state," the basic political unit in ancient Greece.

Prohairesis. Greek for Aristotle's concept of moral choice.

Prakṛti. Sanskrit for the material principle in Sāṃkhya-Yoga philosophy.

Prudentia. Latin for Aquinas's translation of Aristotle's *phronēsis.* Also can mean the virtue of prudence as separate from the faculty of practical reason.

Puruṣa. Sanskrit for "pure individual souls" in Sāṃkhya-Yoga philosophy.

Ren*. Chinese for the highest Confucian virtue, variously translated as "humanity," "humaneness," "human heartedness," "love," and "benevolence." The asterisk is used to distinguish the virtue from the homophonic character that means "human being."

Ru. Chinese for the group of scholars we call Confucians.

Sallekhanā. Sanskrit for the Jain idea of spiritual suicide.

Satyāgraha. Sanskrit for Gandhi's unique idea of "soul force." A *satyāgrahi* is one who practices *satyāgraha.*

Śakti. Sanskrit for feminine cosmic energy, the power of the Hindu Goddess.

Shen. Chinese for "human life" or "divine beings."

Sinngebung. German for the meaning that the cultural-historical world gives to every individual.

Skandhas. Sanskrit for the five constituents of the Buddhist self: body, feeling, perception, disposition, and awareness.

Sōphrōn. Greek for Aristotle's ideal of the person who lives in the mean without any effort. *Wu wei* might be seen as the Chinese equivalent.

Śūnyatā. Sanskrit for Buddhist idea of all things being empty of substance.

Tapasā. Sanskrit for self-suffering of the yogi or Gandhi's *satyagrāhis*.

Technē. Greek for Aristotle's concept of craft knowledge.

Tejas. Sanskrit for male power as a zero-sum game. Contrasts with *śakti* the power that the Hindu Goddess shares with all things.

Theōria. Greek for Aristotle's concept of theoretical knowledge.

Tīrthaṇkara. Sanskrit for the liberated saints of Jainism.

Übermensch. German for Friedrich Nietzsche's concept of the ideal person.

Vedānta. Sanskrit for the Hindu philosophy that is drawn from the Upaniṣadic teachings of Ātman and Brahman.

Vīrya. Sanskrit for "male potency."

Wu wei. Chinese for "no action," but more accurately it means spontaneous action or action in accord with nature.

Xin. Chinese for the Confucian idea of heart-mind.

Zhi. Chinese for the Confucian concept of moral wisdom.

Selected Bibliography

Adams, Robert M. "Saints." *Journal of Philosophy* (July, 1984): 392–401. Excerpted in ed. Christina Sommers and Fred Sommers, 463–74. *Vice and Virtue in Everyday Life*, San Diego: Harcourt Brace Jovanovich, 1989.

Allen, Douglas. "Gandhi's Philosophy: The Struggle over Many Contradictory Philosophies." *Social Theory and Practice* 19, no. 3 (fall 1993): 289–313.

———, ed. *Culture and Self: Philosophical and Religious Perspectives, East and West*. Boulder, Colo. Westview Press, 1997.

Annas, Julia. *The Morality of Happiness*. New York: Oxford University Press, 1993.

Bahm, A. J. *The Philosophy of the Buddha*. New York: Capricorn Books, 1958.

Baier, Annette. "Trust and Anti-Trust." *Ethics* 96 (January 1986): 231–260.

Bayles, Marie B. "The Buddha and the Mahatma." *Gandhi Marg* 6, no. 2 (April 1962): 122–133.

Bedekar, D. K. *Towards Understanding Gandhi*. Ed. R. Gawande. Bombay: Popular Prakashan, 1975.

Bellantoni, Lisa. *Moral Progress: A Process Critique of MacIntyre*. Albany, N.Y.: State University of New York Press, 2000.

Bhargava, N. D. "Some Chief Characteristics of the Jain Concept of Nonviolence." In *The Contribution of Jainism to Indian Culture,* ed. R. C. Divivedi. Delhi: Motilal Banarsidass, 1975, pp. 122–125.

Bondurant, Joan V. *The Conquest of Violence*. New rev. ed. Princeton: Princeton University Press, 1988.

Bose, Nirmal Kumar, ed. *Selections from Gandhi*. 2nd ed. Ahmedabad: Navajivan, 1957.

Chapple, Christopher Key. *Nonviolence to Animals, Earth, and Self in Asian Traditions*. Albany, N.Y.: State University of New York Press, 1993.

Chatterjee, Margaret. *Gandhi's Religious Thought*. Notre Dame, Ind.: Notre Dame University Press, 1983.

Chouduri, Manmohan. *Exploring Gandhi*. New Delhi: Gandhi Peace Foundation, 1989.

Davis, Grady Scott. *Warcraft and the Fragility of Virtue*. Moscow, Idaho: University of Idaho Press, 1992.

Desai, Maganbhai P. "Ends and Means in Politics." *Gandhi Marg* 1, no. 2 (April 1957): 153–157; reprinted in *Facets of Mahātma Gandhi: Ethics, Religion, and*

Culture, ed. S. Mukherjee and S. Ramaswamy, vol. 4 (New Delhi: Deep & Deep, 1996), pp. 26–30.

Eaton, Marcia, *Aesthetics and the Good Life*. Cranbury, N.J.: Farleigh Dickinson University Press, 1989.

Fox, Richard. *Gandhian Utopia: Experiments with Culture*. Boston: Beacon Press, 1989.

Gandhi, Madan. *Gandhian Aesthetics*. Chandigarh: Vikas Bharati, 1969.

———. "Metaphysical Basis for Gandhism." In *New Dimensions and Perspectives in Gandhism*, ed. P. T. Patil, pp. 191–213. New Delhi: Inter-India Publications, 1989.

Gandhi, Mohandas K. *An Autobiography or The Story of My Experiment with Truth* (Ahmedabad: Navajivan, 1927).

———. *Young India*. 11 vols. New York: Viking Press, 1927.

———. *From Yeravda Mandir*. Ahmedabad: Navajivan, 1933.

———. *Harijan*. Ed. M. H. Desai. 25 vols. New York: Garland Publishing Co., 1933–1956.

———. *Non-Violence in Peace and War*. 2 vols. Ahmedabad: Navajivan, 1942.

———. *Truth is God*. Ed. R. K. Prabhu. Ahmedabad: Navajivan, 1955.

———. *The Collected Works of Mahātma Gandhi*. 100 vols. New Delhi: Government of India Publications, 1959.

———. *The Essence of Hinduism*. Ahmedabad: Navajivan, 1987.

———. *Hind Swaraj and Other Writings*. Ed. Anthony Parel. New Delhi: Foundation Books, 1997.

Garfield, Jay L. *Empty Words: Buddhist Philosophy and Cross-Cultural Interpretation*. New York: Oxford University Press, 2002.

Gier, Nicholas F. "Gandhi, *Ahimsa*, and the Self." *Gandhi Marg* 15, no. 1 (April–June 1993): 24–38. Reprinted in Mukherjee and Ramaswamy, *Facets of Mahātma Gandhi*, vol. 4, pp. 108–125.

———. "The Virtue of Non-Violence: A Buddhist Perspective." *Seikyo Times*, February, 1994, pp. 28–36: reprinted in *Living Buddhism* 6, no. 1 (January 2002): 18–30.

———. "*Ahimsa*, the Self, and Postmodernism." *International Philosophical Quarterly* 35, no. 1 (March 1995): 71–86.

———. "Gandhi and Mahayana Buddhism" (in Japanese). *Journal of Oriental Studies* 35, no. 2 (1996): 84–105.

———. "Gandhi: Premodern, Modern, or Postmodern?" *Gandhi Marg* 17, no. 3 (October–December 1996): 261–281.

———. "Gandhi, the Buddha, and Ātman: A Response to Roy." *Gandhi Marg* 21, no. 4 (January–March 2000): 447–459.

———. *Spiritual Titanism: Indian, Chinese, and Western Perspectives*. Albany, N.Y.: State University of New York Press, 2000.

———. "Confucius, Gandhi, and the Aesthetics of Virtue." *Asian Philosophy* 11, no. 1 (March 2001): 41–54.

———. "The Dancing Ru: A Confucian Aesthetics of Virtue." *Philosophy East & West* 51, no. 2 (April 2001): 280–305.

———. "Gandhi and the Virtue of Non-Violence." *Gandhi Marg* 23, no. 3 (October–December 2001): 261–284.

———. "The Virtues of Asian Humanism." *Journal of Oriental Studies* 12 (October 2002): 14–28.

Gomez, Luis O. "Nonviolence and the Self in Early Buddhism." *Inner Peace, World Peace*, ed. Kenneth Kraft, pp. 31–48.

Harvey, Peter. "The Mind-Body Relationship in Pāli Buddhism: A Philosophical Investigation." *Asian Philosophy* 3, no. 1 (1993): 29–41.

Hawley, John S., ed. *Saints and Virtues*. Berkeley, Calif. University of California Press, 1987.

Hay, Stephen N. "Jain Influences on Gandhi's Early Thought." In *Gandhi, India, and the World*, ed. S. Ray, pp. 14–23. Bombay: Nachiketa Publishers, 1970.

———. "Jain Goals and Disciplines in Gandhi's Pursuit of Swaraj." In *Rule, Protest, and Identity*, ed. Peter Robb and David Taylor, pp. 120–132. London: Curzon Press, 1978.

Haydon, Graham. *Values, Virtues, and Violence: Education and the Public Understanding of Morality.* Oxford: Blackwell, 1999.

Hick, John and Lamont C. Hempel, eds. *Gandhi's Significance for Today.* New York: St. Martin's Press, 1989.

Ikeda, Daisaku. *The Living Buddha: An Interpretative Biography.* Trans. Burton Watson. New York: Weatherhill, 1976.

Ivanhoe, Philip. J. "Character Consequentialism: An Early Confucian Contribution to Contemporary Ethical Theory." *Journal of Religious Ethics* 19, no. 1 (spring 1991): 55–70.

Iyer, Raghavan. *The Moral and Political Thought of Mahatma Gandhi.* Oxford: Oxford University Press, 1973.

———. *The Moral and Political Writings of Mahatma Gandhi.* 3 vols. Oxford: Oxford University Press, 1986.

———. "Gandhi on Civilization and Religion." In *Gandhi's Significance for Today,* pp. 122–136.

Jacobson, Nolan Pliny. *The Heart of Buddhist Philosophy.* Carbondale and Edwardsville, Ill. Southern Illinois University Press, 1988.

———. *Buddhism and the Contemporary World: Change and Self-Correction.* Carbondale and Edwardsville, Ill.: Southern Illinois University Press, 1989.

Jaini, P. S. *The Jaina Path of Purification.* New Delhi: Motilal Banarsidass, 1979.

Juergensmeyer, Mark. "Shoring up the Saint: Some Suggestions for Improving Satyagraha." In *Gandhi's Significance for Today,* pp. 36–50.

———. *Fighting Fair: A Non-Violent Strategy for Resolving Everyday Conflict.* New York: Harper & Row, 1985.

Kalelkar, K., ed. *Gandhi's Letters to Ashram Sisters.* Trans. A. L. Mazmudar. 2nd rev. ed. Ahmedabad: Navajivan, 1960.

Kalupahana, David J. *Buddhist Philosophy: A Historical Analysis*. Honolulu University of Hawaii Press, 1976.

———. *A History of Buddhist Philosophy: Continuities and Discontinuities*. Honolulu University of Hawaii Press, 1992.

———. *Ethics in Early Buddhism*. Honolulu University of Hawaii Press, 1995.

Kekes, John. *Moral Wisdom and Good Lives*. Ithaca, N.Y.: Cornell University Press, 1995.

Kelly, Jack. "Virtue and Pleasure." *Mind* 82 (1973): 401–408.

Keown, Damien. "Karma, Character, and Consequentialism." *Journal of Religious Ethics* 24, no. 2 (fall 1996): 329–350.

———. *The Nature of Buddhist Ethics*. New York: St. Martin's Press, 1992.

Khanna, Suman. *Gandhi and the Good Life*. New Delhi: Gandhi Peace Foundation, 1985.

Kotturan, George. *Ahiṃsā: Gautama to Gandhi*. New Delhi: Sterling Publishers, 1973.

Kraft, Kenneth, ed. *Inner Peace, World Peace: Essays on Buddhism and Nonviolence*. Albany, N.Y.: State University of New York Press, 1992.

MacIntyre, Alasdair. *After Virtue*. 2nd ed. Notre Dame, Ind. Notre Dame University Press, 1984.

McKinnon, Christine. *Character, Virtue Theories, and the Vices*. Peterborough, Ontario: Broadview Press, 1999.

Meilaender, George. *The Theory and Practice of Virtue*. Notre Dame, Ind.: Notre Dame University Press, 1984.

Mukherjee, S. and S. Ramaswamy, eds. *Facets of Mahatma Gandhi*. 4 vols. New Delhi: Deep & Deep, 1994.

Nelson, Lance E. "Reverence for Nature or the Irrelevance of Nature? Advaita Vedānta and Ecological Concern." *Journal of Dharma* 16, no.3 (July–Sept. 1991): 282–301.

Nussbaum, Martha. "Non-Relative Virtues." In *Midwest Studies in Philosophy*. vol. 13, pp. 32–53. (Notre Dame, Ind.: Notre Dame University Press, 1988).

Orwell, George, "Reflections on Gandhi." In *Vice and Virtue in Everyday Life*, ed. Christina Sommers and Fred Sommers, pp. 475–484.

Parekh, Bhikhu. *Gandhi's Political Philosophy*. London: Macmillan, 1989.

Parel, Anthony J. "Gandhi's Idea of Nation in *Hind Swaraj*." *Gandhi Marg* 13, no. 3 (October–December 1991): 261–281.

Pathan, B. A. *The Gandhian Concept of Beauty*. New Delhi: Ajanta Books International, 1989.

Patil, V. T., ed. *New Dimensions and Perspectives in Gandhianism*. New Delhi: Inter-India Publications, 1988.

Pinto, Vivek. *Gandhi's Vision and Values*. New Delhi: Sage Publications, 1998.

Porter, Jean. *The Recovery of Virtue: The Relevance of Aquinas for Christian Ethics*. Louisville, Ky.: Westminster/John Knox Press, 1990.

———. "Virtue and Sin: The Connection of the Virtues and the Case of the Flawed Saint." *Journal of Religion* 75, no. 4 (October 1995): 521–539.

Pyarelal, Nair. *Mahatma Gandhi: The Last Phase.* 2nd ed. Ahmedabad: Navajivan, 1966.

Richards, Glyn. *The Philosophy of Gandhi: A Study of His Basic Ideas.* Totowa, N.J.: Curzon Press, 1982.

———. "Gandhi's Concept of Truth and the *Advaita* Tradition." *Religious Studies* 22, no. 1 (March 1986): 1–14.

Roberts, Robert C. "Will Power and the Virtues." *Philosophical Review* (April 1984): 227–247. Excerpted and extensively revised in *Vice and Virtue in Everyday Life,* ed. Christina Sommers and Fred Sommers, pp. 232–253.

Roy, Ramashray. *Self and Society: A Study in Gandhian Thought.* New Delhi: Sage Publications, 1985.

———. *Understanding Gandhi.* New Delhi: Ajanta Publications, 1996.

———, ed. *Contemporary Crisis and Gandhi.* Delhi: Discovery Publishing House, 1986.

Rudolph, Lloyd L. "Contesting Civilizations." *Gandhi Marg* 13, no. 4 (January–March 1992): 419–431.

Rudolph, Susanne Hoeber, and Lloyd L. Rudolph. *The Modernity of Tradition: Political Development in India.* Chicago: University of Chicago Press, 1967, 1983.

———. *Gandhi: Traditional Roots of Charisma.* Part 2 of *The Modernity of Tradition.* Hyderabad: Orient Longman, 1987.

Saxena, Sushil Kumar. *Ever unto God: Essays on Gandhi and Religion.* New Delhi: Indian Council of Philosophical Research, 1988.

Sherman, Nancy. *The Fabric of Character: Aristotle's Theory of Virtue.* Oxford: Oxford University Press, 1989.

Shier, Flint. "Hume and the Aesthetics of Agency." *Proceedings of the Aristotelian Society* 87 (1986–87): 121–135.

Singh, M. Kurti. *Philosophical Import of Gandhism.* Delhi: South Asia Publications, 1994.

Singh, Ramjee. *The Relevance of Gandhian Thought.* New Delhi: Classical Publishing Co., 1983.

———. "Gandhi and the Bodhisattva Ideal." In *New Dimensions and Perspectives in Gandhism*, ed. Patil, pp. 463–473.

Sinha, Shall, ed. *The Words of Wisdom of Mahatma Gandhi.* Edmonton, Alberta: SKS Publishers, 2002.

Slote, Michael. *From Morality to Virtue.* New York: Oxford University Press, 1992.

Smith, Steven A. "Gandhi's Moral Philosophy." In *Gandhi's Significance for Today,* pp. 109–121.

Sommers, Christina and Fred Sommers, eds. *Vice and Virtue in Everyday Life.* San Diego: Harcourt Brace Jovanovich, 1989.

Sondhi, Madhuri S. *Modernity, Morality, and the Mahatma.* New Delhi: Haranand Publications, 1997.

Tähtinen, Unto. *Ahiṃsā: Non-Violence in Indian Tradition.* London: Rider and Company, 1976.

———. "Values, Non-Violence and Ecology: Two Approaches." *Journal of Dharma* 16, no. 3 (July–September 1991): 211–217.

Terchek, Ronald J. "Gandhi and Moral Autonomy." *Gandhi Marg* 13, no. 4 (January–March 1992): 454–465.

———. *Gandhi: Struggling for Autonomy.* Totowa, N.J.: Rowman & Littlefield, 1998.

Verma, Surendra. *The Metaphysical Foundations of Gandhi's Thought.* New Delhi: Orient Longmans, 1970.

Wadhwa, Madhuri. *Gandhi Between Tradition and Modernity.* New Delhi: Deep & Deep, 1991.

Wallace, James D. "Ethics and the Craft Analogy." In *Midwest Studies in Philosophy,* vol. 13, pp. 223–232. Notre Dame, Ind.: Notre Dame University Press, 1988.

Wang, Huiyyun. '"Gandhi's Contesting Discourse." *Gandhi Marg* 17, no. 3 (October–December 1995): 261–285.

White, John D. "God and the World from the Viewpoint of Advaita Vedānta: A Critical Assessment." *International Philosophical Quarterly* 30, no. 2 (June 1981): 185–93.

Williams, Paul. *Mahayana Buddhism: Doctrinal Foundations.* London: Routledge, 1989.

Wolf, Susan. "Moral Saints." *Journal of Philosophy* 79, no. 8 (August 1982): 419–439. Excerpted from *Vice and Virtue in Everyday Life,* ed. Christina Sommers and Fred Sommers, pp. 444–61.

Yearly, Lee. *Mencius and Aquinas: Theories of Virtue and Conceptions of Courage.* Albany, N.Y.: State University of New York Press, 1990.

Yu, Jiyuan. "Virtue: Confucius and Aristotle." *Philosophy East and West* 48, no. 2 (April 1998): 323–347.

Note on Supporting Center

This series is published under the auspices of the Center for Process Studies, a research organization affiliated with the Claremont School of Theology and Claremont Graduate University. It was founded in 1973 by John B. Cobb, Jr., Founding Director, and David Ray Griffin, Executive Director; Marjorie Suchocki is now also a codirector. The center encourages research and reflection on the process philosophy of Alfred North Whitehead, Charles Hartshorne, and related thinkers, and on the application and testing of this viewpoint in all areas of thought and practice. The center sponsors conferences, welcomes visiting scholars to use its library, and publishes a scholarly journal, *Process Studies*, and a newsletter, *Process Perspectives*. Located at 1325 North College, Claremont, CA 91711, it gratefully accepts (tax-deductible) contributions to support its work.

Index

Adams, Robert 161, 162, 163, 166, 168
advaita 3, 5, 10, 14, 32, 33, 36, 39–40, 40, 43, 184, 205
ahiṃsā 1, 5, 28–36, 38, 40, 43, 45, 47, 113, 114, 121, 128, 134, 136, 138, 140, 143–150, 151, 157, 158, 175, 176, 177, 183, 184, 186, 198, 205
akrasia 123
akratēs 68, 123, 126, 176, 205
Analects 6, 69, 71, 73, 84, 87, 89, 90, 101, 102, 103, 105, 106, 109, 190
analogy 40, 41, 45, 46, 47, 87, 91, 94, 100, 111, 173, 197
  body 48,
  cell 25, 48, 50
  craft 95–97
  fine arts 97, 98
  holographic 49
  organic 25, 40, 58
  prism 49, 50
  revised prism 50
anarchism 14, 15–16
anatman (no-self) 61, 205
Anaxagoras 68
anekāntavāda 28, 32–33, 145, 183, 205
Aquinas, Thomas 75, 84, 96, 114, 118, 124, 129, 132, 134, 163, 165, 166, 168, 170, 172
aretē (virtue) 70, 74, 137, 164, 170, 205
Aristotle 4, 12, 14, 26, 36, 44, 45, 66–69, 70, 71, 73, 74, 77, 78, 82, 83, 85, 86, 88, 90, 116–119, 123–126, 129–135, 137, 142, 144–146, 150, 152–155, 160, 165–166, 168, 170, 176, 191, 197, 206, 207
Arjuna 36, 38
art 23, 67, 81, 84, 87, 88, 91, 92, 94, 98, 100, 109–112, 119, 153, 163, 167
  craft 81, 82, 86, 96, 97–98
  fine 81, 82, 86, 96, 97–98
  martial 119
  performance 94
Aryans 35
asceticism 4, 19, 56, 101, 110, 157
Aśoka 49
ātman 2, 20, 22, 33, 35, 39–41, 43–45, 49, 50, 57, 61–63, 74, 80, 86, 126–128, 131, 135, 169, 177, 183, 205, 206, 207
atomism 16, 30
  social 26, 48, 65, 87
Augustine 124, 125, 172
Aurobindo 47
autonomy 10, 14, 17, 19, 21, 22, 33, 39, 41, 42, 48, 49, 65, 83, 85, 88, 102, 128, 141, 162
  situated 182
avidyā 43
axiology 178

Baier, Annette 115, 141
beauty 27, 82, 86, 89, 90, 91, 96, 97, 100, 101, 138, 154, 162, 193
  moral 100–112
Bedekar, D. K. 33, 44, 47, 79, 80, 183
Bentham, Jeremy 25, 138, 141
Bergson, Henri xii, 6
Bhagavad-gītā 29, 31, 36–38, 45, 54, 61
Bodhisattva 52, 58–60
Bondurant, Joan 16, 61
Buddha 3, 9, 19, 21, 22, 25, 27, 31, 32, 39, 49, 51–65, 66, 67, 69, 73–77, 109, 117, 118, 126, 129, 134, 136, 138, 140, 141, 155, 156, 157, 159, 161, 166, 168, 169, 174–176, 178, 179, 186, 189
Buddhism 3, 5, 6, 22, 30, 31, 38, 46, 50, 52–65, 67, 72, 78, 101, 102, 109, 137, 178, 179, 187
  Japanese 109
  Mahāyāna 51, 53, 56, 59, 61, 78, 86, 138, 188
  Nichiren 60
  Pāli 59, 64, 65, 78
  Theravadin 56, 59
  Zen 59, 63
Brahman 9, 19, 36, 37, 40, 41, 43, 49, 169, 174, 205, 206, 207
brahmacharya 5, 11, 58, 108, 126–130, 133, 147, 149, 154, 169, 171, 205
  brahmachāri 7, 108, 121, 170
bravery 93, 109, 133, 136, 145
Buber, Martin 39,

Cartesian 2, 11, 16, 61, 85
caste 48, 128, 161
  caste system 10, 20, 25, 40, 48, 50, 55, 105
categorical imperative 53
cetana 77–78

character 26, 70, 71, 74, 83, 89, 95, 96, 100, 103, 111, 113, 115, 118, 123, 131, 138, 139–140, 143, 144, 146, 163
  consequentialism 4, 7, 24, 94, 137–143, 145, 151, 173
chastity (*brahmacharya*) 10, 26, 120, 129, 131, 132, 144, 205
Chatterjee, Margaret 39, 43, 51, 58
cheng (sincerity) 105, 110
Christ 51, 60, 82, 86, 156, 157, 161, 174–176
Christianity, Christian 5, 6, 10, 44, 50, 54, 60, 61, 81, 82, 86, 115, 123, 124, 125, 127, 134, 135, 161, 162, 164, 168, 175, 176
  ethics 76, 115, 117, 125, 126, 160
  humanism 65
  philosophy 124
  theology 9, 21, 50
  virtues 86, 134
civil disobedience 14
Cobb, John B. 86
Collingwood, R. D. 82, 94, 95
communitarianism 24
compassion 3, 26, 31, 32, 34, 41, 45, 49, 52, 53, 58, 60, 74, 83, 84, 94, 114, 133, 140, 145, 146, 147, 148, 149, 150, 151, 159, 171, 177, 183, 197, 202
conscience 5, 6, 13, 44, 47, 148, 178
consequentialism 32, 136, 137, 138, 160, 173
  character 4, 7, 24, 94, 137–144, 145, 151, 173
  spiritual 138
contextual pragmatism 7, 44, 69, 127, 140, 144, 145, 173
Confucianism 3, 5, 6, 21, 22, 63, 64, 65, 84, 89, 95, 102, 112, 137, 205
Confucius 9, 25, 27, 39, 49, 66, 67, 69, 70, 71, 72, 73, 74, 76, 78, 79, 84–90, 93, 95, 97, 98, 100–109, 110, 111, 116, 117, 123, 126, 129, 131, 134, 141, 166, 178, 193
cosmology 9, 17, 21, 27, 172
courage 7, 26, 53, 60, 64, 70, 71, 73, 77, 94, 104, 107, 109, 111, 114, 119, 121, 122, 128, 129, 130, 133, 134, 137, 138, 140, 146, 147, 149, 150, 151, 159, 163, 164, 165, 166, 168, 169, 171
cowardice 116, 120, 136, 137, 145, 201
craving 21, 32, 38, 56, 65, 77, 78, 79, 118, 140, 169

daimon 5, 33, 178
Dalai Lama 32, 51, 159, 161, 166
Dao 70, 73, 91, 95, 164, 165, 172, 205, 206
Daodejing 119, 165, 170
Daoism 89, 95, 112, 205
Daoist immortals 167, 170, 173
de 74, 75, 95, 103, 105, 106, 107, 118, 121, 122, 134, 157, 159, 162, 164–170, 175, 194–195, 205
Derrida, Jacques xii, 20, 25, 179, 180, 182
determinism 20, 64
  soft 64
Devī 41, 122
Devil 5, 10, 125, 203
dharma 11, 12, 13, 18, 27, 35, 36, 38, 44, 56, 67, 73–76, 122, 130, 137, 146, 163, 166, 170, 174
Dharmakāya 32, 45, 56, 65, 67
divine immutability 56, 175
divine impassivity 197
Doctrine of Double Effect 118
Doniger, Wendy 4, 35
dualism 27, 35, 40, 50, 104, 184
  Cartesian 2, 11
dvaita 32, 43, 184

education 11, 12, 49, 131,133, 134, 154
egalitarianism 25, 30, 49
eight-fold path 63, 67, 74, 76, 77
enkratēs 68, 123, 124, 125, 128, 136, 175, 176
Epictetus 85
Epicurus 152
epistemology 32
ethics 2–5, 8, 12, 13, 22, 23, 25, 27, 30, 35, 36, 38, 44, 50, 54, 56, 67, 71, 76, 80, 88, 98, 99, 101, 105, 106, 108, 115, 118, 131, 133, 134, 136, 142, 146, 159, 162, 163, 167, 186, 187, 189, 197
  Buddhist 27, 52, 74, 77, 78, 79, 99, 149, 173
  Confucian 73, 74, 78, 83, 99, 102
  Christian 76, 78, 129, 162
  Greco-Roman 72, 77, 82, 85, 119
  rule 2, 4, 26, 54, 70, 76, 99, 116–117, 118, 128, 129, 141, 142, 147
  theological 197
  virtue 3, 4, 25, 26, 27, 67, 70, 72, 74, 75, 81, 82, 84, 86, 95, 96, 98, 99, 102, 106, 115, 118, 124, 128, 129, 139, 142, 144, 146, 151, 154, 155, 161, 162, 167, 168, 170, 197
eudaimonsim 36, 67, 157
  Buddhist 56, 73, 150
  nonegoistic 137, 139
euthanasia 53, 54
evil xv, 6, 11, 14, 19, 61, 81, 84, 91, 94, 96, 103, 104, 111, 112, 117, 118, 124, 125, 129, 140, 148, 161, 170, 172, 173, 175, 203

fast, fasting 2, 31, 53, 58, 91, 112, 132, 199
  fast-death (*sallekhanā*) 31, 32, 53, 206
fearlessness 26, 61, 109, 130, 133, 134, 136, 137
feminism xiii, 4, 141
filial piety 26, 104
Foot, Philippa 26
fortitude 119, 146, 147
Foucault, Michel xii, 71, 72, 82, 83, 85, 71, 119

freedom 19, 22, 34, 39, 42, 53, 56, 63–64, 71, 72, 83, 119, 125, 131, 139, 161, 195
  moral 63, 137, 150
free will 64, 172

Gadamer, Hans Georg 6
Galston, William 26
Gandhi, Mohandas K.
  beauty 109–112
  Bhagavad-gītā 34, 37–38, 43, 45, 54
  brahmacharya 5, 108, 129, 144, 149, 169, 205
  Buddhism 3, 22, 32, 35, 38, 44, 47, 50, 110, 117, 126, 129, 131, 137, 141, 146, 148, 181, 187
  character 113, 138
  Christian ethics 103, 127, 126, 134, 135
  Confucius 49, 69, 82, 99, 100–109, 111, 115, 126, 129, 133, 134
  constructive postmodernism 3, 23, 24, 27
  contextual pragmatism 69, 133, 140
  dualism 37, 104
  eudaimonism 56, 137, 155
  fasting 2, 61, 104, 129
  God 1, 12, 22, 56, 60, 105, 110, 112, 114, 181, 189, 203
  Goddess 122–123
  Hinduism 28, 33, 54, 55, 118
  humanism 52, 63–65
  human nature 34, 125, 181, 186
  individualism 12, 22, 25, 39, 42, 47, 65
  Jainism 28, 31–34, 51, 54, 59, 183
  King, M. L. 106, 157, 159, 163, 171, 172, 173, 176
  Manicheanism 10, 37
  mindfulness 3, 51–65
  morality 1, 26, 104
  nirvāṇa 56
  nonviolence 1, 3, 34, 38, 40, 43, 47, 53, 62, 80, 134, 135, 136, 141, 148, 149, 158, 165, 183, 201
  organic holism 42, 47
  pantheism 40, 43, 46
  personal theism 41, 56
  political philosophy 1, 2, 13, 16, 18, 41, 42, 65, 102, 105, 163, 167, 180
  postmodernism 8–27
  prayer 13, 52, 56–57, 110, 187
  Raichandcharya 33
  religion 13
  Ruskin 2, 8
  as saint 156, 157, 159, 161, 163–164, 168, 169, 173, 176
  science 17
  self 39, 41, 42–50, 56–57, 80, 104, 139, 181, 187, 189
  self-suffering 57–61, 102, 121
  Socrates 5, 18, 47, 11, 178
  Tantrism 108
  Thoreau 18, 180
  Tolstoy 18
  truth 1, 13, 35, 56, 66, 79, 100, 110, 111, 127, 144, 148, 149, 158, 183
  untouchables 2, 179
  utilitarianism 74, 110, 136, 138, 140
  Vedānta 3, 10, 12, 20, 33, 39–50, 59, 104, 126, 127, 169, 183, 184
  virility 118–123
  virtue 3, 26, 34, 41, 109, 114, 115, 116, 121, 126–135, 143, 147
  virtue aesthetics 100, 109–112
  vows 114, 123–131, 132, 147
Gandhi, Manubehn 5, 7, 108, 121, 129, 158, 169–170, 171, 172, 173
generosity (*dana*) 58, 78, 93, 105, 202
Gilligan, Carol 141
God xii, 1, 5, 6, 9, 10, 12, 21, 22, 23, 28, 32, 34, 36, 37, 40, 41, 43, 45, 48, 55, 56, 57, 58, 60, 71, 76, 105, 110, 112, 114, 115, 120, 123–127, 129, 133, 141, 148, 157, 161, 162, 172, 174, 175, 176, 181, 184, 189, 195, 197, 201, 203
Goddess 35, 59, 121–122, 175, 207
Griffin, David Ray xi–xv, 182

Hanh, Thich Nhat 63
happiness (*eudaimonia*) xiv, 4, 36, 56, 83, 93, 124, 136, 137, 138, 151–155, 160, 162, 168, 202, 206
Hartshorne, Charles xii, 6, 13
heart-mind (*xin*) 26, 73, 84, 93, 123, 153, 155, 165, 168, 207
heaven (*tian*) 21, 60, 90, 91, 102, 103–104, 105, 109, 110, 115, 133, 165, 166, 169, 172
Hebrew,
  religion 22
  self 62, 169
hedonism 142
  ethical 137, 154, 160
  hedonic calculus 7, 116, 142, 167, 137, 139, 141
Heidegger, Martin xii, 39
Hell 52, 152, 203
Hinduism 2, 3, 4, 5, 10, 12, 13, 18, 20, 21, 28, 30, 33, 34, 35, 36, 43, 51, 54, 55, 56, 57, 63, 64, 86, 107, 108, 110, 118, 120, 121, 122, 124, 126, 127, 129, 131, 159, 172, 183, 184, 207
Hind Swaraj 7, 14, 15, 17, 18, 25, 26, 132, 180
humanism 17, 56, 64
  Buddhist 52, 63–65
  Christian 65
  Chinese 63, 91
  European 63–64
Hume, David 61, 62, 64, 74, 97, 141, 157, 189
humility 114, 130, 132, 134, 135, 159, 161, 162, 168

individualism xiii, 5, 12, 22, 23, 41, 42, 51, 65
individuation 12, 46, 62

integrity 7, 12, 14, 21, 25, 30, 37, 50, 62, 65, 85, 86, 101, 128, 133, 139, 140, 143, 159, 173
Iyer, Raghavan 3, 5, 7, 51, 133
Islam 33

Jainism 3, 5, 12, 19, 21, 28–34, 36, 38, 45, 51, 52, 53, 54, 56, 59, 61, 64, 74, 80, 145, 151, 157, 174, 175, 183, 205, 206, 207
Jaini, P. S. 33
James, William xii, 67, 13, 62
Jesus 51, 158, 160, 168, 174, 176
jīva 3, 30, 32, 33, 45, 53, 62, 74, 86, 131, 135, 169, 205, 206
joy 83, 90, 112, 137, 150, 151–155, 166
Juergensmeyer, Mark 2
junzi 69, 70, 71, 81, 85, 87, 89, 90, 106, 107, 173, 206
justice xii, 3, 26, 41, 45, 71, 103, 110, 116, 117, 119, 146, 147, 148, 151, 171, 175, 181, 197

Kant 2, 4, 7, 13, 22, 26, 27, 87, 88, 98, 115, 116, 124, 125, 127, 139, 141, 150, 156, 159, 161, 162, 167, 178, 181
karma 10 12, 31, 38, 40, 44, 58, 105, 179
karuṇā (compassion) 53, 74
King, Martin Luther 106, 151, 156, 157, 159, 163, 170, 171, 172, 173, 176
kingdom of ends 87, 98, 141
Kohlberg, Laurence 141
Kṛṣṇa 36, 37, 38, 174

Laozi 95
law 12, 15, 48, 56, 58, 69, 70, 71, 74, 88, 98, 102, 104, 105, 117, 124, 152, 161, 186, 190
  of contradiction 70
  divine 114,
  of excluded middle 77
  moral 114, 115, 116, 118, 125, 206
  physical, 39, 48, 197
li 66, 70, 71, 72, 84, 87, 89, 90, 91, 92, 98, 99, 103, 105, 206
liberalism
  classical 26, 48
logos 11, 23, 82, 86, 92, 206
Lotus Sūtra 78, 79
love 8, 31, 32, 34, 37, 41, 45, 51, 53, 60, 61, 68, 71, 102, 103, 107, 113, 114, 128, 133, 134, 140, 141, 143, 145, 146, 148, 151, 153, 156, 157, 158, 160, 163, 164, 175, 176, 186, 197, 198, 206
  Christian 134
  filial 84
  graded 103, 104
  self-love 83, 85
lying 78

MacIntyre, Alaisdair 4, 25, 190, 203
Mahābhārata, 36
mahātma 52, 58, 157, 168–169
Mahāvīra 28, 29, 175
maitri (friendliness), 53
Manicheanism 6, 10, 11, 29, 37, 104
Maritain, Jacques 42
Marx, Karl 39, 46
matter 28, 32, 44, 45, 53, 54
māyā 39, 40, 43, 185, 206
Mead, George Herbert 22, 39
means/ends 24–25, 27, 33–34, 69, 97, 133, 136, 137, 138, 142–149, 154, 160, 178, 183
Mencius 71, 72, 73, 84, 89, 90, 91, 92, 104, 106, 109, 112, 119, 165, 166, 190
Merleau-Ponty, Maurice 21, 22, 39, 72
metaphysics xii, 13, 21, 41, 44, 63, 64, 65, 79, 118, 122, 181
Middle Way 4, 5, 38, 55, 56, 62, 73–77, 117, 127, 129
Mill, John Stuart 27, 64, 115, 138, 142, 160
mindfulness 7, 58, 75, 77, 78, 119, 138, 148, 151
modernism xi–xv, 8, 10, 11, 13, 14, 17–18, 21, 24, 26
Mother Theresa 158
monism 30, 40, 41, 43, 50, 65
  absolute 41, 49, 182, 185, 205
  Vedāntist 21, 41, 65, 104, 126, 175
moral laws 4, 113, 116, 118, 119, 161, 166, 197
moral rules 26, 113, 114, 117, 119, 137, 152, 167, 203
Muslims 7
mysticism 41, 112
mythos 11, 23

Nāgārjuna 179
Neanderthals 114
Nehru, Jawaharlal 102, 112, 167
Neo-Vedanta 41
Neville, Robert 158, 159, 163, 164
Nichiren 57, 60, 65, 188
Nicomachean Ethics 83
Nietzsche, Friedrich 98, 160, 168
  Three Metamorphoses 107
  Thus Spake Zarathustra 107
nihilism 22, 24, 56, 61
nirvāṇa 56, 59, 74, 79, 179
nominalism 114
nondualism (*advaita*) 41, 50, 205
nonviolence (*ahiṃsā*) 1, 4, 10, 15, 16, 18, 24, 26, 29, 30–32, 34, 40, 43, 49, 50, 51, 54–55, 59–60, 62, 65, 80, 101, 106–107, 120, 121, 126, 129, 131, 133, 134, 141, 146, 157, 165, 167, 171, 176, 177, 187, 198
  absolute 29–31, 34
  pragmatic 51
  relative 34, 35, 38
  virtue of 52, 112, 123, 131, 136–155, 176
norms xii, 66, 70, 71, 98, 113, 147, 164
nous 66, 67, 68, 69, 88, 206
Nussbaum, Martha 113, 115, 116, 152, 168

objectivism 17
ethical 26
omnipotence 125
omniscience 175, 183
ontology 5, 30, 62, 95, 178
order 27, 49, 91, 105, 206
aesthetic 82, 86–89, 97, 193
rational 86–89, 198
organic holism 21, 41, 42, 43, 47, 48, 50, 62, 65, 74, 88
Orientalism 6
Orwell, George 126, 141, 156, 157, 159, 178

pain 35, 54, 60, 138, 145, 150, 151, 152, 154, 157, 173, 197
pantheism 33, 40, 42, 445, 46, 56
Parekh, Bhikhu 11, 15, 17, 40, 40–42
Partition 102, 162, 163, 167
passive nonresistance 140, 145, 146, 147, 149, 150
patience 53, 121, 129
penance 48, 55, 57, 58, 60, 104, 106, 121, 161, 170
phronēsis 66, 67–82, 86, 92, 93, 97, 118, 130, 132, 151, 167, 168, 190, 206
pleasure 4, 7, 83, 90, 124, 126, 137, 138, 142, 146, 147, 148, 150, 151–155, 199
poēsis (making) 82, 93, 96, 97, 206
political philosophy 8, 15, 17, 18, 41, 42, 101
postmodernism xi–xv, 8–27, 197
constructive xi–xv, 2, 3, 4, 6, 11, 13, 16, 18, 20, 21, 23, 24, 27
deconstructive xi–xv, 8, 22, 24, 27
Potter, Karl 19
pragmatism xii, 6, 21, 22
Buddhist 38, 76
contextual 7, 44, 69, 127, 140, 144, 145, 173
prajñā 74
praxis 82, 93, 96, 97, 191
prayer 13, 36, 52, 56, 57, 64, 110, 187
premodernism xii, xiv, 8–10, 21, 24, 27
pride (*megalopsychia*) 67, 83, 132, 134, 168, 172
process philosophy 6, 21, 22, 25, 45, 46, 76
propositions 118
analytic 118
synthetic 118
synthetic a priori 132
Protagoras 13
Protestantism 54
prudentia 75, 84, 118, 206
Purāṇas 36
puruṣa 30, 35, 36, 37, 45, 74, 169, 174, 206

Raichandcharya 29, 33, 183
Rāma 13, 36, 60, 105, 120, 127
Rāmānuja 25, 43, 45, 50
Rāmayāna 13
reason xii, xiv, 14, 16, 21, 23, 38, 41, 64, 68, 81–85, 88, 114, 118, 119, 124, 170, 178, 180, 197, 206
analytic 23, 86–92
practical (*phronēsis*) 2, 66, 67–82, 97, 114, 118, 130, 132, 134, 139, 144, 151, 161, 165, 168, 206
synthetic 23, 82, 86–92, 97, 193
reciprocity 30
reductionism 4, 16
relations 23, 24, 25, 28, 31, 33, 42, 43, 45, 48, 50, 55, 56, 62, 63, 73, 74, 84, 85, 93, 101, 102, 106, 107, 108, 113, 119, 133, 136, 137, 140, 141, 142, 148, 157
asymmetrical 149
external 30, 88, 149
internal 30, 62, 74, 88, 149
means/ends 142–144, 154
symmetrical 30, 149
relativism xii, 6, 12, 13, 24, 75, 152, 182
ren 62, 70, 72, 73, 79, 83, 84, 88, 90, 102, 106, 109, 134, 169, 190, 191, 206
Roman Catholicism 54
Rorty, Richard xii, 8
Roy, Ramashray 17, 42–49
Ruskin, John 2, 18, 19, 33

sage 63, 76, 90, 91, 95, 97, 99, 102, 104, 105, 106, 107, 112, 121, 133, 163, 165, 166, 169, 173
saint 19, 29, 31, 47, 97, 107, 122, 133, 156–176
charismatic 164–168
Śaivite 36
śakti 121, 123, 168, 169, 172
Salt March 149
Śaṇkara 9, 25, 36, 40, 41, 43, 44, 45, 46, 48, 49, 50, 59, 179, 184, 205
Śāntideva 32, 60
Sartre, Jean Paul 46
sarvōdaya 10, 28, 125
Satan 172, 175
satyā 2, 28, 32, 110
satyāgraha 2, 3, 16, 18, 129, 206
Schweitzer, Albert 51
science xii, xiii, 9, 10, 12, 16, 17, 67, 68, 100
self xii, xiv, 3, 4, 5, 6, 8, 9, 13, 14, 15, 20, 21, 22, 27, 30, 31, 32, 33, 35, 36, 37, 39, 43–45, 48–50, 53, 55, 56–57, 80, 82, 84–86, 96, 104, 107, 111, 117, 118, 124, 126, 128, 131, 134, 135, 140, 165, 168–169, 173, 181, 182, 183, 185, 189, 205, 206
Buddhist 3, 5, 52, 61–63, 118, 177, 207
Confucian 26, 42, 62, 65
no-self (*anatman*) 61, 46, 205
self-control 58, 121, 125, 129, 133, 146, 147, 148, 149, 150, 171
self-suffering (*tapas*) 5, 16, 40, 52, 57, 58, 60, 61, 102, 121, 143, 185, 207
siddhas 173
śilā (virtue) 74
sincerity (*cheng*) 7, 61, 105, 110, 133, 143, 159
Singer, Peter 116
Śiva 37, 41, 90
skandhas 62, 169

Slote, Michael 4, 137
Socrates 5, 12, 18, 25, 42, 69, 70, 71, 82, 104, 111, 151, 178
Soka Gakkei 65, 138
sophia 66–68, 74, 206
Sophists 12, 19
sōphrōn 68, 123, 125, 126, 127, 133, 169, 176, 207
soul 2, 10, 14, 20, 21, 28–34, 37, 39, 40–41, 44, 50, 51, 56, 62, 63, 65, 67, 68, 77, 83–85, 89, 99 104, 111, 120, 124–126, 152–153, 156, 158, 168, 173, 183, 186, 205, 206
soul force (*satyāgraha*) 2, 18, 24
subjectivism 17, 98
  ethical 26
substance 3, 6, 9, 21, 44, 46, 62, 85, 92, 122, 146, 169, 205, 207
śūnyatā 57
swadeshi 128
sympathy 30, 31, 74, 146, 147
sympathetic continuum 30
synthetic a priori 132

Tähntinen, Uno 34, 35
Tantrism 11, 108
tapas 58, 57
Taylor, Charles 173–174
temperance 132, 133, 146, 168
Thales 68
theosophy 121
Thomism 159
Thoreau, Henry David 18, 19, 23, 33, 180
Tīrthaṇkara 33, 207
Titanism 17, 19, 21, 64, 107
Tolstoy, Leo 18, 19, 23, 33, 180
Trinity 114
truth xii, 2, 6, 10, 11, 16, 23, 25, 26, 32, 34, 35, 40, 51, 56, 57, 65, 66, 68, 74, 75, 77, 78, 100, 101, 105, 109, 110, 111, 112, 114, 118, 129, 131, 132, 134, 138, 143, 146, 147, 148, 149, 150, 156, 157, 158, 159, 171, 175
  absolute 13, 44, 66
  experiments in 3, 7, 12, 19, 20, 54, 66–80, 99, 108, 115, 127, 130, 132, 133, 144
  final xi
  finite 42, 44, 79
  personal 42, 44, 66, 75
  relative 13, 32, 66

Übermensch 107
untouchability 10, 128
Upaniṣads 19, 22, 36, 37, 43, 45, 61, 63, 205
  Chāndogya 35
  Katha 36
  Māndūkhya 36
  Muṇdaka 36
  Śvetāśvātara 37
utilitarianism 2, 4, 6, 7, 24, 25, 136–140, 142, 159–161

Vaiṣṇava 6, 18, 35, 36, 60
Vedas 36, 37
  Vedic peoples 35
Vedānta 3, 19, 20, 30, 32, 33, 34, 39–50, 126, 128, 131, 178, 183, 205, 207
  Advaita 5, 10, 12, 33, 39–50, 205, 206
vice 25, 67, 91, 97, 103, 109, 144, 123, 129, 135, 136, 144, 145, 168, 170
village republicanism 10, 14–15, 24, 102, 105
violence 7, 9, 27, 32, 34, 35, 37, 38, 46, 52, 53, 54, 55, 58, 61, 91, 103, 113, 121, 122, 129, 140, 141, 143, 144, 147, 148, 151, 164, 167, 186–187, 201
virility 114, 118, 119–120
virtue 1, 5, 7, 10, 18, 23–27, 31, 33–36, 52–54, 60, 67–80, 83, 84, 85–88, 90, 92–97, 101–104, 106, 108, 109, 111, 112, 113–135, 136–154, 156–161, 163–176, 190, 193, 194, 203, 205, 206
  aesthetics 27, 72, 81–99, 109–112, 134, 154, 165, 195
  cardinal 36, 146, 170
  divine 114, 197
  duress 124, 126, 157, 174–176
  enabling 34, 137, 146–149
  ethics 24, 26, 67, 70, 72, 74, 81–82, 84, 86, 95, 96, 98, 99, 102, 106, 115, 117, 124, 125, 126, 131, 137, 142, 144, 149, 152, 153, 159, 160, 165, 168, 170, 197
  intellectual 66, 67–69, 88, 92
  moral 67–70, 73, 75, 118, 132, 152
  natural 126, 175–76
  substantive 137, 143, 146–149
  theory 34, 116, 129, 136, 137, 139–141, 143, 146, 150, 152, 166, 167, 173, 203
Viṣṇu 13, 36, 41, 47, 105
vows 10, 59, 112, 113, 114, 123–133, 147, 187, 199

Whitehead, Alfred North xii, 6, 13, 22, 25, 81, 197
Wilde, Oscar 98
wisdom 10, 26, 37, 53, 67, 69, 73–74, 92, 102, 146, 167, 207
Wittgenstein, Ludwig xii, 72
Wolf, Susan 156, 159, 160–163, 166, 175

xin (heart-mind) 73, 84, 92, 153, 165, 207
Xunzi 84, 91

yi 66, 69–73, 88, 89, 92, 95, 99, 102, 109, 151, 165, 167, 190, 191, 193
yoga
  bhakti 12
  karma 31, 38
Yoga-Sūtra 130, 157

Zaehner, R. C. 37, 43
Zhuangzi 9
Zimmer, Heinrich 19

SUNY series in Constructive Postmodern Thought

David Ray Griffin, series editor

David Ray Griffin, editor, *The Reenchantment of Science: Postmodern Proposals*

David Ray Griffin, editor, *Spirituality and Society: Postmodern Visions*

David Ray Griffin, *God and Religion in the Postmodern World: Essays in Postmodern Theology*

David Ray Griffin, William A. Beardslee, and Joe Holland, *Varieties of Postmodern Theology*

David Ray Griffin and Huston Smith, *Primordial Truth and Postmodern Theology*

David Ray Griffin, editor, *Sacred Interconnections: Postmodern Spirituality, Political Economy, and Art*

Robert Inchausti, *The Ignorant Perfection of Ordinary People*

David W. Orr, *Ecological Literacy: Education and the Transition to a Postmodern World*

David Ray Griffin, John B. Cobb Jr., Marcus P. Ford, Pete A. Y. Gunter, and Peter Ochs, *Founders of Constructive Postmodern Philosophy: Peirce, James, Bergson, Whitehead, and Hartshorne*

David Ray Griffin and Richard A. Falk, editors, *Postmodern Politics for a Planet in Crisis: Policy, Process, and Presidential Vision*

Steve Odin, *The Social Self in Zen and American Pragmatism*

Frederick Ferré, *Being and Value: Toward a Constructive Postmodern Metaphysics*

Sandra B. Lubarsky and David Ray Griffin, editors, *Jewish Theology and Process Thought*

J. Baird Callicott and Fernando J. R. da Rocha, editors, *Earth Summit Ethics: Toward a Reconstructive Postmodern Philosophy of Environmental Education*

David Ray Griffin, *Parapsychology, Philosophy, and Spirituality: A Postmodern Exploration*

Jay Earley, *Transforming Human Culture: Social Evolution and the Planetary Crisis*

Daniel A. Dombrowski, *Kazantzakis and God*

E. M. Adams, *A Society Fit for Human Beings*

Frederick Ferré, *Knowing and Value: Toward a Constructive Postmodern Epistemology*

Jerry H. Gill, *The Tacit Mode: Michael Polanyi's Postmodern Philosophy*

Nicholas F. Gier, *Spiritual Titanism: Indian, Chinese, and Western Perspectives*

David Ray Griffin, *Religion and Scientific Naturalism: Overcoming the Conflicts*

John A. Jungerman, *World in Process: Creativity and Interconnection in the New Physics*

Frederick Ferré, *Living and Value: Toward a Constructive Postmodern Ethics*

Laurence Foss, *The End of Modern Medicine: Biomedical Science Under a Microscope*

John B. Cobb Jr., *Postmodernism and Public Policy: Reframing Religion, Culture, Education, Sexuality, Class, Race, Politics, and the Economy*

Catherine Keller and Anne Daniell, editors, *Process and Difference: Between Cosmological and Poststructuralist Postmodernisms*

Timothy E. Eastman and Hank Keeton, editors, *Physics and Whitehead: Quantum, Process, and Experience*

Nicholas F. Gier, *The Virtue of Nonviolence: From Gautama to Gandhi*